THE NOTORIOUS LIFE
OF NED BUNTLINE

*A Tale of Murder, Betrayal,
and the Creation of Buffalo Bill*

JULIA BRICKLIN

TWODOT®

GUILFORD, CONNECTICUT
HELENA, MONTANA

For my dad

A · TWODOT® · BOOK
An imprint and registered trademark of The Rowman & Littlefield Publishing Group, Inc.
4501 Forbes Blvd., Ste. 200
Lanham, MD 20706
www.rowman.com

Distributed by NATIONAL BOOK NETWORK

British Library Cataloguing in Publication Information available

Library of Congress Cataloging-in-Publication Data

Names: Bricklin, Julia, 1970- author.
Title: The notorious life of Ned Buntline : a tale of murder, betrayal, and the creation of Buffalo Bill / Julia Bricklin.
Description: Lanham, MD : TwoDot, [2020] | "Distributed by NATIONAL BOOK NETWORK" —T.p. verso. | Includes bibliographical references and index. | Summary: "Edward Zane Carroll Judson aka Ned Buntline (1821–1886) was responsible for creating a highly romantic and often misleading image of the American West, albeit one that the masses found irresistible in the mid- to late nineteenth century. The Notorious Life of Ned Buntline captures the likeness of a man who sparked an American legend but whose own scandalous life somehow escaped history's limelight"—Provided by publisher.
Identifiers: LCCN 2019039432 | ISBN 9781493047536 (hardback) | ISBN 9781493047543 (epub)
Subjects: LCSH: Buntline, Ned, 1822 or 1823-1886. | Authors, American—Biography.
Classification: LCC PS2156.J2 Z55 2020 | DDC 813/.3 [B]—dc23
LC record available at https://lccn.loc.gov/2019039432

♾™ The paper used in this publication meets the minimum requirements of American National Standard for Information Sciences—Permanence of Paper for Printed Library Materials, ANSI/NISO Z39.48-1992.

CONTENTS

Acknowledgments

Dr. David Haas
Stuart Rosebrook, PhD
Westchester Historical Society
Adirondack Experience
Stamford Historical Society
Claire Prechtel-Kluskens
Sarah C. Smith
Dianne Thibodo
Wayne County Historical Society
New Castle, New York, Historical Society
Dr. Robert D. Pepper
Carol Renick Monroe
Denise McAllister

Special thanks goes to Dr. Clay Reynolds, author of *The Hero of a Hundred Fights: Ned Buntline*, who patiently and thoroughly answered my questions about Ned Buntline's literary contributions.

Author's Note

Kevin S. Blake, when writing about author Zane Grey, said: "When dime novels acquired a trashy reputation toward the end of the nineteenth century, eastern publishers searched for a writer who could address the colorful characters of the West more seriously." The search culminated in 1902 with Owen Wister, "a Pennsylvanian who sat in South Carolina to write a book about a Virginian living in Wyoming." His popular novel, *The Virginian*, praised the action and romance of the frontier that, according to this tale and to Frederick Jackson Turner's 1893 frontier thesis, had just disappeared. "Wister's innovative combination of cowboys versus rustlers," wrote Blake, "the transforming power of good woman's love, and the main-street shootout changed the course of stories about the West, but the main significance of 'The Virginian' was that it paved the way for Zane Grey."[1]

Who, then, paved the way for Owen Wister and Zane Grey?

Without a doubt, it was Edward Zane Carroll Judson. His fiction, says historian and writer Clay Reynolds, "is utterly horrid," but it is typical of the period: "corny, over-written, tritely plotted, naive, ill-informed and highly romantic." Nonetheless, Judson constitutes an important literary bridge between the early frontier novels of Cooper and the "first western" of Owen Wister, with only a few writers—Mark Twain, Bret Harte, Artemis Ward, et al.—in between. There were others, not the least of whom was Prentiss Ingraham, who were no less prolific and no less popular. But even Ingraham called Judson "The King of the Dime Novel," probably with some grudging envy. We owe him a huge debt for establishing so many of the archetypes, plot lines, and even western clichés ("Head 'Em Off at the Pass . . ." among many others) that generations grew up believing came from the authentic West, but which actually found their genesis in Judson's imagination.[2]

Of course, acknowledging Judson's contributions to the myth of the American West is not giving him full credit. While he is best known for his creation of the celebrity "Buffalo Bill" and, to a lesser extent, "Wild Bill Hickok" and "Texas Jack" and any number of other heroes and heroines, Judson was more famous during his lifetime for his seafaring adventures and his urban crime fiction—in which Anglos won battles with exotic peoples who threatened white America and in which Protestant values won battles against amoral life in the big city. In some ways, Judson can be given credit for bridging the work of Washington Irving with that of Edgar Rice Burroughs, or even for inspiring the work of Upton Sinclair.

From his youthful exploits as a stowaway and sailor to his brief career as a midshipman, a kind of mountebank and raconteur on riverboats, to a supporter of Cuban revolution, champion of the Seminoles, to duelist and accused and lynched murderer to broadside pundit to instigator of major city riots, to temperance leader to drunk, loyal family man and bigot, braggart, master of disguise, soldier, nativist, political pundit, patriot, adventurer, impresario, actor, outdoorsman, politician, journalist, philanthropist, and tireless author, he was like a dozen or more individuals all rolled into one.[3] Nonetheless, Judson will always be best known for creating Buffalo Bill, who, by the turn of the twentieth century, was arguably the most famous American in the world.

* * *

It would be impossible to write a book about Edward Zane Carroll Judson, aka "Ned Buntline," without mentioning the "Buntline Special." This term refers to five 10-inch-barrel Colt Single Action Army revolvers that Judson supposedly presented to ex–buffalo hunters Wyatt Earp, Bat Masterson, Bill Tilghman, Neil Brown, and Charlie Bassett. Stuart N. Lake first described these guns in his 1931 biography of Earp, entitled *Wyatt Earp: Frontier Marshal*.

According to Lake, Judson offered these metallic tokens to the Dodge City lawmen to thank them for supplying him with "material for hundreds of frontier yarns." After its publication, various Colt revolvers with long (10-inch or 16-inch) barrels were called Colt Buntlines or Buntline Specials. Colt manufactured the pistol among its second-generation revolvers produced after 1956.

The notion that Judson commissioned the guns for the peacekeepers has been widely debunked. My research leads me to reject the idea too, for the same reasons outlined by William B. Shillingberg, author of *Wyatt Earp & the "Buntline Special" Myth* (Tucson, AZ: Blaine Publishing Co., 1976). Shillingberg's main contentions are that 1876 was too soon for any of these men to be considered as having any official peacekeeping position, and that Judson's "Western" output was then limited only to his Buffalo Bill dime novel and newspaper series, and the play he wrote and starred in with Cody—*Scouts of the Prairie*—and a few related pieces using ancillary characters. While Judson's creation of Buffalo Bill would become one of the biggest cultural success stories in American history, the author simply did not have an interest in limiting himself to an evolving genre—though he certainly helped create it. Moreover, purported stories that Judson supposedly wrote about Earp have yet to be discovered—he certainly did not publicize any. And though some historians have posited that Judson gave these gentlemen such gifts as a bribe to replace Cody, "Texas Jack" Omohundro, and Wild Bill Hickok in his stage play, I could find no evidence that he was interested in reviving his traveling Western show in 1876.

I could not find any evidence that Judson ever left the eastern seaboard in 1876. For that matter, he never went west of Cincinnati after 1869, when he returned to his home state of New York after his temperance tour in California—including that fateful stopover in North Platte, Nebraska, where he met Cody for the first time. Anna Fuller Judson, the writer's wife from 1873 until his death in 1886, wrote of accompanying her husband on his travels with Cody—surely she would also have mentioned his travels to Kansas City to see such illustrious men. She did not. Most importantly, though, is the fact that Judson's personality dictates that he would have made sure that every paper in the United States carried news of such an expensive and magnanimous act as having guns made for these gentlemen and hand-delivering them to Dodge City. He did not.

Still, myths become myths because they have some kernel (maybe many kernels) of intrigue. Though Lake's biography is accepted as highly fictional, he deserves some credit for creating a scenario with which Judson himself would be delighted. I suggest the following reading for more about the Buntline Special:

William B. Shillingberg, "Wyatt Earp and the Buntline Special Myth," *The Kansas Historical Society* Vol. 42, No. 2 (Summer 1976), 113–154.
Lee A. Silva, *Wyatt Earp: A Biography of the Legend, Vol. II, Part I: Tombstone Before the Earps* (Santa Ana, CA: Graphic Publishers, 2010).
Jon Guttman, "Did Wyatt Earp Carry a Buntline Special?" Ask Mr. History column, HistoryNet: www.historynet.com/did-wyatt-earp-carry-a-buntline-special.htm.

For thorough bibliographies of Edward Zane Carroll Judson's works, please see the appendixes provided by Jay Monaghan and R. Clay Reynolds. (I say "thorough" as opposed to "complete" because Judson was so prolific and wrote under many noms de plume—it would surprise no one if new stories were discovered.) They can be found in their books:

Jay Monaghan, *The Great Rascal: The Life and Adventures of Ned Buntline* paperback reprint (San Bernardino, CA: Ulan Press, 2012).
R. Clay Reynolds, *The Hero of a Hundred Fights: Collected Stories from the Dime Novel King, From Buffalo Bill to Wild Bill Hickok* (New York: Union Square Press, 2011).

INTRODUCTION

AROUND ONE O'CLOCK IN THE MORNING ON MAY 11, 1849, FOUR MEN rushed into the main entrance of the imposing brick hospital on a bluff directly above the East River. Their stretcher held William Harmer, who had immigrated to New York City from New Brunswick the year before. He worked as a butcher on Third Avenue and Eighth Street. Harmer screamed in agony and clutched his abdomen. The men who brought him in tried to hold him flat down and at the same time tried to hold kerchiefs over their mouths and noses, afraid of the cholera germs that had already killed three thousand New Yorkers that year. There was no ether contraption available because so many wounded had been pouring in since ten o'clock the night before, but a nurse managed to place a filthy chloroform rag over his mouth and provide some relief. A doctor worked feverishly to remove the musket ball but could not do so without further damage to Harmer's intestines. He cut his losses, hastily sewed the patient up, and moved onto the next. Harmer lingered until four o'clock that afternoon, when he mercifully died. He was fifteen years old.

The teen was a victim of New York City's bloodiest riot. The day before, at half past six o'clock in the evening, people began to assemble around the theater at Lafayette Street in lower Manhattan. Within half an hour, crowds wended their way to it from other parts of the city. By 7:30 p.m. several hundred people had gathered in the street in front of the brick and stone structure with imperious colonnades. Horses and carriages could no longer get through from Astor Place or East Eighth Street, the roads on either side of the venue. The evening's performance of *Macbeth* was already sold out, but still the crowd grew bigger. By 7:45 there were so many people packed around the Astor Opera House that on adjacent Broadway dozens stood precariously at the top of an earthen mound dug for a sewer line. Inside the hall, patrons jostled and bumped and cursed to get to their seats. Policemen pulled out the rowdiest hooters and hecklers and locked them in rooms beneath the box seats.

A hush fell over the audience when the play officially opened at 8:00. The theater remained silent during the first two scenes featuring actor C. W. Clarke as Macduff. But when the third scene opened and British actor Charles Macready appeared on stage, a group of men shouted, groaned, and hissed; some cried, "Out with him! Out with him!" Police and other patrons subdued the worst offenders. The play went on, and while there was a constant low hum of excitement, all of the performers could be heard clearly.

Some minutes later, the smell of smoke began to permeate the gallery. The four prisoners in the temporary prison underneath the boxes had funneled wood shavings and pieces onto gas lights and started a fire. Policemen opened the doors and put the men in irons, but not before oily smoke spread throughout the hall. Patrons put handkerchiefs over their faces and fanned themselves, but most planned to keep watching the program—until some viewers began hurling chairs upon the stage, and all heard the sound of breaking glass. Macready and the other actors scurried off the stage and into the safety of their carriages, waiting out back. Volley after volley of large paving stones smashed through the windows on all sides of the theater, and the showgoers erupted into a mass of confusion. Their screams of panic and pain as some fell under the fleeing limbs of others were juxtaposed against those of one man outside yelling, "STONE THE BUILDING!" The windows, sans glass, held for a few minutes, but the mob outside succeeded in splintering open the frames and tossing in even more stone and bottle projectiles.

Cooler heads inside the Astor building managed to corral many of the women away from the windows and flying shards of glass. But panic ensued again minutes later when a rumor began circulating that there was a bomb inside the building and that a fire had been set to it on the outside. "Where is the military? Where is the mayor?" wailed patrons. A few men tapped out the remnants of glass in one frame, hoisted the theater's fire hose outside of it, and sprayed the mob in an effort to get it to disperse. But this just inflamed the angry masses even more, and they gathered more flagstones to hurl against the structure. A dozen or so men from the mob took turns battering the main entrance, and just as they succeeded, an equal dozen or so policemen burst out of a side door and began pulling the offenders all the way in, clubbing them as they did so.

Things were direr outside the venue. At about 9:15, a company of mounted troops with drawn swords riding two abreast on white horses approached the swirling cabal. These were followed by two divisions of National Guard infantry, marching with fixed bayonets raised high. As the procession reached the corner of the Bowery and turned down Eighth Street, rioters began showering the animals and their riders with rocks, and some of the horses tossed off their riders. Those who maintained their seats turned around and galloped back to a safe distance. The infantry quickly filled their vacated spots on the street and marched resolutely toward the Opera House. The 7th Regiment was a very disciplined group, and it began to clear a path between Broadway and the Bowery. It seemed that the crowd might finally disperse when shots rang out; one captain took a bullet to the leg while another took one to the cheek. After dozens of men fell hurt out of the ranks, their colonel finally ordered them to fire warning shots above the crowd.

When a minute or two passed and no rioters appeared hurt, the mob thought wrongly that the infantry was using blank cartridges. Encouraged, the violent crowd rushed the troops, each caught up in the shared consciousness that he could crush the peacemakers—without collectively questioning why. At this point, the militia fired directly upon it, and even as rioters fell back wounded or killed, the mass of people still pushed forward. In the dark, flashes of gunfire highlighted men and boys scrambling every which way, tumbling over each other and getting sucked under the roiling stew of humanity. A general drew his men up and ordered them to turn their fire toward the intersection of the Bowery and Fourth Avenue, where some thousand or so rioters congregated.[1] At last the murderous gang of thousands started to break up and retreat.

When the smoke cleared, hundreds of people lay on the streets dead, dying, or maimed. Most were injured by thrown rocks or other debris or had been trampled. Scores were wounded by the pocket pistols of the rioters or the guns fired by the National Guard. Young William Harmer and at least twenty-two others were killed by the infantry's fire. Many of the killed and wounded were merely passersby or spectators who had taken no part in the riot. Judge Charles P. Daly, who would preside over the eventual case against the primary perpetrators of the violence, recounted some of the human carnage: "A woman walking with her husband on Broadway was shot dead; a man was killed instantly by a musket ball while stepping from a Harlem railroad car; an eminent merchant was wounded in the neck by a ball while standing in the Bowery; and another person was severely wounded by a shot in St. Mark's Place, two blocks from the scene of the riot. A Mr. Gedney was shot dead while looking at the riot from the corner of Astor and Lafayette places, and his own brother was a member of the platoon that had fired the volley."[2]

Citizens quickly dubbed the madness of this evening the Astor Place Riot. It was the bloodiest event to occur in New York City history at that time. The instigator of it all was Edward Zane Carroll Judson.

* * *

At Judson's trial that September of 1849, his brother-in-law Frank Bennett recounted how he had been duped into accompanying Judson that evening. Judson picked him up from work in his carriage, and on the route home he said that the editors of the *Courier and Enquirer*, for whom he worked, wanted him to head a riot that evening. Astonished, Bennett asked him why anyone would demand such a thing of their employee. "The authorities have ordered out the troops," Judson said, "and I consider it an insult to the American people!" Bennett still did not quite understand why the mayor would order troops for something that had not happened yet. But he knew Judson had visited with American-born actor Edwin Forrest the day before, and that night his brother-in-law's gray eyes flashed with anger as he bellowed about the injustice of Macready, a Brit, taking on the Shakespearean role that should have gone to Forrest.[3]

The young Bennett felt compelled to watch over his sister's husband. His mother knew Judson was up to something and bade her twenty-three-year-old son to follow him closely. Anna Bennett, Judson's wife, got on her knees and begged him not to go out, but he ignored her and instead walked upstairs and put on Frank's white sack coat and Tom Hyer cap, which covered most of his flaming red hair. He also put two pistols in the coat pocket and a dagger in a pants pocket.

At dusk the pair took a carriage from the Bennett home on Abingdon Square and clip-clopped down Twelfth Street. "Let's go down to the Opera House," Judson said to Frank. "I heard there's going to be a sport there."[4] First, though, he insisted on stopping at a pub at the junction of Twelfth Street and Broadway. There he insisted Frank take one of his pistols. He explained that some of his enemies—gamblers—would likely be there, and he needed his brother-in-law to watch out for any trouble. After Judson downed several shots of whiskey, he and Frank headed down Fourth Avenue to Eighth Street and Lafayette.[5]

Judson drove around the opera house once, appraising it. Finally, the two disembarked and walked toward the small crowd. "Are there any Americans here?" Judson roared. "The ground is your own and you have a right to it, and I will assist you in defending your right!" The response was tepid, Bennett recounted later, so Judson complained to the group that it needed to work "in concert" to get anything done. "Couldn't you get up the cry of fire?" Judson bellowed. "Gather some shavings, boys!"[6]

People in the crowd began to recognize Judson. He was, they realized, Ned Buntline, the famous author, adventurer, and provocateur. Only twenty-six years old, the man was already famous throughout the eastern seaboard. He had been editor of the *Western Literary Review* and had written smashing adventures for *Knickerbocker* magazine. He had founded his own paper, *Ned Buntline's Magazine*, and was the author of *Mysteries and Miseries of New York*, the sensational volume about gamblers, prostitutes, child-snatchers, thieves, and murderers who prowled the underbelly of their city. In *Mysteries and Miseries* and his other dime novels, there were murders, drunken brawls, suicide attempts, blackmail, ravished virgins, adulterous wives and husbands, golden-hearted prostitutes, abortions, marauding scions, daring escapes, Bowery folk heroes, and everything else you can think of in a page-turning guilty pleasure.

* * *

Judson was a celebrity in part because his written works were so popular, but also because his real—rather, his reported—life exploits were no less exciting and notorious. He left his father's home in Philadelphia at age fifteen and joined the navy. He received a midshipman's commission after purportedly saving seventeen men from drowning in a boat crash in the Staten Island harbor. After he had served a couple of years on vessels in the ports of Philadelphia, Brooklyn, and Boston, Judson joined the US man-of-war *Levant* and sailed for the Caribbean. After a short time patrolling against French blockades of Veracruz, Mexico, the navy sent him to Pensacola, Florida, where the stocky teen was assigned to a cutter that patrolled southern Florida, battling Seminoles who tried to tear down US military installations there. He created the pen name "Ned Buntline" (a buntline is one of the ropes attached to the foot of a square sail) and related his swashbuckling experiences in such stories as "A Chase in the Everglades."

Judson detached from the navy in 1845. The writer recounted his next adventure in his *Knickerbocker* magazine: He traveled to Eddyville, Kentucky, where in November 1845 he supposedly captured two murderers who were hiding in some woods, an accomplishment that won him six hundred dollars. Restless, Judson moved on to Nashville, where he hoped to make some money as a freelance writer and perhaps find investors for a new magazine. On March 14, 1846, he shot and killed Robert Porterfield, husband of a teen with whom he allegedly had been having "criminal intercourse."[7] A mob tried to lynch Judson for what he had done, but the rope broke and he managed to escape the city. He took the first steamer available to Pittsburgh, where his father lived, and when his name no longer appeared in the newspapers for the Nashville incident, he moved to New York City. Here, he wrote *The Maid of Monterey: A Tale of the Mexican War*, *Virgin of the Sun*, *The Red Revenger*, and dozens of other novels that turned him into a household name and a wealthy man.

At the time of the Astor Place Riot, Judson was married to Annie Abigail Bennett, a beautiful woman from a very respectable mercantile family in lower Manhattan. Annie became pregnant, and the pair took an apartment in her family's large home on Abingdon Square.

Despite Annie's and her family's best efforts, Judson's dark side surpassed his amiable one and his true nature soon became public knowledge. He drank to excess for days at a time and then spent an equal number of days completely sober, unable to stop violently chastising any family or friends who dared have so much as a brandy after dinner. On April 9, 1849, Judson's wife suffered the ultimate humiliation when a well-known madam named Kate Hastings accosted her husband in the middle of Broadway. "You dirty, mean, sneaking, paltry sonofabitch! How dare you publish me in your paper!" Hastings hollered, then pulled out a horse whip and thrashed him until he needed medical attention for his wounds. Though Hastings had no compunction whatsoever about running a house of prostitution, she took exception to Buntline's description of her as "the infamous cast-off mistress of a deceased gambler, known as 'gallows Kate Hastings,' the keeper of a low house of prostitution on Leonard-Street."[8]

Judson took Hastings to court for the assault, and won, but this only served to publicize the fact that he was a frequent visitor to Hastings's house of prostitution. The judge was forced to find in the writer's favor based on point of law, but he was so outraged at Judson's behavior that he fined Hastings a mere six cents. Between this trial in April 1849 and the one in September of that same year that found the writer guilty of instigating the bloodiest riot known in recent memory, Annie Bennett had had enough. She divorced Judson in October 1849, a few weeks after Judson was sent to prison at Blackwell's Island.[9]

For most souls, being imprisoned in Blackwell's Island for a year would be enough motivation to pursue a more bucolic lifestyle. But prison just seemed to give Edward Judson time to come up with more ideas for books and escapades. On the day of his release, rowdy friends met him with a band playing "Hail to the Chief." He spent the next twenty years crisscrossing the United States as the human embodiment of contradictions. He delivered fiery temperance lectures and drank ambitiously. He proclaimed the virtues of public peace, but in addition to causing the Astor Place Riot, he stirred up another one in St. Louis, which killed at least three men. He despaired of social injustice but only reluctantly spoke or wrote against slavery. He admired strong and independent women but held suffragists in nearly satiric contempt. He professed a sanctimonious devotion to the institutions of chastity and marriage—but married at least nine women, sometimes two, even three at a time. He was apparently areligious but treated the faithful (including Indians and their "pagan beliefs") with respect, and once considered embracing Spiritualism.[10] He fashioned an isolated existence in the Adirondack Mountains, churning out some hundred novels in just a couple of years, and then abandoned this retreat for crowded barracks as a Civil War private. In turn, his real and imagined experiences in the war inspired dozens more bestsellers about Rebel privateers, cavalry scouts, villains, female Union spies, and battles with Native Americans on the more western fringes of the rebellion.

* * *

Twenty years after the Astor Place Riot, Judson "discovered" William Cody by accident while briefly exploring these more western regions in person. In the late summer of 1869, the populist writer headed to Fort McPherson, Nebraska, on his way back from a temperance tour in California. He was looking for heroes of a conflict known as the Battle of Summit Springs.[11] On July 11 the US Army's 5th Cavalry had attacked a village of Cheyenne Dog Soldiers. The Cheyennes had two white captives, and during the fight one of them was killed by one of the Cheyennes. Major Frank J. North of the US Army's white soldiers and his band of Pawnee scouts tricked and then killed Tall Bull, leader of the Cheyennes. What better "hero" for Judson to write about?[12]

Major North had no interest in becoming Judson's hero. In fact, he did not care for writers in general. "If you want a man to fill that bill," he told Judson, "he's over there under the wagon."[13] The writer, so the story goes, stumbled over, where recuperating soldiers were trying to sleep in the fly-infested heat. He poked beneath a wagon, perhaps looking for shade, and found a "young giant" with sleepy eyes and straw in his long hair.

William Frederick Cody was twenty-three years old and already well-known in frontier circles when he and Judson met. Too young to enlist in the formal army when the Civil War broke out, Cody rode for the "Kansas Redlegs," an antislavery militia. He enlisted with the 7th Kansas Cavalry in 1864. After the war ended, he married and then worked as an army scout and dispatch carrier in Fort Ellsworth, Kansas. In 1867, Cody got work hunting buffalo to feed the construction crews of the Kansas Pacific Railroad. According to Cody, he killed 4,280 head of buffalo within seventeen months. Whatever the actual number, it was this trade and his wholesale slaughter within it that earned him the nickname "Buffalo Bill." In 1868 Cody returned to his work for the army, where General Philip Sheridan made him chief scout for the 5th Cavalry. He took part in sixteen battles, including the Cheyenne defeat at Summit Springs. Cody even took credit for killing Tall Bull, though evidence suggests otherwise.

Whatever the case, Cody knew all of the details of the fight at Summit Springs and all of its participants. Edward Judson found the scout to be engaging, talkative, and believable. Most importantly, he found Cody to be the perfect embodiment of righteousness, adventure, and gallantry. With delight he accepted Cody's invitation to ride with him to scout for Indians, something Judson claimed he had done as a teenager when fighting the Seminoles in Florida. Also, Judson claimed, he had used similar techniques during the recent Civil War to ferret Confederates from their nests in the woods of Virginia.

Judson spent several days—weeks, perhaps—on the platte with Cody, but they encountered no hostile Indians. His vacation over, the writer returned to New York with his head full of stories.[14] On December 7, 1869, Judson—as Ned Buntline—published his first story about Cody in *Street and Smith's New York Weekly*. It was entitled *Buffalo Bill, The King of the Border-Men*, and it was printed in installments between the last few weeks of 1869 and March 1870. It featured the exploits of hero Buffalo Bill and his erstwhile sidekick, Wild Bill Hickok, and villains like Jake M'Kandlas (a misspelling of McCanles), a proslavery Missouri bushwhacker. Naturally,

Cody and Hickok smote all villains by the end of the story, and Buntline left his readers breathless for the next novel. In 1872 Judson convinced Cody to travel east and star in a play he had written featuring him called *Scouts of the Prairie*. The show was outrageously popular along the eastern seaboard and introduced the world to the showman Buffalo Bill, "Texas Jack" Omohundro and also James Butler "Wild Bill" Hickok. *Scouts* was the template from which Cody developed his fantastically popular Wild West show. "No one could have known," wrote William H. and William N. Goetzmann, "that 'The Scouts of the Prairie' was a performance that would change American entertainment forever—it was the first 'Western.'"[15]

Judson's and Cody's stage partnership ended in June 1873, when, after their last appearance together in upstate New York, Omohundro and Cody decided they could manage the show on their own. Omohundro and Cody realized that Judson's character was replaceable while their personal appearances were not.[16]

Cody and Judson eventually repaired their awkward relationship and remained friends until Judson passed away in 1886. The explosive popularity of the *true* Buffalo Bill could not be surpassed—and never would be again. Judson's discovery of Cody and his immediate exploitation of him created a Western hero unparalleled in his era. Neither Judson nor his publisher, *Street and Smith's New York Weekly*, could have appreciated the magnitude of what they were creating, or how enduring the legend of Buffalo Bill would become. In fact, Judson wrote only five novelettes featuring Buffalo Bill. Other authors, including Prentiss Ingraham, W. Bert Foster, William Wallace Cook, and the Reverend John Harvey Whitson, picked up the mantle in the 1870s and wrote hundreds more throughout the following decades. John Burke and others took over Cody's performance career, but Judson will forever retain credit for discovering the American legend of Buffalo Bill.

* * *

When Judson's experiment with Cody and live entertainment foundered in the fall of 1874, he retreated to his beloved mansion in Stamford, New York, a tiny hamlet nestled in the Catskill Mountains. He was not upset about his situation because it was merely the latest in scores of adventures, and it gave him ideas for many more. By this time, he was earning between $10,000 and $20,000 a year from the hundreds of adventure stories he had written before he had ever met Cody and Hickok and the rest. This amount would place him squarely within millionaire status today.[17]

In truth, Judson had far more pressing issues. His wife of two years, Anna Fuller, desperately wished to start a family. He owed money to the attorney who had helped bail him out of a St. Louis jail in January 1874, when he arrived there with his troupe and was immediately arrested for skipping out on court twenty years prior on the St. Louis riot charge. He was wanted in Maine for an 1873 incident, when he had a *Scouts* troupe member in charge of ammunitions arrested for stealing guns—now this man successfully sued him for false complaint in absentia and won a $1,000 verdict.

More stressful for Judson was the fact that an odd woman kept coming around the village and asking people about him and his wife and his home. Her name was Lovanche Kelsey Swart, and she claimed to have been married to Edward in 1853 and again in 1863. This woman, forty-five, asked strangers whether the Judsons had any children and when they had wed and how old Anna was and, according to Anna, any number of other "deep and designing" questions meant to cast aspersion on the writer and his much younger bride.[18]

But Lovanche Swart was not trying to defame Judson or his bride. It would be difficult to do so, as the writer had been a notorious womanizer since he was a teen. Some of his marriages were bigamous, and Judson at times agreed to them merely to keep one step ahead of an angry father who might believe his daughter had been seduced. And in the mid- to late nineteenth century, some newspapers were often too polite or too embarrassed to report what we would today call rape: Some of Judson's wives, including a few he had children with, were girls as young as fifteen—and some had been servants in his household.

Judson's marriages and sexual proclivities were viewed negatively, but it is important to put his liaisons into context. To be sure, most of them were opportunistic, ill conceived, and criminal. But, it should be noted that two of Judson's driving forces throughout his whole life were the ideas of reinvention and legitimacy, which were sometimes at direct odds with each other; marriage was a primary way for him to achieve both. He moved from city to town to hamlet, east to west, urban to rural and back again, chasing adventure and income. He met many, many different kinds of women—and, in his own corrupted or contorted way, thought a marriage ceremony would bring validity to his liaisons—both for him and his partners. And though he truly found his intellectual match with at least two of these wives, the others should not be relegated to a much lower status; he had a genuine affection for their exoticism, energy, ability to be a good helpmeet, or some combination of all of these things.

As for Lovanche: She was merely trying to get the financial support she so badly needed from the man who married her at least twice, and who had made her a number of promises over the previous twenty-two years. Lovanche knew him better than any other woman Judson had married—and there were at least nine others. He had confided in her about his oppressive father and how Levi Judson's raging morality pushed Edward to join the navy as a youth. And she knew about at least some of Edward's illegitimate children—evidence shows he had at least four, besides the five to whom he gave his last name.

Swart knew about Judson's gifts, too. After all, they were the reasons she had been drawn to him in 1851 after her husband died. He could be protective and paternal: He promised he would take care of her and be a father to her toddler son, Frank. He was humorous, solicitous, charming, well-groomed, and generous. Swart was a novice writer herself and enjoyed literary pursuits. Judson's biggest detractors had to concede that he had no equal when it came to writing stories that appealed to the masses, and he could write them in just days—Mark Twain patterned some of his works after Judson's pulp fiction and even referenced his vigilante pirate tome *The Black Avenger of the Spanish Main* in *The Adventures of Tom Sawyer*. There is some evidence to suggest that Lovanche may have helped Judson with some of his stories.

Whether Lovanche was in love with Judson or simply in love with his money is beside the point. When she challenged Anna Fuller Judson's claim for his pension upon his death in 1886, she instigated a twenty-year legal investigation of Ned Buntline. The five hundred–page investigation file contains testimonials from Judson's last three wives, military colleagues, friends, enemies, even the writer himself. (Sister Irene handed over letters that she and her brother had written back and forth during the Civil War.) It is starkly and sharply honest, as people are wont to be when a celebrity in their midst passes away. It provides the best material for analyzing the man who created Buffalo Bill, Wild Bill Hickok, and any number of other frontier stereotypes.

Two of Judson's biographers, Jay Monaghan and Albert Johannsen, sourced this pension file—probably the originals in the National Archives. Both refer to "Pension File 906598," and Monaghan even quotes from several of the original letters it contains. But as scholar Robert David Pepper, late professor of English at San Jose State, wrote, "Neither man had the time or inclination, circa 1950, to read over those hundreds of pages of legal forms and handwritten depositions, in search of facts not already known. The file has been, until now, an under-mined treasure."[19]

* * *

Monaghan's *The Great Rascal: The Life and Adventures of Ned Buntline*, published in 1952, remains the most recent and comprehensive biography of the ruffian. It is meticulously researched using materials available to Monaghan at the time and recounts Judson's fantastic and uproarious career. The scholar painstakingly corroborated what he could of Judson's own highly colored accounts of his own life, but as Robert Pepper notes, "even this indefatigable researcher was unable to illuminate every dark corner." Johannsen's 1950 *The House of Beadle and Adams and Its Dime and Nickel Novels* gives some superficial accounts of Judson's life as pertinent to his literary career.

Adirondacks expert and scholar Harold K. Hochschild's 1961 *Township 34* provides a lively account of Judson's five years at Hamilton Lake in the Adirondacks, where he sequestered himself in a successful attempt to churn out more books and in an unsuccessful attempt to stay sober and chaste. Regional and family historians from Delaware and Hamilton Counties in New York, along with some from St. Louis, Pittsburgh, Philadelphia, Nashville, and Broward, Florida, have over the years provided snippets of Judson lore from the times he created home or havoc in their cities. And Robert Pepper wrote several incisive articles about Judson in the 1980s and 1990s but passed away before he could publish anything comprehensive.

Judson's published works during the first half of his life were at least partially inspired by the Leatherstocking Tales of James Fenimore Cooper, which emphasized tensions between the wild frontier and encroaching civilization. After the Civil War, the writer's short stories and novels emphasized conquest and subordination of nature and Native Americans that reflected the ideas of Manifest Destiny. Judson's literature demonstrated the necessity of an unwritten code of honor in the lawless Wild West—a West he never saw save for long train rides to and from California in 1868–1869. He had a remarkable knack for prose style and command of vocabulary, especially for a man with no formal education. Judson was, writes Reynolds, exceedingly erudite and rhetorically astute.[20]

Edward Zane Carroll Judson once wrote a succinct explanation for his life's course: "I might have paved for myself a far different career in letters, but my early lot was cast among rough men on the border; they became my comrades and when I made my name as a teller of stories about Indians, pirates and scouts, it seemed too late to begin over again. Besides, I made more money than any Bohemian in New York or Boston." Indeed, he made (and lost) a lot of money. But what Judson missed in his self-analysis—what he could not possibly have known unless he had lived a couple of decades longer—is how much his writing would whet the country's appetite for stories from that great expanse of frontier loosely referred to as the American West. The popularity of his pulp fiction spurred an estimated eleven million individual titles of "dime novels," or "yellow-backs," as they were sometimes derisively called.

For Judson, summarizes Clay Reynolds, the line between fiction and fact was always blurred, just as the line between Edward Z. C. Judson and Ned Buntline was always blurred.[21] He would be proud of the way historians have treated him, for many have had no choice but to repeat the fictionalized versions of his life that he himself promoted. He was certainly a philanthropist, bibliophile, naturalist, proponent of law and order, and supporter of civic institutions. But there is no doubt he was also a bigamist, slanderer, blackmailer, liar, deadbeat, philanderer, murderer, and fugitive from justice. "Ned Buntline" was the human embodiment of America's complicated past and its struggles with racism, its treatment of native peoples and women, and its efforts to both tame and conserve natural resources.

Judson's Westerns were a small part of his output, but they were the most enduring. In fact, his works like *Dashing Charlie: A Texas Whirlwind*, *Buffalo Bill's Best Shot*, and *The Seven Scouts* are, stylistically, a bridge between Cooper and the modern-day Western novel or film, according to Reynolds. And of course, his play *Scouts of the Prairie* and the popularity of his Buffalo Bill tales spurred the creation of the longest-running Wild West shows in the world. "It sounds like an exaggeration," said Reynolds in one interview, "but I honestly believe that Judson is wholly responsible for the career that William F. Cody built for himself." The publicity that Judson gave Cody as an "authentic character" of the West, Reynolds continued, "provided Cody with a platform from which he could launch his larger and more dynamic talents, first as a stage performer, then as a politician, ultimately as a showman of the first order, and finally as an icon of the American West who became, quite literally, a legend in his own time."[22]

Buffalo Bill, one of America's brightest stars, came from one of its darkest minds.

CHAPTER ONE

Death of a Legend Maker

*It is evident from the numerous widows that have appeared that
E. Z. C. Judson was a Buntline which had frequently been spliced.*
—LONDON AMERICAN REGISTER, AUGUST 21, 1886

EDWARD ZANE CARROLL JUDSON DIED OF HEART FAILURE AT 4:20 IN
the afternoon on July 16, 1886. According to the *New York Times*, more
than eight hundred people attended the funeral, held two days later. It
was, said the paper, the largest funeral ever held in Stamford, New York.
Special trains were run on the Ulster and Delaware Railroad, bringing
friends and spectators from New York City, Westchester, counties of
the Catskills region, and even Pittsburgh, Pennsylvania. One of Judson's
Hambletonian horses was ushered behind his casket, wearing an empty
saddle and boots reversed in the stirrups. Nearly two hundred members
of local Grand Army of the Republic posts marched in line to the cemetery and said their goodbyes to the writer known as "Ned Buntline."

Judson was buried in a family plot under the shadow of Mount
Utsayantha near his home in the Catskills. After the service, family,
friends, and neighbors trudged up to Judson's beloved estate, Eagle's
Nest, where he had taken his last breaths. Mourners walked up gravelly
pathways until the sprawling lawn of the estate suddenly appeared, the
twenty-room Second Empire–style mansion with mansard roof made
from eleven tons of Vermont slate looming ahead. In front of the stately
home, a huge American flag flapped in the breeze, and to the side was a
carriage house for Judson's six fine horses and as many carriages. Undu-
lating around this grandeur was a 120-acre farm.

In all likelihood, Judson was buried in one of the dark suits he was fond of wearing in his later years, with about twenty or so gold medals and badges of secret societies pinned to its lapel. The novelist's headstone was just a few feet away from that of his little daughter Irene, whose image had been crafted from Italian marble. "He was a model of muscular vigor up until the day of his death," Judson's syndicated obituary said. He had, it claimed, probably more wounds in his body than any other living being at that time, with a bullet forever lodged in his right knee and twelve other wounds inflicted by sword, shell, or gun.[1]

Almost as soon as Judson was in the ground, tongues began to wag about how much money he had made in his lifetime, how much his estate was worth. Depending on who was guessing, his salary had been anywhere from twelve thousand to sixty thousand dollars a year, but most people concurred he had earned an average of twenty thousand per year for at least half his life (equivalent to about five hundred thousand dollars today—more in purchasing power). Eagle's Nest was rumored to have cost twenty thousand dollars to build—and that had been fifteen years earlier.[2]

Just one day after Judson's death, letters started to arrive at the Delaware County Surrogate's Court. The first, dated July 17, came from an attorney in Westchester:

> *I find by the* New York World *of this date that Edward Z. C. Judson of Stamford in your county died suddenly. At the request of Mrs. Kate M. Judson who claims to be his widow and the mother of four children by the said Judson whose names are as follows:*
>
> > *Mary Carrollita Judson, age 24 years*
> > *Irene Elizabeth Judson, age 22 years*
> > *Alexander M. Judson, age 20 years*
> > *Edwardina Judson, age 18 years*
>
> *The said Edward Z. C. Judson abandoned his family here in April 1869 and went to California and has ever since 1872 neglected to provide for his family here except once in a while he would send them a little money. Mrs. Judson wishes me to write you and say that*

if any will made by the said Judson is offered to probate or if any person applies to your Court for Letters of Administration, of the Estate of said Judson, that she and her children may be before you, and make said motions or file such objections as they may be advised.[3]

Next, on July 21, was one from a Sydney Algernon Bennett of New York City:

Dear Sir,

Will you kindly have me advised if any will is offered in letters of administration sought on estate of E. Z. C. Judson, deceased. I believe that my mother to whom he was married in '47 is lawfully entitled to dower in any real estate and would therefore like to appear in case probate is sought.[4]

One woman even came to Stamford in person to inquire about the writer's estate. On or about July 25, 1886, fifty-five-year-old Lovanche Kelsey Swart Judson arrived there from the hamlet of Acra, in nearby Greene County. The trip was forty miles by carriage and likely financed by friends, since she was very poor. It is likely friends paid for the attorney she hired too. This lawyer met with Lovanche and agreed to investigate her claim on the writer's estate, spurring local reporters and even a *New York Times* correspondent to take notice: "Ned Buntline's Estate: Two Widows in the Field for the Property" was one of its front page headlines on July 30. The "two widows" referred to Lovanche and the woman married to Edward when he died, Anna Fuller Judson.

It was natural for those who had known him—and those who had known *of* him, and millions did—to wonder how Edward Z. C. Judson had managed his affairs in life and in death. Between 1838 and 1886 he'd produced a seemingly endless number of books: *Mysteries and Miseries of New York; Sea Waif, or, the Terror of the Coast; Merciless Ben, the Hair-Lifter; Quaker Saul, the Idiot Spy; Old Sib Cone: The Mountain Trapper*, and on and on. Though he had owned (and lost) several literary magazines and wrote for newspapers, Judson's Western thrillers written for publishers Beadle & Adams proved to be extremely lucrative. As one historian said of the company's paperbacks, "They were more truly a gold mine than most of the mineral discoveries in the West," and Judson—writing, of course, as Ned Buntline—was quick to exploit this reputation.[5] Somewhere along the way, he earned the title "King of the Dime Novel."

Hyperbole aside, most scholars agree that Buntline was at least one of the top three or four most popular American writers of fiction of his time. While his works did not display the literary artistry of Mark Twain or Nathaniel Hawthorne, they certainly rivaled or even beat Twain or Hawthorne in terms of contemporary readership.[6] His fame was most certainly equal to that of Bret Harte or humorist Artemus Ward. "He was," said historian Clay Reynolds, "pretty much a 'household name' during his own lifetime, widely read and phenomenally popular."[7] Judson himself acknowledged that although he had set out to write highbrow works in his early years, he quickly came to another conclusion: "In my case, I found that to *make a living* I must write 'trash' for the masses, for he who endeavors to write for the critical few, and do his genius justice, will go hungry if he has no other means of support."[8]

Judson brought the American frontier into focus for the first time for many people with his tales of untamed lands west of the Mississippi and south to the Mexico border. He fed a growing reading public's love of the sensational by drawing on his past military service at sea, in the Seminole Indian War, and in the Civil War, and on various adventures in between. His themes were fairly simple. Guns spit fire and Indians drop. Wild rides through storms and danger brought rescue in the nick of time. His heroes were brave, keen, strong, and able to overcome insurmountable odds. His villains were entirely despicable, his heroines brave, beautiful, and entirely feminine.[9]

Judson's most famous creation was the folk hero Buffalo Bill. In late summer 1869, the writer met then-unknown scout William F. Cody in Nebraska on his way home from a temperance tour in California. He was looking for the officer who had defeated Cheyenne chief Tall Bull in the Battle of Summit Springs—an officer who was now recuperating at Fort McPherson. But the colonel did not wish to speak to any writers; undaunted, Judson went looking for someone else to take on the role of hero. He found him in a handsome twenty-three-year-old army scout named William Frederick Cody, whose life Judson portrayed in a series of "true" stories, starting with *Buffalo Bill: King of the Border Men*. "So cleverly did Buntline interweave fact with fiction," said one historian, "that even commanding generals testified to the truth of his accounts."[10]

According to legend, Buffalo Bill was a "straight-shooting, hard-riding, milk-drinking hero" who was the epitome of all virtue.[11] Cody himself admitted that he was intoxicated when he joined the army and that he had spurious claims to success at the battle of Summit Springs, where he took one of the shots that killed Tall Bull. But the American public was not interested in the truth, whatever it was. The masses had a new hero to love, and Ned Buntline was ready to capitalize even further. Seizing on inspiration, he wrote a play entitled *Scouts of the Prairie* as a starring vehicle for Cody. The play was savaged by critics (one Chicago reviewer called it "intolerable stench"), but for two years every performance in the Midwest and up and down the eastern seaboard sold out, with thousands attending each one. The publicity and authenticity that Judson created for Cody launched the scout's career in entertainment, and the stories and plays he wrote for Cody served as a template for Cody's later Wild West shows.

The men and women who inquired after Judson's estate that summer of 1886 had every reason to believe that he had reaped the financial rewards of an illustrious and prolific career. They also had reason to believe he might be benefitting from pension money—money earned from new legislation that allowed Civil War veterans to apply for a lump sum to help cover the loss of income by the inability to work because of illness or injury incurred during the conflict. "The hero of three wars and literally riddled with bullets," the *Pittsburgh Post* said of Judson in 1884, "he routinely resolutely declines to be placed on the pension list, and is content to pass the remainder of his days with rod and gun at 'Eagle's Nest,' one of the cosiest homes in this mountain-environed and surpassingly lovely village."[12]

But Judson did apply for an "invalid pension," though only a week before he died. According to his application, he had earned this annuity because he had been wounded in the groin and the head while serving in the navy in Key West in 1838–1840 and had also contracted yellow fever while there. Also, he purportedly suffered from wounds received during the Civil War.

Judson was too sick in July 1886 to do anything but scrawl a signature on the invalid pension application. Rather than the "model of muscular vigor" described by his obituaries, he was about two hundred pounds at five feet, eight inches tall. For months he had suffered from a weak heart, asthma, and edema so severe he was confined to a special chair.[13] The cost of his medical care may have been one reason his wife, Anna Fuller Judson, insisted he apply for the pension, late though it was.

Another reason was surely that Ned Buntline's fortune was considerably less than the public believed. At the time of his death, according to Anna, he left no personal property. In fact, she said, she had to borrow from friends to pay for his funeral. Judson listed a life insurance policy in his will, but it was false, Anna later testified—there was no policy, or at least he had never paid any premiums. To be sure, there was the mansion and all its furnishings and land . . . but Eagle's Nest was an expensive farm to maintain.

But Ned Buntline had been one of the most prolific writers in America, and his grandfather had been a substantial landholder, so naturally people assumed Anna would inherit a sizable amount. More importantly, Judson had made many promises of support to many women. He had married at least nine women and neglected to lawfully part ways with some while wed to others. At the time of his death, three were long dead; one was proudly divorced from him and would not even give their child his last name; and two simply remarried and never spoke of him again. But the last three wives—Lovanche, Kate, and Anna—all had good reason to battle over the writer's estate. All three of them had been emotionally and financially dependent on the novelist for decades. He had hurt all three of them emotionally and financially.

The *New York Times* headline about Lovanche and Anna compelled one anonymous citizen from Elizabeth, New Jersey, to write the Delaware court and explain that Lovanche's case should be dismissed immediately, for Lovanche had married Edward Judson long ago, and it was under false pretenses. The headline also spurred Kate, mother of four of Buntline's children, to bypass her attorney's niceties and pen a direct request on August 10, 1886:

> *I will promise to you that I am the only lawful wife of Edward Z. C. Judson. He married me from Chappaqua. . . . I do not <u>nor never did</u> think it an honor to be his wife. I wish to have my children rited. I have 1 boy and three girls & sent a man to go to your office last week. Instead, he went to Stamford and did not bring me the information.*

Moreover, Kate wrote, the woman "Lovantia [*sic*] Swart, styling herself Judson's wife, is a blackmailer and a bad egg."[14]

Anna, Judson's wife when he died, did not take kindly to either Lovanche or Kate when they came poking around for money after her husband's death. She believed her husband to have been properly divorced from both women and, moreover, that Judson had been paying Lovanche fifty dollars a month out of his good graces to just leave them alone. Anna had lived with Judson for the last fifteen years of his life, and the last ten of those were the most peaceful years of his existence. She gave him two children: daughter Irene, who died when she was four, and Eddie Jr., on whom the writer doted incessantly until the day he died. Though Anna was thirty years younger than her husband and not exactly his contemporary, the Fullers and the Judsons had lived in Stamford together for generations—they were constant attendees at each other's harvests, baptisms, weddings, and funerals. At times the Judsons and Fullers served as executors for one another's wills.

The would-be money-grubbers bothered Anna, but she was particularly angry at Lovanche. "The woman Lovanche L. Swart who claimed to have been married to my late husband Edward Z. C. Judson—he always said [she] was not his legal wife. She blackmailed him and did a great many things to annoy him and came here to Stamford after we were married and in fact wanted me to give her my husband's invalid chair after his death."[15] Moreover, Anna maintained, her late husband led her to believe that neither of his marriage ceremonies to Lovanche were legal ones. And it was Anna who had supported Judson's career with William Cody, not these other women. It was she who had supervised the building of their home in 1871 while Judson labored over stories of his new muse, Cody, and she who traveled the show circuit with the two of them.[16] And it was Anna who had nursed Judson when he got gout and heart problems the last five years of his life. While money was a pressing issue for Anna, she felt that her reputation and that of her dead husband and their living child were even more important.

Soon after Judson's death and after all the lookie-loos left Stamford, Anna thought she might have found a way to both preserve her husband's legacy and also derive some cash from his intellectual property. An old friend of Judson called on Anna sometime in August 1886. Eben Locke Mason, an antiques dealer and onetime publisher of *Ned Buntline's Own* magazine, convinced her that he could publish Judson's unfinished works and perhaps write a biography of the "deceased lion," which would include: "Sensations upon sensations—riots, rowdies, shootings, hangings, speeches, duels, fights, prisons (North and South), travels, dramas, yachts, wives, divorces, marriages, quarreling and a thousand and one condiments of this character will go together to spice a life that will furnish a dish for lovers of wild scenes among Indians, rough experiences on sea, and startling episodes ashore."[17]

Mason never published anything, but he did marry Anna. Apparently, Mason thought Anna had money and Anna thought Mason had money. They were both wrong. They went to Europe on their honeymoon and found that between them, they barely had enough money for the return trip.[18] Edward Judson's prolific and complicated past would continue to dog Anna Fuller even after her second husband and son, Eddie Jr., passed away.

Chapter Two

Creation of a Legend Maker

NEAR THE VILLAGE OF STAMFORD, NEW YORK, LIES MOUNT UTSAYANtha. It rises more than three thousand feet above sea level. Delaware tribes that inhabited the region said the peak got its name from the legend of a local Indian maiden and that it meant "beautiful spring." The maiden was said to have borne a child whose father was white, something that made her father, the chief, so furious he buried a tomahawk in the white man's skull and rowed with the baby to the center of a nearby lake and drowned it. Utsayantha followed her father to the lake and, in her despair, drowned herself too. Upon discovering what she had done, the legend says, the chief recovered her body and carried her up the mountain, where he buried her.[1]

The maiden's lone little grave was discovered in 1862, and so the story of Utsayantha was fresh in the minds of Stamford residents ten years later when the New York, Kingston & Syracuse Railroad built all the way through to the village. In the summer, the rail brought a constant stream of tourists and health seekers from Hartford, Providence, Boston, and New York City. Many who vacationed in Stamford hiked to see Utsayantha's grave marker because it was only two miles from the center of town, and was something to write about in a letter. From the peak of Utsayantha, with a good eyeglass, one could see Albany, and maybe even the Green Mountains of Vermont. Looking closer one would see strips of yellow birch, purple sugar maple, and green American beech stretching out for miles.

Stamford's high altitude gave it a remarkably healthy climate. In summertime the temperature was ten to fifteen degrees lower than New York City, without the seaboard humidity. The nights were always cool and free of fog. But the village was an unlikely destination before the rails got there because it was so far from the city or Albany or Buffalo. It was seventy-two miles from Kingston, a major depot at the entry to the Catskills, and not nearly as famous as the same-named city in Connecticut. Located near the source of the East Branch of the Delaware River, the village lay at the head of a broad agricultural valley.

This fertile valley in Stamford is what attracted E. Z. C. Judson's grandfather, Samuel, who purchased farmland there in 1789 and relocated his family from nearby Dutchess County. He was, by one account, an old-style farmer—"plain and homely" in his dress, and extremely thrifty. Here, in Stamford, seven years later, Judson's father, Levi Carroll, was born. Little is known about his younger years, but records show that he enlisted as a private in the War of 1812 and served with distinction.[2]

On May 1, 1817, the elder Judson married eighteen-year-old Sarah Ann Collings, a granddaughter of Richard Collings and Esther Zane, early settlers of Collingswood, New Jersey. Unfortunately, Sarah passed away just a few days after the pair's first anniversary. Shortly thereafter, Levi married Elizabeth Goodrich of Delaware County.

There really is no way to know whether Edward's mother was Collings or Goodrich. His name would seem to suggest the former, and it is possible she died giving birth to him. A marriage record has yet to be found for Levi and Goodrich, but it is well documented that by 1820, after a brief residence in Waterloo, New York, the senior Judson had moved with her to Stamford, where he found work as a schoolteacher and perhaps the financial security of being near relatives.

Both Edward Judson and his younger sister, Irene, took liberties with their birth dates over their lifetimes. The best estimate for Edward is sometime in the year 1821, probably March, and sometime in 1823–24 for Irene.[3] Regardless of what the date actually was, Judson liked to recall later in life that it was one wracked by a terrible storm, offering his own foreshadowing of a turbulent biography.

In the early 1820s, when the Judson children were tiny, Stamford was hardly more than a settlement, with a few houses, maybe a store and a wagon shop or two. Part of the village was called the "Devil's Half-Acre" because unscrupulous innkeepers charged outrageous prices, and because of the behavior of the rough men who traveled the turnpike on business, enjoying the tavern barrooms while stopping for the night.[4] Edward and Irene's life was not much different from that of their grandfather when he got there a quarter-century earlier. Homes sheltering families with twelve children were smaller than many "cottages" built by wealthy summer visitors in later years. Ed and Irene's mother did her cooking in the fireplace, while their father read and wrote by the light of homemade candles. To keep the people of Stamford in touch with the world outside the mountains, the stagecoaches and post riders brought newspapers with week-old news. Those who wished to bank their money also had to go by stage or horseback all the way to Catskill or Kingston.[5]

Levi had little interest in working his father's farmland. He tinkered with public works development projects in Delaware. He also dreamed of becoming an author, but by 1826 nothing he wrote had been accepted by a publisher, so he moved the family to Bethany, Pennsylvania, where he had been offered the job as principal for the Beech Woods Academy, a public school.[6] Levi purchased eight hundred acres of land next to a spot on the Lackawaxen River and built his family a modest house. The four Judsons plus Elizabeth's two maiden sisters traveled southwest for five days in a caravan consisting of two large wagons and four-horse teams, with most of the family tucked into a two-horse carriage in front. Young, redheaded Edward insisted on riding with one of the furniture wagons in the rear, riding up top with their trusted teamster friend, Mr. Champlain.[7]

The Judson's new home in Wayne County was ideal—it had a large, natural cold spring in which Edward learned to fish. The previous owner had built a sawmill near the house, which Levi used to clear the cherry and maple trees on his land—he sold this wood for extra money along with the oats and potatoes he grew on the land. When he was a little bigger, Levi took Edward to bigger streams and taught him how to cast a fly rod made of slender, well-seasoned ash with its bark peeled. Trout fishing remained a favorite pastime for Judson for the rest of his life. He also loved to spot the plentiful wildlife on their property, which included bears, deer, panthers, wolves, and his favorite, elk. He never stopped praising the majesty of these animals, even when he was once almost trampled by them when taking wheat to the gristmill for his father.[8]

Levi was strict—even by nineteenth-century standards—and whipped Edward often. The future writer was, by his own accounts, a spirited little boy (biographer Jay Monaghan aptly labeled him "cyclonic" at this age), but Levi was also distracted by his own pursuits and had little patience for his children. More than anything, Levi wanted to write books about the glory of the War of Independence, with which he was obsessed. Edward remembered a Fourth of July on the Bethany village green when his father assembled men to portray Revolutionary figures. "Papa Judson," wrote Monaghan, "stood on a platform, haranguing against redcoats, taxation without representation, and the tyranny 'that tried the souls of the patriots of '76.'"[9]

It seemed that the elder Judson also had a bit of a cruel streak. Edward recalled that when he was about six or seven years old, he and his Aunt Ann narrowly missed being mauled by a bear they had accidentally come upon. A few days later, Levi hid behind some hemlocks about a half mile from home, where he knew his son would pass on the bridle path that took the youngster to and from a post office miles away. When Edward passed by at dusk, Levi growled loudly and shook the bushes. Paralyzed with fear, the boy decided he could not run or go around the bushes, for surely the bear would catch him. "I brought my steel pointed cane down to a bayonet charge, and pushed right in spite of another terrific growl. The next instant when I was close up to the black looking object, my father burst out in a loud laugh." In fairness to Levi, this may have been a perfectly acceptable, nineteenth-century way to teach his dauntless son how to be more cautious.[10]

The Judsons loosely adhered to Presbyterianism—Levi's cousin was even a famous missionary who was routinely featured in major newspapers—but for the most part the elder Judson followed the tenets of Freemasonry. This caused some grief for the rest of the Judson family, because poor settlers in Bethany who could not afford membership in the fraternity complained that Masonic secrets were undemocratic— un-American, even—and they pointed to the Judsons as public nuisances, out of touch with hardworking Democrats.[11] Levi wrote articles for the local paper defending Masonry, and impressed upon his family that the Anti-Masonic Party that had formed in Wayne County was its enemy. The Judsons were, he maintained, fifth- and sixth-generation New Englanders, and therefore a superior people.[12]

In addition to teaching at Beech Woods, Levi made a little money growing millet for livestock. But apparently these endeavors were not enough to cover the land payments for his farm, and in 1834, when Edward was just on the verge of puberty, Levi had to declare bankruptcy.[13] He decided to move his family again—this time to Philadelphia, where he could study law. This was somewhat traumatic for Edward and Irene who, in spite of having few non-animal friends and being teased for being children of a Mason, cherished their freedom to roam. Later, during the Civil War, Edward wrote his sister wistfully from his camp in Scranton, Pennsylvania: "It is about 40 miles from here to the old Beech Woods farm where we spent our happiest days."[14]

In the early 1830s the Judsons removed to an elegant mansion on Girard Square, on Chestnut Street in Philadelphia. Edward later recalled that his father could often be found in his study, a room lined with shelves bending under the weight of "yellow-backed folios." [15] The elder Judson studied law and passed a test given by the Philadelphia Bar Association. He started practicing law in 1833 or 1834.

One cold morning in 1834 stayed with Edward the rest of his life. The youth and Levi got into an argument about whether Edward would continue his studies and follow him into law. The argument escalated into a blowup, ending with Edward throwing Levi's new set of law books into the lighted coal-grate in front of him. Levi allegedly responded by striking him hard across the face, recounted by Judson with flourish and his usual third-person form, popular at that time:

As you have seen a fleecy fore-running cloud, before a storm, linger an instant, then give place to one dark and ominous, so that first look left the father's face, giving place to one as black as the veil of Envy's soul; and his upraised hand came crushingly down on the youth's cheek, as falls the gardener's mattock on the fragile wild-flower. The boy tottered and fell at his father's feet, the blood gushing from between his pearly teeth, like the red wine from a marble press.

In return, Judson's story goes, he bade his father farewell.[16]

In truth, Judson would not say goodbye to his parents and sister for another three years or so. Records show that on August 4, 1837, he joined the US Navy as an apprentice on the frigate *Macedonia*.[17] He would have been sixteen or seventeen and not thirteen, as he claimed in later accounts. A short while later, in February 1838, Judson was a fully commissioned officer at the rank of midshipman.[18]

Judson's formal entry into the navy as a midshipman was a perfectly acceptable life path for a young, boisterous man who had little interest in formal schooling. But this was changing—in 1838 the US Navy began requiring men to attend the US Naval Academy (then in Philadelphia) and then serve two years as apprentices before they were eligible to become midshipmen. Without a doubt, Levi called in a favor to secure this position for his son, knowing these extra requirements would soon be implemented. This was a usual practice for men of influence who wanted a gentlemanly option for a child who may have had few other ones. Judson himself spent a great deal of time perpetuating the myth of how he acquired his midshipman status, most likely to distance himself from the notion that he did not exactly "run away" from an overbearing father. Perhaps the best retelling of Judson's early navy days was done by a friend, who pretended to interview a retired admiral who had allegedly served with Judson:

We were all boys together then, but Judson was the youngest of the lot and ought to have received more consideration. He was only thirteen years old when he was made a midshipman and sent among us. He had been a mere boy before the mast and had been promoted to be an officer. That's what made the trouble. The navy was very aristocratic—five times as aristocratic as it is now. Boys were appointed because their fathers were rich or distinguished or influential in some way, and it was rumored around that young Judson's folks weren't anybody, and that he had been appointed a midshipman for coolness and judgment in saving life when his gig was run over by a Fulton [New York] ferry-boat and he only a common sailor.[19]

The "ferry-boat" refers to an oft-repeated story about Judson's bravery that earned him the midshipman's commission. The story originated in Frederick Pond's biography:

He was large for his age, strong as a horse, and precocious. One day a boat for which he was coxswain was run over by a Fulton-ferry boat on the East river [New York], and upset in floating ice. She drifted down toward Governor's Island, in New York bay, and Judson managed to get ashore with the whole crew. Then he fainted under his injuries and was taken back to the Macedonian unconscious. The crew were so loud in their praises for rescuing a couple of them, that the officers united in a request to have him made a midshipman, and President [Martin] Van Buren sent on the commission within a fortnight.[20]

There's no mention of this act of bravery in Judson's military files, and no mention of a commission from President Van Buren. Nonetheless, Judson spent the next three years fighting courageously against Seminole Indians in Florida, engaging in many hazardous naval enterprises along its east and west coasts. These Seminole War experiences deeply affected the impressionable Judson. Some of his most popular, early literary examples were derived from this wartime service.[21] And it was during this time that Judson decided to acquire a nom de plume that linked him with this service and also allowed him to use a title separate from his father's surname: "Ned," a nickname for Edward, and "Buntline," a rope at the bottom of a square sail.

CHAPTER THREE

The Seminole War

Soon after the sun came up from his visit to the nether world, we entered into the "Pai-ha-okee" or "grass water," as it is termed by the Indians; which is an immense sea or level field of sawgrass, covered with fresh water, varying from eighteen inches to four feet in depth, rising from the innumerable springs in all parts of its vast extent.[1]

AT SOME POINT IN EARLY 1838, JUDSON TRANSFERRED FROM THE SHIP *Macedonian* to the *Levant* and set sail for Florida. Affairs along the southeast coast of this state in late 1838 had a decided effect on Edward Judson's writing career. They also gave him some personal experiences that formed his public character.

In all probability, neither the young Judson nor his various shipmates knew much about the complicated history of this southern tip of the continent that brought about the Second Seminole War and the navy's involvement there. This conflict was the last major one fought on US soil before the Civil War, and the early battlefield success of the Seminoles unnerved US generals, who worried it would spark a rebellion among Indians newly displaced by President Andrew Jackson's removal policies that forced them into central Florida.[2]

When Judson arrived in Pensacola in the spring of 1838, the military situation looked dismal to the United States' military personnel. By midsummer 1839, the majority of Seminole warriors in Florida had migrated to the Everglades region but still posed a danger to the military establishments along the coast and the keys.[3] They raided ships head-quartered on the New River, stealing food and supplies and murdering castaway crews and passengers. The most horrific encounter between the indigenous people and whites occurred in July 1839, when a band of Indians massacred a small detachment of Colonel William S. Harney's troops stationed on the west coast near the mouth of the Caloosahatchee River. Harney proclaimed that he would hang an Indian in retaliation for each of his killed men.

These atrocities strengthened the determination of the American government to rid Florida of the Seminoles. Thus the US Navy directed Lieutenant John T. McLaughlin to organize the Florida Squadron to protect mercantile interests along the southeast Florida coast and assist the army along inland waterways there. He established headquarters first at Tea Table Key and later at Indian Key, two tiny isles between the southern tip of Florida and Cuba. McLaughlin named his largest schooners *Wave, Flirt,* and *Otsego;* young Judson spent some time on all three ships but most of his three and a half years in the navy aboard the *Otsego.* He joined forays into the Everglades, which had never before been explored by whites.[4]

Judson wrote about some of these adventures a few years later, in the literary magazine he cofounded, the *Western Literary Journal and Monthly Magazine.* He would borrow from his Florida adventures for the rest of his life (all his stories that had to do with the sea can be directly or indirectly attributed to his time here), but the ones he drew most from personal experience were five that appeared in the *Journal.*[5] In two of these, Judson describes his experiences with Harney in a second expedition into the Everglades, commencing New Year's Day 1841. One of these was "A Chase in the Everglades":

> *For several days we passed through the "grassy water," without meeting anything worthy of particular note, except occasional signs of the cunning and ever watchful enemy, and had apparently reached the centre of the glade, as neither the main land or any islands were visible around us; not a speck in the green horizon to relieve*

the tiresome sameness of the prospect, save one tall palmetto tree, which stood alone, like a solitary watch tower in the desert rearing its leaf-crowned head and branchless trunk far above the level of the glades. . . . After some time, we began to perceive the superiority of our long oars, which, from having a fulcrum in the row-locks of the boat, enabled our men to work with more ease than the Indians could with their short paddles, thus, in a long race giving us a decided advantage. We had gained sufficiently upon them to observe and distinguish their force. From each canoe, the crimson-trimmed scalp-locks of three warriors waved tauntingly in the breeze, while the heads of several women and children peered up from over the low wales of the canoes.[6]

In "Indian Key: Its Rise, Progress and Destruction," Judson described another conflict, and also the natural environment in which it took place:

Formerly it was a barren rock, but, from its peculiar situation, having a fine "wrecker's" harbor, it was chosen for a residence by one Jacob Housman, who spent such care upon its improvements, that it soon became a miniature Eden. From its low moonlike surface, the lofty cocoa-nut tree arose, a green crowned monarch of tropical forestry— the date and fig trees blossomed and paid tribute, as did the orange and lemon; while, as man's rough footsteps crushed o'er grass and flowers, their perfume rose and mingled with the sweet sea breeze. The little island once but a coral rock, now lies in its acquired beauty, a variegated jewel in the pale green ocean, looking like a butterfly in a mud pond, a pretty portrait in a moldy frame, a lovely face in a dirty night cap, or, as a poet would say, an oasis in a desert, or a peerless gem in a leaden setting.[7]

In this particular story, Judson goes on to describe the attempted murder of Jacob Housman—a ship parts salvager—who had cheated the Seminole for years in trade and barely escaped with his life during a raid on his home on August 7, 1840. Judson is fairly sympathetic toward the Seminole and his own men alike in his recounting:

The Indians plundered the stores and buildings, and then set them on fire, burning all to the ground. They carried off several negroes belonging to Capt. Housman, and also some belonging to Charles Howe, Esq., the Postmaster of the place, and a worthy man. The attacking party was led by Chico and Chikika, two celebrated and bloody chiefs. They were supposed to consist of from two hundred to two hundred and fifty or three hundred in number.

I cannot pass by the gallant conduct of Francis Key Murray, a midshipman of the US Navy, who was left on Tea Table Key, one mile from Indian Key, in charge of the sick men, belonging to the Flirt. He had only eleven men with him, and all these were on the sick list, yet, as soon as he heard the alarm, he manned a barge on which was mounted a small four pounder, and taking a position near the island, opened fire upon the Indians, which killing one and wounded several others, caused the enemy to take their departure, immediately after having set fire to the houses. Mr. M. would undoubtedly have damaged the enemy much more, but on the third discharge of his gun it recoiled overboard, and he was compelled to retire. He aided in rescuing all that were saved of the inhabitants, and acted in the most humane and generous manner towards the destitute sufferers. His action, that of running a boat manned by only eleven men with the fire of two or three hundred Indians, impelled as he was by noble impulse and a wish to save all that he could from savage violence, should give him a lofty place in the consideration of his countrymen. In his boat, one man was mortally wounded and several others badly injured.

Indian Key was afterwards chosen as a government depot by Lieut. Com. J. T. McLaughlin, and occupied during the duration of the war.

Capt. Housman was killed about two months after the destruction of the island, while attempting to go on board a wrecked vessel in a heavy sea-way; being crushed between his boat and the side of the vessel.

Thus he lost his ill-gotten property and his own life, leaving behind nothing of any great value, not even a good name.[8]

Jacob Hausman's ordeal in Indian Key (the Indians set fire to his home, and his family barely escaped with their lives) brought McLaughlin's fleet there, and then to St. Augustine, where the family was treated. Judson was almost certainly with this emergency crew pulled from the *Flirt* and placed on the *Otsego* to help with the tensions in this colonial city. It was in St. Augustine that sailor Judson met the beautiful young woman who would become his first wife. The daughter of Francisco Marin, Severina Tecla was one of nine siblings and the granddaughter of Menorcans—colonists from the Balearic Islands located in the Mediterranean Sea and belonging to Spain. Judson took a leave of absence in the fall of 1841 to attend to some matters in New York. From there he wrote his commanding officer to ask for an extension of leave in order to visit a "relative" in St. Augustine who was "dangerously ill." He was granted the extension, and then married Severina on December 18, 1841, at the St. Augustine Courthouse. Judson was somewhere between eighteen and twenty years old, his bride a couple weeks shy of twenty-two years old.[9] Judson described Severina to readers a couple of years later:

Reader, I was about to conclude my yarn, but there is a little witch looking over my shoulder, who bothers me so that I cannot write. I'll describe her. As all of the witching kind does, she appears in the shape of a woman. In the first place, she's between eighteen and twenty years of age; tall—no she is not tall, nor is she short; but she is just a VENUSIAN height, her figure like that unto which Nature modeled, and then in anger broke the mould which formed it, because it excelled herself.

"Confound it, Madam!—good Lord! Mrs. Buntline!—let me alone!" There, reader, she has capsized the inkstand and pulled my

ears. My tale must close; there! she has blown out the light. God bless the ladies![10]

Judson resigned from the navy in May 1842 and took Severina north. He regretted leaving so soon, as evidenced by the letter he wrote the navy, begging to be reinstated:

Brooklyn, Long Island, NY
June 8, 1842

Sir,
I regret very much to trouble you again with my correspondence, but I have not yet received any answer to my former communication, the first of which was written on the 14th of May.

I beg to state that this delay subjects me to the greatest inconvenience inasmuch as I am living here at considerable expense without any income and am unable to form or execute any means of business until informed of the decision by the Department.

I am in a state of great anxiety and suspense, and my health is such that my physicians insist on a change of climate immediately, advising me to visit Florida or Cuba. If it is not too late to do so. I would most respectfully beg leave to withdraw my resignation as [I am] now obliged to look at my profession for support, having lately met with issues which thrown me upon my own exertions for the support of myself and my wife. I hope, sir, that my situation will excuse my troubling you so much, and by leave to express & hope that the Department will end my suspense by informing me of its decision.

I have the honor to be very respectfully,
Edward Z. C. Judson[11]

The navy declined to answer; Judson's honorable discharge stood.

As Florida historian Cooper Kirk aptly explains, Judson's lurid stories about the Second Seminole War "teemed with clichés, awful quotations, incorrect punctuation, irritating digressions, and downright fabrications."[12] But Kirk concedes that some of Judson's accounts of

Harney's expedition and events leading up to it can be corroborated by other sources, and also that he was able to include informative details that might otherwise have been lost to posterity.[13]

Judson's service was capable enough that the navy promoted him to acting lieutenant on the *Otsego* in late 1839, after he recovered from a debilitating case of yellow fever.[14] According to Judson, he needed to command respect from his shipmates because he was promoted to midshipman at such a young age. He reminisced about this time with biographer Pond:

> *They oftentimes insulted me and refused to mess [eat] with me because I had worked my way up. I never was a man disposed to command respect through love and fawning. If one, two, or three insulted me, I would knock them down. If they kept out of my way I would challenge them to a fight in the first harbor we landed. Often the very fact of the challenge commanded their respect and they would take measures to apologize before we reached a port. I have, however, been forced to command the respect of seven of my equals by meeting them in mortal combat, four of whom I wounded; with three others I exchanged shots, unharming or unharmed, but in every case receiving their apology.[15]*

There's nothing to support this and later accounts that Judson engaged in duels with his shipmates.[16] But it may be that hindsight is the best evidence: His lifetime was rife with quick-tempered, often violent actions, followed by little consequence.

CHAPTER FOUR

"The Captain's Pig" and a Problem in Nashville

JUDSON AND HIS FATHER SEEMED TO HAVE HAD A RECONCILIATION OF sorts after the former left the navy, because the fledgling writer surfaced in Pittsburgh in 1843. Levi had moved to Pittsburgh a couple of years earlier, where he began practicing law and finally published his own book. The younger Judson formed a surveying and engineering business with a friend; it dissolved within months.

Monaghan posits that Edward moved back into his father's household and the two pooled their resources to publish *Ned Buntline's Magazine*, which featured work from the two men. Levi's contributions were dry character studies of Revolutionary War figures; Edward's were more sensational tales from the sea. "The Captain's Pig"—a wild story that, if not entirely true, was at least partially based on his experiences in Florida—delighted readers with a comic narration of how the captain of his ship was ready to eat the pig he'd brought onboard, before Buntline tricked the captain and ate the pig himself.

Judson noticed that several publications were being printed in Cincinnati, and so in mid-1844 he left his father's home and took a boat down the Ohio River to seek opportunities there. Before he left, the fledgling writer sent copies of his self-published magazine to Lewis Gaylord Clark, the illustrious and snooty editor of *The Knickerbocker*, a literary magazine in New York City devoted to the arts, and one of the earliest vehicles for communication about the United States' "vanishing wilderness." [1] Clark had turned down "The Captain's Pig" a year earlier, but reconsidered when he saw the work in Judson's newspaper. "Take with you gentle winds your sails to swell, Mr. Buntline; and if the 'Old Knick' can serve your interests at any time, let him know the *how* and the *when*. That you will *deserve* encouragement and substantial patronage, is quite certain." *The Knickerbocker* subsequently picked up Edward's story "Running the Blockade," and seemingly overnight, he became a minor literary sensation in the city.[2]

In Cincinnati, Judson met Lucius A. Hine, a law student. Four years Judson's senior, Hine also wanted to become part of a more upper echelon of literary society. For months he had been editing a magazine that, for all its serious patriotic intent, had failed to make money. The two men saw an opportunity to combine their talents—Judson's more sensational, entertaining style that sold copies with Hine's more serious political analysis. It was time, Judson thought, for a Western city to have a more serious journal to compete against those of the eastern seaboard. A decade earlier, Edgar Allan Poe had capitalized on sectional pride by starting the *Southern Literary Journal*; why shouldn't the Ohio Valley have one? Hine agreed to supply one thousand dollars to start the venture, while Judson agreed to supply his name and five hundred dollars—as soon as he could raise it.[3] The paper born of this union was the *Western Literary Journal and Monthly Review*, which debuted in November 1844.

The *Western Literary Journal* was aimed at the casual reader, devoted more to literature, poetry, and art than toward politics. Between contributions by more established, erudite writers, Judson—writing as Ned Buntline—placed some of his own stories, nautical in nature. Monaghan notes that "The Last of the Buccaneers; a Yarn of the Eighteenth Century" must have seemed to readers like a title copied from the contemporary *Last of the Barons* by Edward Bulwer-Lytton and the *Last of the Mohicans* by James Fenimore Cooper.[4] Judson and Hine made an effort to feature female writers whenever possible; for example, they helped Julia L. Dumont gain recognition as a premier writer of the Mississippi Valley.[5] Writing as E. Z. C. Judson, he either praised writers or trashed their works, as he did with J. H. Ingraham and his new book, *The Midshipman; or, the Corvette and Brigantine*. "Ned Buntline, at twenty-one," observed Monaghan, "was enough of a writer to know that no man could turn out so many books—except rubbish."[6]

Judson was restless after the excitement of publishing the first issue of the *Journal* (it would take at least a month for reviews to come in). Severina still had not joined him from Pittsburgh; also, he faced the specter of not yet having enough subscribers to the *Journal* to make it profitable. He decided to again hop a riverboat and sail down to Eddyville and Smithland, Kentucky, where he would presumably find more subscribers, or investors, or excitement, or all of this. He most certainly made his way down to Nashville for a spell, where he picked up third investor Hudson Kidd, a recent college graduate who wanted to be in the magazine business. Kidd must have sufficiently contributed financially, because he ordered that the *Journal* move its headquarters from Cincinnati to Nashville; Hine and Judson accommodated this request. Meanwhile, Judson had Severina move from Pittsburgh to Smithland, where he checked her into the Gower House, a 1780s inn at the junction of the Cumberland and Ohio Rivers.

On January 25, 1846, friend George Allen stopped in Smithland, on his way back to Cincinnati from Nashville on his steamboat *Cicero*. Here he learned about the passing of Severina, Edward's wife:

> *Just passed Smithland—I went up for Mrs. Judson & they told me <u>she was dead</u>—What a change—a few days ago I spoke so cheeringly to her of her visit to our home—and now she is gone—"Truly thy ways are inscrutable Oh God"—I shall always remember with satisfaction my friendship for her—I can truly say now in this place that I always endeavored to act kindly towards her—I can imagine I saw her at Cincinnati at Dr Waldos and I never went up there at any hour of the night that I found her setting up by Edward's side.[7]*

Judson did not travel back to Kentucky for any funeral or memorial for Severina. The Allens' letters of condolence to him went unanswered until finally Edward wrote to George Allen to explain why he could not provide any details: "I cannot write to you now—<u>for my heart is in my wife's grave and I cannot dig it up</u>."[8] William Allen's journal entry from about the same time notes that in spite of his grief, Judson wrote some "good pieces" for his paper, though he was distracted and tired, and told another passenger that he was sorry he'd neglected Severina.[9]

The Allens probably buried Severina at some cost, which may have tested the limits of their friendship with Judson. Rumor had it that Severina had either borne Judson a son or was pregnant with one—this rumor is substantiated by the recollection and testimony of Judson's second-to-last wife, Kate Myers. Some hundred years later, former slave Frank Leffler of Smithland told a newspaper reporter friend of his about a macabre incident from his youth. Cemetery authorities hired Leffler and an older friend of his to dig graves, and once while doing so, the pair came upon an older coffin in an unmarked spot. They opened it in order to try to figure out whose body they needed to move elsewhere. Leffler noted that the remains were fairly well preserved. They were female and still had long, dark hair and some jewelry and clothing. Leffler remembered the tragic stories of Mrs. Judson that he had heard as a little boy in his tiny town and recalled the rumor that she had been buried on this particular hillside. Fearing they would lose their pay if they did not bury her in a timely manner, the pair decided just to dig the hole a little deeper and pack the newer body on top of Severina's.[10]

Judson decided to make Nashville his new home. It was an exciting place to be in the 1840s. Judson may have been there when Andrew Jackson died at his plantation, The Hermitage, on June 8, 1845, and he might have been in town when city officials laid the cornerstone for the new, permanent capitol building on July 4, 1845. This building would, within a few years, become symbolic of Nashville's maturing culture. Nashville then boasted turnpikes, stagecoaches, and steamboats, and sometimes the luxury of ice shipped in from western lakes. Travelers could get from Nashville to New York City in a record-breaking six days.[11] On summer evenings the streets were crowded with people, some on horseback, some in expensive carriages, others in plain buggies, but all well-dressed.[12] Judson liked to socialize at the famous City Hotel in Nashville proper, where, thirty years before, Missouri senator Thomas Hart Benton and Andrew Jackson had fought viciously.

At age twenty-four, Ned Buntline now needed to reinvent himself. He had already made and buried a family and had failed twice in the newspaper business (The *Journal* had failed financially, and he had left Hine and Kidd with the bills.) In March 1846 a story appeared in *The Knickerbocker* that served as an explanation, or distraction, for why he was not with Severina during her decline. It was submitted by an anonymous "new contributor" writing from Nashville and dated November 25, 1845:

> By the way, NED passed through here this morning, on his way to Gallatin [Tennessee], thirty miles distant. Being on a visit to Eddyville (Ky.,) a few days since, he heard that three persons, charged with having committed an atrocious murder near Gallatin some point since, were in the woods in the neighborhood. Arming himself, NED "put out" in pursuit of them, alone. He soon overtook them, when two of them surrendered, after a short resistance. These he tied to trees, and then went on in pursuit of the other, who had absconded in the meantime. But the fellow had too good a start; and NED, after firing one or two shots after him, gave up the chase. He arrived here with his two captives last night in the steamer, and as I said before, went on to Gallatin with them this morning. He has entitled himself to the reward of six hundred dollars which had been offered for their apprehension.[13]

It is highly likely that Judson himself was this "new correspondent" and that the story was fiction. The story of the three criminals' capture appears in the *Tri-Weekly Nashville Union*, but it does not mention the novelist.[14]

While he still published occasional articles in *The Knickerbocker*, Judson needed more money on which to live and decided to resurrect a version of *Ned Buntline's Magazine* with new features that would make it "the sensation of the age."[15] Nashville could be his fresh start. At steamboat wharves he posted broadsides announcing his new publication, *Ned Buntline's Own*. One of the features he planned for this new paper was a guide to help travelers avoid gambling pitfalls and confidence games. It would not be a series of cautionary tales but rather a column in which he promised to print the names of notorious gamblers, the details of their crooked games, and the names of the steamboats on which they operated. "This was dangerous business," wrote Jay Monaghan, "but Ned professed not to care what the gamblers might do to him."[16]

Fortunately for Edward, his blackmail scheme did not result in any bodily harm. But he soon found trouble of a different nature.

Judson seemed to have just enough money at this time to buy some flashy clothing and swagger around the social scenes of downtown Nashville. One evening during the week of Christmas in 1845, the writer sauntered into a church bazaar wearing an unseasonable but lovely Spanish cloak and Panama hat. Here, Mary Figures Porterfield, the nineteen-year-old wife of an auctioneer's assistant, presided over a picture gallery, charging twenty-five cents for the benefit of the First Baptist Church.[17] She was beautiful, and Judson immediately started chatting with her in the hopes of getting some news for his magazine.

Those who testified in the criminal trial of Edward Judson in March 1846 and in the church's trial of Mary Porterfield in July 1846 recounted the events that followed over the next few months. Both Judson and Porterfield strongly denied many of these accounts.

It all began shortly after Judson and Mrs. Porterfield met at the church fund-raiser. At that time, Robert and Mary Porterfield were lodging at the home of Charles Clay Trabue, a wealthy American banker, Whig politician, and, until a few years prior, mayor of Nashville. Trabue's son, Anthony, then twenty, recalled that Mary had asked him to introduce her to young men as if she were a single woman, and that Judson had been one of those young men. She wished, according to Anthony, to talk about literature with someone, especially the works of Thomas Moore and George Gordon, Lord Byron.[18]

During the holidays, Nashville people "masked" in the streets, wearing costumes and reveling in public avenues, similar to Mardi Gras in New Orleans today. At Trabue's boardinghouse, the guests noticed that sometimes Mrs. Porterfield joined the merrymakers without her husband. Monaghan's account is a good summary of what happened over the next couple of weeks:

Later he sent still another [letter] to Mary, signed El Strangero—she relished Spanish as he taught it to her. Some nights later boys found Ned with a woman in the alley behind the Episcopal church. They pelted the couple with rocks. Ned covered his companion with his cloak and escaped. The boys were not sure that the woman was young Mrs. Porterfield, but the story set the neighbors' tongues wagging.[19]

Judson tried to join parties at the Trabue household disguised as a fortune-teller, but Clay and Julia Trabue already felt that the novelist might have designs on Mary Porterfield and refused to let him in. Over the next couple of months, rumors reached the point that Robert Porterfield could no longer ignore them. On March 11, 1846, the twenty-four-year-old Porterfield waited on Capitol Hill, a main thoroughfare Judson was likely to cross at some point during his day. The young husband pulled out a pistol, pointed it at Judson, and accused the writer of improper relations with his wife. Edward vigorously denied the charge, and passersby overpowered Porterfield and helped calm him down.[20] But later that night at the Porterfield home—they had left the boardinghouse—Robert sat in the parlor with the minister of their Baptist church, Reverend Isaac Paul. Outside in the dark they heard someone whistling a "merry air." They also heard Mary's steps hurrying along the hall toward the door. Robert called out to her; she stopped and came into the lighted room. Her husband and the minister both lectured her sternly, even as she pleaded innocence to hearing the whistling outside.[21]

According to Paul, who later testified against Mary Porterfield's virtue, it was the next day—Thursday, March 12, 1846—when Mary and Judson's assignations became very clear to him. He and a friend noticed Judson walking over a hill with a female, so they followed the same path and came upon the novelist and Mary standing face to face in the city graveyard in deep conversation. He described this particular section of the cemetery as very remote, with high cedar picketing on either side so that it was difficult for people to see in, and he considered it "a very much out-of-the-way place." Paul cleared his throat a bit to make his presence known, he recalled, and the pair whirled away and began walking toward the back of the graveyard toward town, "their elbows and clothes touching," until they separated at the Nashville turnpike. Paul followed Mary, and when she arrived at a friend's house, he lectured her about spending time with Judson. "I told her I was fearful that this evening's work would settle in the minds of the people her guilt, and that it was a most unfortunate and imprudent thing for her; for I believed the people were beginning to think favorably of her but now they would settle down in their minds that she was guilty" of adultery.[22]

Paul gave Mary the benefit of the doubt. She told him she was going to talk to her husband about all of these misunderstandings. After all, she reminded him, their baby daughter, who had died of smallpox in February, was buried there—she went there often. Paul implored her not to speak with Robert about all these misunderstandings. In fact, when Porterfield asked Paul if he had ever seen anything improper between the two, the reverend said "No!" It was so unfortunate, Porterfield remarked to the older man, that Judson continued to follow his wife around and throw himself in her path. After all, he had no doubt as to her innocence, and even gave her a ring with the word "confidence" engraved on it.[23]

Mary ignored Paul's warnings and approached her husband about the topic after he came home from work on Friday, March 13. Robert believed her. And Paul reassured him that townspeople would surely expel "the wretch" Judson eventually.

No one really knows exactly what led up to the murder the next day. According to Monaghan, a group of Porterfield's friends, including his brother John, came to his house and urged him to kill Edward. Other reports say that after thinking about things, Porterfield decided he simply did not believe his wife.[24] Whatever the case, on the evening of March 14, Porterfield took a pistol down to Sulphur Spring, a popular area for picnicking and recreation about a mile from the capitol building. It could not have been coincidence that Judson was there with two pistols.

Porterfield shot at Judson three times, while his companions applauded. None of the bullets hit their mark. Judson fired once, and Robert Porterfield fell face down in the dirt. He was not quite dead yet, but the bullet had pierced his forehead right above his right eye—it was just a matter of time. John Porterfield and his friends carried Robert to town. Some reports say Judson gave himself up to the sheriff; others say he hid but was found. Either way, he was arrested. Shortly after that, around eleven o'clock that evening, Robert Porterfield mercifully passed away. The news of Porterfield's death spread through Nashville like wildfire:

> *The public mind, wound up to a pitch of deep and maddening excitement, was in a condition to be thrown off its balance. Here was a young man in the prime of manhood (he was not yet thirty years of age), the dutiful and affectionate son of a widowed mother—a tender, confiding and devoted husband—most exemplary and highly esteemed in all the relations of life—first stricken to the heart by his wife's dishonor, as was believed, and then shot through the head by the author of the destroyer of his happiness.*[25]

That same evening of March 14, 1846—or perhaps in the early hours of March 15—Sheriff Churchill Lanier brought Judson to the courthouse for examination by Isaiah Ferriss, justice of the peace for Davidson County. Furious and curious onlookers packed the room and anterooms, even at this late hour.

Just as Ferriss started to ask some questions, a man in the crowd cried out, "Make way for John Porterfield! Let him kill Judson!"[26] Robert's brother jumped over the railing behind the bar and headed toward the clerk's box, where Lanier held Judson. The sheriff jumped out of the box to head off Porterfield, but the latter pushed his way through the throngs and fired twice at Judson with his revolver. He missed both times, but the crowd became even more aroused, and Judson—no fool—took advantage of the chaos and ran as fast as he could out of the courthouse, his red locks flying behind him.

John Porterfield chased the writer down the steps of the city building, firing every so often. One bullet grazed Judson's head but just scratched him. Judson ran to the City Hotel, and even though some men tried to block Porterfield, he kept fairly close behind. Judson ran up the hotel's staircase but, once he reached the third floor, realized he had nowhere else to go.[27] He tried to escape by sliding down the posts of a balcony, but he slipped and fell to the ground. He broke one leg and slipped into unconsciousness for a few minutes.[28] The sheriff caught up to Judson while he lay in front of the hotel and, with the help of a couple of other men, took him to jail. It seemed that Judson was probably near death, so keeping him comfortable and confined was the best thing to do at this point.

John Porterfield and his mob did not agree. As soon as Judson was locked up again, a bunch of men broke into the jail, stripped Judson of his clothes, and hauled him out to the city square, intending to hang him. The writer begged for a minister and also for a gentleman to please shoot him instead of subjecting him to such a painful ordeal. The mob ignored both requests, put a noose around his neck, dragged him to a nearby building, and threw the other end of the rope over the awning. According to some accounts, someone friendly toward Judson either cut him down or pre-cut the rope so that it snapped with Judson's weight. Whatever the case, Judson fell unhanged, and the mob's adrenaline dissipated. Deputies took Judson back to jail to recover for a second time. This time, he was left alone.[29]

Mary Porterfield was not so lucky—at least not emotionally. The First Baptist Church of Nashville, of which she had been a member since she was a little girl, deemed it necessary to investigate the case insofar as her reputation was concerned. "During the excitement," wrote the *Nashville Union*, "which prevailed in the popular mind in consequence of the lamented death of Mr. Robert R. Porterfield, by the hands of E. C. Z. [*sic*] Judson, the newspapers contained many allusions to the causes of that unfortunate and tragical affair, which were well calculated to fix a stain upon the character of Mrs. Porterfield."[30] Her friends, according to the article, found it prudent to wait until public discourse about the events quieted down.

On June 4, 1846, Mary Porterfield wrote to her church from rural Logan County, Kentucky, where she had moved temporarily to avoid the notoriety that came with her husband's murder and all the related events. She was despondent over the church's announcement that it was planning a trial of its own to decide whether she should remain within its membership for engaging in "falsehood" and "improper intimacy with E. Z. C. Judson," which resulted in the death of her husband. It read, in part:

> *I am wholly at a loss to know what "falsehood" it is, that is to be arrayed against me. I do not claim for myself, that I never uttered a falsehood, but I do deny, most positively, ever to have uttered a falsehood, with the wicked and malicious desire, of stamping infamy, or disgrace upon another; and had others, learned in the same school, in which I have been taught, to bridle their tongues, and refrain from malice, envy,* evil surmising, *and evil speaking, I should not have fallen as their unfortunate victim. . . . As to the charge of improper intimacy, with Mr. Judson, I only have to say, that I regret, exceedingly regret, that I ever saw the man, but being introduced to me, as he was, as a gentleman of high literary attainments, and observing him hold converse with gentlemen, and visiting families of high moral character, and standing in society, and all my life, having had a partiality for literary characters, I was imperceptibly led (not conscious at the time that harm* could *grow out of it) to tolerate, and receive such attention from him . . . in this I erred, for which I am heartily sorry, and with confidence, do appeal to my Brethren and Sisters . . . and sorely regret, that I ever saw the man (Judson). . . . I deny most positively any criminal intercourse with him (or any other man) either in thought, word, or deed.*[31]

Pitifully, Mary pleaded for church elders to return her son, Frank—her only remaining child—whom they took from her "by stratagem and wicked device" and refused to give back to her. Frank's paternal grandmother raised him to adulthood.

On April 16, 1846, the Tennessee state attorney general ordered Judson released from prison in Nashville. The bulk of the criminal court files from the city at this time are no longer extant but for a summary in an index that says no prosecutor appeared to present a case against him. Given Judson's constant exhortations that he shot Porterfield in self-defense and the fact that he had been so injured by John Porterfield's actions, it seems likely that a jury might not have convicted him anyway. Even more likely, the city may have decided another riot might occur if Judson were the center of another spectacle. Whatever the case, "Ned Buntline" quietly and immediately slipped out of town on the steamboat *California* bound for Pittsburgh, where his father resided.

Mary Porterfield gave birth to a baby girl on October 6, 1846. Assuming she was full term, the baby would have been conceived in early to mid-January 1846. Mary gave her baby the Porterfield surname, but she did not introduce the little one to her husband's family—either because she was afraid they would take the baby or because she did not resemble her father, or both.

CHAPTER FIVE

"That Odious Rascal"

AFTER THE EVENTS OF NASHVILLE, JUDSON SPENT A FEW WEEKS IN
Pittsburgh with his family. He had only seen sister Irene briefly since she
got married there in 1843, and he needed to rest the leg he had broken
in his fall from the Nashville hotel. He also carried his left arm in a sling.
Judson noticed that the Eastern papers were arguing about his escapade
in Tennessee, but one profusely defended his actions: the *Spirit of the
Times*, a sports and entertainment paper headquartered in New York.
Judson decided to meet the editors of this popular periodical, as well
as Lewis Gaylord Clark, editor of *The Knickerbocker*, who had started
exclaiming the merits of Judson's stories.

According to one source, Judson first went to Philadelphia with
friends, on a yacht he claimed to own. "Upon landing he proceeded to
Guy's famous drinking house, in Seventh-street, above Chestnut, and
there he announced himself Ned Buntline. 'Gentlemen,' he said, 'I am
Buntline, and if any body wants to see me particularly, why, you may
just say that I'm here.'"[1] But he wasn't for long. The fledgling novelist
sailed his new vessel to New York Harbor and moored it there. "The
Ned Buntline," wrote the *New London Democrat*, "is said to be one of the
finest Schooners ever built in this vicinity. Success to her, and may she
float as triumphantly upon the saline wave as does her namesake upon
the wave of popular literature."[2]

In New York, Judson wined and dined with the "new" class of writers
and editors, but still found himself outclassed. These new acquaintances—
Clark, sports editor William T. Porter, British novelist Henry William
"Frank Forester" Herbert—talked in the "leisurely language of Pope and
Addison," and used Shakespeare and Milton to express every idea.[3]

The redheaded writer wandered around the city looking for things to write about. His father had just written a new book that contained homespun philosophy and emphasized the correct way to raise boys and the importance of religion, virtue, and discipline. It also contained dry biographies of the signers of the Declaration of Independence. "Ned" wondered if this was what he should be writing about, and experimented by writing a poem about Aaron Burr.[4] He experimented in the *Spirit of the Times*, proffering futuristic visions of technology such as the "electric telegraph," which would prevent "rogues and highwaymen" from escaping: "I wonder," he concluded, "if we will not have *conversation wires* before long, instead of being obliged to send written communications."[5] Still, no ardent following.

In his Judson biography *The Great Rascal*, Monaghan posits that Judson must have asked himself how others made a living at writing. Could it be that they pirated from one another and followed certain patterns? Edgar Allen Poe, for example, had written a great crime story called "The Mystery of Marie Rogêt" after a real cigar salesgirl, Mary Rogers, had been murdered at the St. Nicholas Hotel in 1842. Two years later, Joseph Holt Ingraham had written one of his novelettes about a similar cigar girl—so popular that he wrote a sequel the next year. And Poe followed his up with *The Murders in the Rue Morgue*. "Impossible realism was what the people wanted, it seemed" Monaghan theorized, "but Ned hesitated to debase himself. He would struggle along with the 'letter.'"[6]

Still, Judson preferred not to chase literati and the classics so much as talk to soldiers milling around the city—soldiers preparing to head southwest to fight in the Mexican-American War. He took copious notes. He also studied the clerks and common workers who went to "reading rooms"—informal libraries—before and after work and saw that they were crowded with poorly-dressed, unfussy people who read tattered, cheaply printed books. Lastly, Judson noticed that novelists George Lippard, Jasper C. Neal, and Ingraham—who wrote about the debauchery of big cities and the plight of working-class men—seemed to be selling books faster than they could write them.

And so, in early 1847, having burned most of his financial and ethical bridges in the Ohio River Valley and the South—and thus far unable to find a book publisher for himself in New York—Judson decided to make his way to Boston. There, he thought, he could start fresh, present his ideas to its publishing houses, and explore a career writing less-serious works.

By all accounts, Judson's move to Boston was a good one for his literary career. He sold a few nautical-themed short stories to local papers, and—encouraged—sat down to write *The Last Days of Calleo; or, the Doomed City of Sin*, which the Jones Publishing House sold to soldiers, who put it in their knapsacks to take with them to Tampico or Veracruz. A month later, Gleason House publishers announced they'd print Ned Buntline's *The King of the Sea: A Tale of the Fearless and Free*, which proved to be so popular that it was printed and reprinted over and over until 1860 and even pirated by a British publishing company.[7]

Continuing to capitalize on his service with the navy, Judson wrote what must have been a scathing rebuke of Commodore Matthew C. Perry in the short-lived New York *Daily Mail*. In March 1847 Perry had begun court martial proceedings against an officer for advancing too quickly upon the city of Alvarado in Mexico, allowing its residents to burn all its supply houses, set its horses free, and flee before the US fleet could arrive and fully capture the city. It was a rather big scandal in the spring of that year, and no doubt Judson wished to weigh in for his readers. In response, naval captain John H. Aulick circulated a report that called Judson "a broken midshipman," guilty of misconduct before the enemy, and "slanderous." Aulick's most egregious charge against Judson's writing, though, was that he tried to remain "anonymous" by hiding behind a nom de plume.

In a move that was either bizarre or brilliant, Judson angrily wrote Aulick, demanding that the latter open a court of inquiry against him so that he could present evidence that showed his article to be solidly reported. Furthermore, he said:

I am no anonymous scribbler—the name of "Ned Buntline" has appeared in the best magazines and reviews of the times for the last four years, and in numerous works of romance—his pen has fought steadily and long in the columns of the Boston Times, *and other* *sterling <u>administration</u> papers for the cause of democracy—and I am as well known under that <u>nom de plume</u> as I am under my own name. Besides Sir, the private letters written to yourself, Com. Perry, etc., were written in the presence of several of the first literary men of this city—seen and mailed with the postage <u>paid</u> by the publisher of the* Mail; *this certainly does not look as if I wished to shield myself under an anonymous signature.*[8]

No doubt this was a publicity ploy for Judson. Had the navy acquiesced to this demand, the writer would have been hard pressed to provide any inside knowledge of the events of which he wrote, but his name would have been in every newspaper. He was counting on the fact that the military would ignore him, which they did, and Judson would then have license to say they were afraid of his inquiries—which he likely did.

Judson had another reason for all these machinations. He sent copies of all the correspondence between him and Aulick to John Y. Mason, secretary of the navy, in Washington, DC. He requested "to have a copy of anything and everything that is filed on the records of the Department in regard to myself, favorable or unfavorable. . . . I am determined now, sir, since so much has been said and done in this matter, that the <u>true</u> life of the whole affair shall come out. I regret to trouble you so much—but <u>justice</u> to all parties involved demands this course."[9] Judson's copy of the letter he sent Aulick contained a not-so-subtle threat to Mason: "I must say that either you or the records or both are in error in regard to my resignation from the Navy. I shall at once take means to ascertain the nature of those records and through my excellent friend and <u>then</u> Commander, Captain [James McKay] McIntosh to have them corrected if they are not so."[10] In his letter to Aulick, Judson emphatically denied any misconduct before the enemy during his naval service—clearly, he was afraid his resignation in the files might be supplemented with such an accusation.[11]

In 1847 the Boston publisher and dime-novel author Maturin Murray Ballou paid Judson one hundred dollars to write *The Black Avenger of the Spanish Main; or, The Fiend of Blood: A Thrilling Tale of Buccaneer Times,* a melodramatic and violent pirate novel. This sold so well that Ballou contracted with Judson with for a similar one: *The Red Revenger; or, The*

Pirate King of the Floridas: A Romance of the Gulf and Its Islands. Both stories were still being printed forty years later; Mark Twain even put one of them in *The Adventures of Tom Sawyer,* in which his boy hero imagined he could run away to find adventure in the far corners of the world, and then come back home to the wonder of all his family and neighbors:

> *How his name would fill the world, and make people shudder! How gloriously he would go plowing the dancing seas, in his long, low, black-hulled racer,* the Spirit of the Storm, *with his grisly flag flying at the fore! And at the zenith of his fame, how he would suddenly appear at the old village and stalk into church, brown and weather-beaten, in his black velvet doublet and trunks, his great jack-boots, his crimson sash, his belt bristling with horse-pistols, his crime-rusted cutlass at his side, his slouch hat with waving plumes, his black flag unfurled, with the skull and crossbones on it, and hear with swelling ecstasy, the whisperings, "It's Tom Sawyer the Pirate!—the Black Avenger of the Spanish Main!"*[12]

Gleason House picked up Judson's novelette *The Volunteer, Or, The Maid of Monterrey,* which featured a protagonist who disguises herself as a soldier during the Mexican War and falls in love with another soldier from Kentucky. In *The Volunteer,* Judson gave his male hero the name "Blakey," an homage to Mary Porterfield's defense attorney in Nashville. Throughout the rest of his career, Judson peppered his works with personal references meant to reward those who supported him in some way or whom he admired—or punish those who spoke against him.

These works and various poems and short stories were the extent of Judson's involvement in the Mexican War, despite claims of some biographers that he served in the military there. It's easy to understand the confusion, given that he generated so many works set against the backdrop of both the Seminole Wars and the Mexican War, and the fact that decades later, two decorated veterans "remembered" serving in the same regiment with him.[13] In 1848 Judson capped off the bulk of his seafaring adventures with a compilation of all his "yarns" in that genre. *Cruisings, Afloat and Ashore, from the Private Log of Ned Buntline* was a whopping

380 pages, yet so compact and printed on such thin, cheap paper that it could still fit into a man's pocket. "Compact as a brickbat," *Cruisings* contained variations of "The Captain's Pig," "The Race on the Bahama Banks," and many more nautical tales, plus a few new poems and sketches like "The March-Born" and "Who the De'il is Buntline?" which extolled the importance of the author and was meant to build up his name in the minds of the reading public.[14]

In fact, Ned Buntline was already well known to the general public by the end of 1847. While he had been carving out a fiefdom within the "literature for the masses" genre, Judson had also been flirting with a woman named "Laura Lovell" in the *Boston Daily Times*. One of his poems— "Things I'd Love," about a humble man looking for a humble life and wife and family in Boston—earned some romantic prose in response from Lovell. On October 14, 1847, Buntline responded to Laura in the *Times*, bemoaning the fact that his serious writing earned "so scant a sum to me 'twould scarcely buy my pony's grain," and therefore he would not be able to properly support a family.[15]

It was likely lack of funds that drove Judson back to New York City in November 1847. One contemporary source maintains that the writer neglected to pay his hotel bill in Boston and, moreover, squired a young woman back with him, only to desert her and leave her with the room bill.[16] But Judson now had a significant portfolio of writing under his belt and was popular enough that he felt he could approach New York publishing houses with confidence and steer his career. He rented an office at 309½ Broadway and began writing.

The first week of January 1848, Judson self-published the first of five installments of *The Mysteries and Miseries of New York: A Story of Real Life*. He wrote these volumes to explore and exploit his interest in social reform and to build on his rapidly growing celebrity. He did this, as cultural historian Michael Denning puts it, "by telling tales of criminal underworlds, urban squalor, and elite luxury and decadence." As part of that project, Buntline represented poor sewing girls persecuted by "fashionable young *gentlemen*, sons of the 'first families'"; a prostitute with a heart of gold; a clerk who is tempted to embezzle from his employer to support his gambling habit; and a dizzying array of other urban types. In order to condemn urbanization, he also singled out for particular criticism spaces in which working-class blacks and whites mingled, included several representations of foreign-born criminals, and added an appendix that blamed immigrants for increases in urban crime.[17] Part exposé, part diatribe, but mostly melodramatic hyperbole loosely based on facts, his announced intention was to warn the general public about the deadly pitfalls of various gambling and drinking establishments in Manhattan.[18] His detractors begged to differ:

> *The* pretence *for such a literature has been* "reform," *while the* real *object has been* "Black Mail." *Granting, however, that reform* was really *intended, we have yet to ascertain how it was to be accomplished by pointing out to young men* where *gambling is carried on, or to wives and daughters,* where *assignation houses are located? Can any really reflecting mind believe that such dreadful evils are compensated by the hypothetical good these reformers jabber about?*[19]

This critic missed the point: *Mysteries*, like most of Ned Buntline's works, was not meant to be a primer, like his father's books. It was meant to entertain while delivering a message. Judson didn't even pretend that his book's title was original—it was clearly patterned after Eugène Sue's *Mysteries of Paris* or maybe one called *Ada; or, the Mysteries of Low Life in London.* Still, it was the first time anything like it had appeared in the United States, or at least the first time anything like it sold an astounding one hundred thousand copies and was translated for sales in Europe.[20] These paperbacks sold for twenty-five cents each; while this was no tiny sum in those days, it was small enough so that after several people had read the story, the pulpy book could simply be thrown away when there were enough holes and smears in it. In these muckraking, urban-gothic novels—and the sequels he wrote over the next couple of years, like *Three Years After* (1849) and *The B'hoys of New York and The G'hals of New York* (1850)—Judson developed the white working-class characters of Mose and Lize.

Bedford and Company publishing house quickly offered Judson a deal, and with this partnership, Judson wrote four more volumes. In addition, stage manager and producer Benjamin Baker used *Mysteries and Miseries* as the basis for his melodrama; there's no record of whether he paid Judson for his characters or whether Judson simply thought of the play as good publicity for his novels. The play highlighted the plague of urban poverty and promoted stereotypes about immigrants living in the city: "The dressing of the various characters is most admirably done," wrote one reviewer, "the slouchy, seedy pickpocket, the bluff burglar, the muddle-headed Dutchman out on a spree, and especially the low Irish represented in the scene, in the old Brewery, are all most perfectly costumed."[21]

During this time, in July 1848, and intermittently for many years afterward, Judson edited his own newspaper, *Ned Buntline's Own*, for which he claimed thirty thousand readers. They were drawn to his sensational stories as well as, presumably, his notices for meetings of nativist organizations such as the Order of United Americans and the Order of United American Mechanics that appeared in its columns.[22] The writer provided his readers with a glossary of terms that they would have to learn if they were to have a proper appreciation of his current and forthcoming works. Among these terms were:

> *Bender—To go upon a (drinking) spree*
> *Coppers—Officers of the police; also termed "pigs," "nabs," etc.*
> *Jug—The prison*
> *Mountain-dew—Scotch whiskey*
> *Swag—Plunder or booty*
> *Swell-head—a bloated drunkard*[23]

Judson's anti-immigrant messages in *Ned Buntline's Own* did not extend to his personal life. According to one account, rewritten more eloquently by Jay Monaghan, the writer met nineteen-year-old Annie Abigail Bennett, who had recently moved to New York from Britain, at a New Year's Eve festival in 1848:

> *Full of mischief and sherry cobblers, he mingled with soldiers just back from Mexico in formal shakos and striped trousers. One day he met*

an old friend, Lieutenant Potter, who was glad to be home again. The two drank together and planned a practical joke. Potter offered to introduce Ned to a young lady of his acquaintance, Annie Abigail Bennett, a real-life heroine like his Angelina, except that Annie had money. Ned beamed, suggested that he dress in cloak and sword. His curled red mustache and broad hat with an ostrich feather made him look like a Spanish grandee, his Nashville role. Potter agreed to introduce him as a Castilian count.[24]

The pair married on January 28, 1848, just two weeks after the second installment of *Mysteries and Miseries*. The *Flag of the Union* cheered its favorite author: "Miss Bennett, now Mrs. Judson, is a very sweet and beautiful lady—one who is intelligent, beautiful and wealthy. She is young, but very womanly. . . . Readers, we wish we could hand you all a piece of the wedding cake—for we know Ned is a great favorite with you all."[25]

The Bennett family was, indeed, wealthy. Anne's father, Thomas, was a retail merchant. The family, including her mother, Sarah, and three older brothers, immigrated to the US when the bride was about five years old. Judson immediately moved into her family's home at its toney 16 Abingdon Square address and commenced writing *Ned Buntline's Own* from there.

Almost immediately, Judson pulled his in-laws into his frenetic world. In his paper he raged against vice in the city. But in real life he participated in the very immoral behavior he stridently opposed with his pen—and may have even blackmailed those who did it with him. The *Sunday Courier* summed up the irony of *Ned Buntline's Own* and its owner:

It is, on the contrary, a species of misanthropic one, for it proceeds from a deeply diseased mind—instead of taking a "stand against vice and immorality," he is secretly aiding them, and living . . . upon the wages of prostitution. His name is "a terror to evil-doers" only when they have no money to purchase his silence, and we have no doubt that he is so steeped in infamy as to be capable of leading a man into a disgraceful action, and then extort money to save him from exposure.[26]

In fact, during the first week of September 1848, Judson printed up handbills advertising the story he would write in a mid-month issue of *Ned Buntline's Own*. It was to feature a wealthy grain merchant named Samuel Suydam, and Judson planned to expose him as an inveterate gambler. Suydam threated to shoot Judson if he dared to repost the bills on Broadway, and Judson replied that he would protect his bills with his life if it became necessary. Worried about this public escalation of tempers, Thomas Bennett had both men arrested "to prevent a contemplated breach of the peace." Both men posted substantial bail to be released— Judson's portion likely came from his father-in-law, who was managing the paper's books and delivery boys, in addition to his own business.[27]

More problematic for the Bennetts was Judson's attempted and successful blackmail of prostitutes. His "Bawdy House Directory" column in *Buntline's Own* sold a lot of papers, but it also served as a reminder to readers that the proprietor seemed to know quite a bit about the houses of ill repute that he wrote about. For example, he wrote columns assessing the legal outcome of a perfunctory legal matter involving a prostitute named Mary Fowler; in reality, the neighborhood would never even have heard of her or known her house was one of "ill fame" but for Ned Buntline's column. The reason for this, according to a contemporary rival, publisher Thomas V. Paterson, was that Fowler refused to pay Judson blackmail money. Moreover, Paterson wrote, Judson removed another prostitute from his rolls of infamy because she exchanged sexual favors with him—favors she provided in the Bennett home while Anne was pregnant with their child.[28]

Ned Buntline's Own did not limit its exposés to prostitutes. It frequently threatened to print suggestive material about subscribers who might be thinking of letting their accounts lapse. Taking things one step further, Judson sometimes wrote blackmail threats against himself— signed by fictitious people—to make it seem that he was under attack by rival papers. In fact, a rival scandal sheet—fed up with Judson's subtle and not-so-subtle barbs against its editor and those of other papers—did offer a ten-dollar reward for any information about a "red mustached libertine" who kept a mistress at a certain whorehouse. "Ned's wife and father-in-law," wrote Monaghan, "must have looked at Ned's red mustache, read the dispatches, and wondered. Could the new member of their family be guilty?"[29] Judson started to wear disguises when he left the house, owing to threats of violence against him.

Judson did not let constant libel charges and threats of violence against him stop *Ned Buntline's Own*. By late 1848 the paper was selling out its weekly runs in New York City, Binghamton, and Albany, and even some cities in Pennsylvania like Honesdale and Philadelphia. He was earning upwards of one thousand dollars per month.

Buntline's Own also gave Judson a platform for his coalescing political views. The election of 1848 provided him ample fuel for his anti-immigrant sentiment. In the aftermath of the Mexican-American War, some Democrats wished to expand slavery into the massive territories won; others did not, and switched to the new Free Soil Party. Before Whig Zachary Taylor won the presidency, Democrats made a desperate attempt to hold their majority by enlisting thousands of immigrant Irishmen who had fled their country's potato famine. The Democrats also appealed to immigrant radicals who had recently escaped Europe's widespread revolution, and who eagerly accepted low wages and usurped the jobs of American-born workers.

It isn't clear why Judson would feel personally threatened by (mostly) Irish and German Catholic immigrants. There's no obvious seminal moment in his childhood or young adulthood that would point to a personal or financial loss due to an influx of foreigners. He'd had no reservations about marrying Severina, who was Catholic—though notably they did not marry in the Church. Anne Bennett was, as noted, British, and his future wives would run the gamut of Catholic to Jewish to Dutch Lutheran to Methodist to Presbyterian. "America for Americans!" was a rallying cry Judson used to whip up various crowds at his lectures.

American nativism in the mid-nineteenth century walked hand in hand with temperance. Immigrants were stereotyped as being constantly drunk—Irish with their whiskey, Germans with their beer—thus drinking alcohol became synonymous with social ills and even the threat of an overthrow of the American republic by some monarch. On or about September 23, 1848, Judson attended a Daughters of Temperance meeting in lower Manhattan, probably to get some material for

Buntline's Own—and to catch a glimpse of the then-famous phrenologist Lorenzo N. Fowler, who was doing brisk business publishing studies about the shape and size of the cranium as a supposed indication of character and mental abilities. Fowler was to present the women's organization with a Bible; since Judson was the only other male there, participants noisily urged him to accept the Bible on their behalf. "Here was a scrape for a moderate drinker," the *New-York Organ & Temperance Safeguard* reported. "Nothing daunted, however, Mr. Judson, as the readiest way of getting honorably out of it, called for the pledge, affixed his name, and then received the precious gift, in a manner highly satisfactory to the ladies. We see by the last number of his paper, that he has raised the temperance flag, and attacks the Sunday grog shops with a vigorous hand."[30]

Presumably, the novelist adhered to nativism on the same philosophical level as other Protestants, which is that he feared that Catholics were more loyal to the pope than to the United States. He may have been aware—from his time in Cincinnati—of the large numbers of Catholics there who opposed paying taxes to finance public schools. In all likelihood, though, cleaving to nativism simply gave him an enemy upon which to fixate for society's ills, and a way to enter politics in the form of the Native American Party. Judson's attempt to lead this organization would result in the deadliest conflict on the streets of New York since the Revolutionary War.

This lithograph by Augustus Köllner portrays the New York City in which Judson lived. Broadway Barnum's American Museum (left), Trinity Church (center background), Brady's Daguerreian Miniature Gallery (distant right), St. Paul's Chapel (middle right), and finally the Astor House (far right) frame the frenzied street scene that defined the intersection in the 1850s. METROPOLITAN MUSEUM OF ART

View of the lakeshore that once held "Eagle's Nest," Judson's cabin on Eagle Lake in the Adirondacks. This photo was taken around 1890, some years after Judson's rebuilt cabin was torn down. ADIRONDACK EXPERIENCE

Artist's rendering of the Astor Place Riot, primarily instigated by E. Z. C. Judson. The affray caused the deaths of at least twenty-two people, perhaps as many as thirty-five, and injured about one hundred. LIBRARY OF CONGRESS

Kate Myers, Judson's eighth wife and mother of at least four of his children. ADIRONDACK EXPERIENCE

Judson dressed for some formal occasion, perhaps his marriage to Kate Myers.
ADIRONDACK EXPERIENCE

Judson posing in Civil War dress. LIBRARY OF CONGRESS

An occasional songwriter, Judson wrote "The Rainbow Temperance Song" to underscore the evils of drinking alcohol. Gaining popularity in the 1840s, the Sons of Temperance and the Good Templars of the United States promoted fraternity and mutual support. LIBRARY OF CONGRESS

Publicity photo for *Scouts of the Prairie*, a play written by Edward Z. C. Judson (aka Ned Buntline) featuring a new celebrity, Buffalo Bill. From left to right: Judson as "Cale Durg," a trapper; William F. "Buffalo Bill" Cody as himself; and John Baker "Texas Jack" Omohundro.

Publicity photo for either *Scouts of the Prairie* or Judson's subsequent traveling production.
WESTCHESTER HISTORICAL SOCIETY

Judson's daughter Irene Elizabeth, born to him and wife Kate Myers Judson and named for his sister. The writer would later have another daughter with wife Anna Fuller, also named Irene. WESTCHESTER HISTORICAL SOCIETY

CHAPTER SIX

Libel, Nativism, and
the Astor Place Riot

By October 1848, *Godey's Lady's Book* announced that the news-paper of its sometime-contributor Ned Buntline was commanding the largest circulation of any weekly in New York City and its environs.[1] His new novelettes, *The Queen of the Sea, or, Our Lady of the Ocean*; *The Curse: A Tale of Crime and Retribution*; *Magic Figure Head*; and *The Virgin of the Sun*, to name just a few, were doing exceptionally brisk business, as were his *Mysteries and Miseries* installments and his semiautobiographical *Ned Buntline's Life-Yarn*, which was now being sold as a stand-alone novelette. Judson's titles often made up one-third to one-half of any bookseller's listings each month for the years 1848 and 1849. He struck up a close friendship with Marcus Cicero Stanley, a reporter for the *United States Police Gazette*. Stanley funneled Judson stories of arrests and investiga-tions throughout the city upon which he could model some stories in return for *Gazette* promotions in *Buntline's Own*.

The more successful Judson became on the literary scene, though, the more he failed at sobriety and humility. He was a fixture at Palmo's saloon on Broadway, where he liked to have people buy him wine, sarsaparilla, and brandy. Thomas Bennett, Judson's father-in-law, noticed that he was drinking brandy and wine virtually nonstop for days at a time, and when he pointed this out to Judson, the writer contended that he could not write or do business without it. For the first six months of his marriage to Anne, Bennett later recalled, Judson was able to stop drinking for short periods of time: Just when it was becoming intolerable to those in the house, he would abstain for a week or two.[2] But it was difficult for

Judson to go "cold turkey" for very long, and invariably he would get into a barroom brawl or print something especially vitriolic.

Such was the case with Katherine Hastings, a high-class call girl who kept a house of prostitution in the Chelsea neighborhood of New York City. In early April 1849, Judson printed one of his diatribes against Samuel Suydam, the very-married merchant who had nearly come to blows with Judson. In it he told readers that if they had any interest in seeing just how unattractive Suydam was, they had only to go to his "den" at No. 14 Barclay Street, where "his *chere amie* is the infamous cast-off mistress of a deceased gambler, known as gallows Kate Hastings, the keeper of a low house of prostitution in Leonard-Street. Sam dances attendance to this strumpet when called on."[3] According to a letter from Hastings printed in the *Herald*, Hastings learned about the article the day after its publication, while she was shopping in a store on Ann Street. Hastings stated that the article was "derogatory to my own character and the character of my house. . . . I immediately said I would cowhide Ned Buntline the first time I caught him in a public street." Just as Hastings declared this to her acquaintants, Judson passed the store; Hastings followed and caught him by the arm. She told him she would cowhide him (whip him with braided leather) for the insult the next time she met him, and she would wait on Broadway until the opportunity arose.

Five days later, after waiting an hour on the corner near Judson's office, Hastings found her opportunity. As Judson walked down the street with friends, she gave him two blows on the head, to the great amusement of onlookers on the busy thoroughfare. Hastings said she "didn't stop to see if he was much hurt and didn't care."[4] Mortified, Judson immediately had her arrested. The pair went to trial on April 4, 1849. Hastings held her head up high and told the truth of what she had done: that she was simply tired of Judson besmirching her character in his paper. She insisted that Judson's unsavory behavior warranted the cowhiding, and to support this claim, she produced two letters that had been sent to her the day after the assault. One was signed by Judson:

> *You are an infernal dirty bitch and if you ever attempt to do to me a similar act you may consider yourself shot. Take warning by this you*

dirty whore. My paper is mine and I am able to be responsible for any articles contained therein.

  E. Z. C. Judson

The other was signed "One Who Knows Something" but which appeared to be in Judson's handwriting. It justified the actions of Judson and accused Hastings of being a destroyer of youthful morals and lives. She was, it said, a "damd [*sic*] whore . . . [who is] fucked every night by sporting men." The letter ended with the warning: "Woe be to you cursed whore. Look out!"[5] Judson did not appear in court for the matter; the judge simply told Hastings to keep her hands off him and fined her six cents.

Ned Buntline's libel of Miss Georgiana C. Crean was even more serious. Crean was the sister-in-law of James Gordon Bennett (no relation to Thomas Bennett), the founder, editor, and publisher of the *New York Herald*. When Judson read the *Herald*'s in-depth coverage of his suit with Hastings—with emphasis on the cowhiding and snickers from bystanders—he charged straight into his office burning with rage. According to his then-assistant Thomas Paterson, Judson reached for pen and paper and said, "I will rip up the character of the whore of a sister of that cockeyed villain Bennett next week." He then wrote an article that intimated that Miss Crean had been seen at various houses of "ill-fame" in the city for the purposes of prostitution.[6] Authorities arrested Judson on May 4, 1849, and held him for two thousand dollars' bail, which his friends furnished. The judge set a court date for a few weeks later so that Crean could present her case for libel. As it turned out, a much bigger case against Judson would have to take priority—though the Crean affair was partly to blame for what came next.

On May 10, 1849, an explosion of class tensions brought about by a bitter feud between two Shakespearean actors turned into one of the most violent public outbursts in New York history. Major General Charles Sandford recalled the scene at the Astor Place Opera House, which was about a fifteen-minute walk east of the Bennett residence at Abingdon Square. Sandford, a general in the New York Militia, wrote: "I have never seen a mob so violent as the one on that evening. I never before had occasion to give the order to fire."[7] Edward Zane Carroll Judson was the primary instigator of this bloody affray.

Judson may have been grateful that his supporters kept him out of jail for the Crean affair, but if he was, it was buried deep beneath his rage against James Gordon Bennett. How dare this British man get the better of him, a native-born citizen! As luck would have it, Judson had an event toward which he could channel his anger: a theatrical performance of Shakespeare's *Macbeth*, which was to take place at the Astor Place Opera House the evening of May 11, 1849. William Charles Macready was set to play Macbeth, which was perfectly acceptable to most theatergoers in America. Macready was a fine actor, classically trained, complete with fey handkerchief-waving, and during the first half of the nineteenth century, US audiences were used to European actors taking center stage in major cities. But as the populations of major cities grew, so did the number and prominence of theaters—which became venues not only for plays but also for political discourse and (usually peaceful) protest.

Macready, though, had been quarreling bitterly with American actor Edwin Forrest since 1844. That year, James Knox Polk ran for president on a vehemently anti-British platform, determined to wrest the Oregon Territory from that country. Some Americans preferred Forrest's Shakespearean acting—it was less rigid, less nuanced, and more athletic, with important passages punctuated with expressive movement. Forrest followed Macready on his American tour in 1844 and 1845; reviews for both were either favorable or dismissive, depending on whether the audience preferred American or European talent. The rivalry extended across the Atlantic too. Macready's supporters ensured that Forrest's performances received tepid coverage from the British press, sabotaging his obsession with global fame. In retaliation, Forrest made it hard for his rival to play in the states without a competitive booking or a rowdy house. At a Macready performance in Cincinnati, patrons in the gallery went so far as to throw half a dead sheep onstage.[8]

As Forrest and Macready sniped in the press, the sensational back-and-forth came to symbolize class warfare in America: the wealthy, Anglophile establishment (labeled the "Upper Ten," a 1-percenter nickname referring to the city's ten thousand wealthiest residents) against the broad masses; native-born Americans against a rising tide of immigrants; and low-wage workers against nearly anyone better off.[9] As Monaghan summarized, "Mechanics, workmen, Bowery 'b'hoys,' all Buntline's people, classed Macready, Britishers, and aristocrats as common enemies of their America. Didn't rich people want immigration from abroad to supply cheap labor, which took bread from the mouths of American workers' children?"[10] Now, four years later, as Macready rehearsed for a return engagement to the New York stage, Judson plotted.

On the morning of May 9, 1849, before dawn broke, several youths ran around lower Manhattan, pasting on fences and handing out handbills that had been printed by Judson the night before. They read:

> **WORKING MEN**
> *Shall Americans or English Rule! In this City!*
> *The crew of the British Steamer, have threatened all Americans who shall dare to express their opinions this night at the ENGLISH ARISTOCRATIC! OPERA HOUSE!*
> *We advocate no violence but a free expression of opinion to all public men.*
> *Workingmen! Freemen!*
> *Stand by your lawful rights!*
> *   ~ The American Committee*

In addition to these bills, Judson printed a report that the officers and crews of the British vessels and steamers in the harbor would assemble at the theater to show their support of Macready. The mayor, hearing rumors of potential conflict, advised the managers of the opera house to close for the evening of the 10th. But the managers insisted that it was their right to open the theater and perform, and likely did not want to lose revenue from ticket sales.[11] Also, newspapers like the *Herald* reported that citizens need not fear rioting, for New York's police had easily quelled other potent political gatherings in recent days and months. "The conduct of the rioters, on Monday night, has roused the feelings of order and propriety in the community, to such an extent as will render all attempts at riot utterly ineffectual and impracticable."[12] How wrong they would turn out to be.

On the night of May 10, 1849—hours before the performance started—the Opera House had sold every ticket and the streets surrounding it were crowded with murmuring but subdued crowds. It was a sold-out show, but curiosity seekers tried to sneak in or bribe guards to let them in. Being cautious, New York chief of police George Matsell placed two hundred officers around the Opera House vicinity, and another seventy-five officers at the stables and estate opposite the structure.[13] At dusk, city workers began carving away the paving stones that had been raised for the purpose of constructing a sewer near the theater, which was located on Lafayette Street between Astor Place and East Eighth Street. After they were done with this, the workers also nailed pieces of wood across the delicate frames of the windows facing the street. Finally, at half past seven o'clock, the doors were closed and barricaded on all sides; inside the theater, the curtain rose.

The first scene of *Macbeth* went fairly smoothly, with no deliberate interruption but with some nervous twitters from the audience, which was still collectively anxious because of the crowds it knew were outside. But during the second scene, when Macready appeared on stage for the first time, there was "overwhelming" and "protracted" applause that demonstrated that the clear majority of the theatergoers were quite all right with the British actor on their stage. But about fifty people stationed throughout the hall, mostly right at the foot of the stage, began hissing and booing. One reporter described it: "Their noise and insulting remarks, directed at both Mr. Macready and his assistants on the stage, and particularly Mrs. Pope, who supported the character of Lady Macbeth with surprising fortitude, became more and more intolerable, as the evening wore, until the last scene of the first act." Police plucked out the hecklers they could find, but by the end of the first act, it was clear that the troublesome minority was not going to stop. The stage manager signaled for all the security guards present to take out the chief disturbers en masse, and they placed them in holding cells located underneath the stage.

Unfortunately, removing the agitators in the audience did not quell the commotion outside; it only stirred it up when the police were seen running into the theater. Rioters began throwing stones and paving bricks from the sewer project and pushing on the doors. Several were successful, and the mob outside was able to push its way into the Opera House, hurling objects while they did so. This caused the crowd inside to start trampling one another in an effort to get outside and avoid harm. Large numbers of policemen were trampled or hurt by the missiles.

The mob, Chief Matsell later said, "got the better of the police," but he was willing to let it take over in hopes that the violence would naturally die out from exhaustion. But two things happened after the anti-Macready horde incited enough bloodshed and confusion to stop the police: Someone started a fire under the stage, and a contingent of the military arrived. Stagehands were able to quickly put out the fire before any harm came to patrons, but the smoke added to the urgency felt by Major General Sandford of the New York Militia: "During a period of thirty-five years of service," he reflected during the Astor Place trials two months later, "I have never seen a mob so violent as the one on that evening. I never before had occasion to give the order to fire."[14]

Sandford and General William Hall ordered their lines of foot soldiers and cavalry to approach from the north and south of the Opera House, with the goal of dispersing the crowds and subduing the violent offenders. But they were met with emboldened rioters, who turned their stones and sticks on the soldiers and even their horses. Both generals managed to get their well-trained militia to hold still, even in the face of this violence against them, but shouted to the crowd to disperse or they would have to use their weapons. When the mob still wouldn't untangle, they gave the orders to fire blank cartridges, but to do so just once or twice well over the heads of the people in the crowd, in order to scare them into submission and to disperse.

These warning volleys did not work. Shouts of "blank cartridges" rang out from the melee, which encouraged the mob to attack the military even more violently. In fact, the militia had already started loading lethal ammunition when it appeared that the mob was not dispersing. Finally, the troops—fearing for their lives and presumably those of others—fired directly upon the crowd.

The recollections of some of the victims—which included not only innocent bystanders but police and militiamen as well—were horrifying:

> I was standing on the corner of Mrs. Langdon's house when the first discharge took place. A man fell; I laughed, and so did others, as we thought it was only blank cartridges to scare them. I heard a man say, "My God, look at this—he's shot!" This was at the first discharge of musketry. I heard no notice given to disperse; they might have done so. After this I started down. . . . I was so frightened. . . . I stood there until I heard another banging of muskets, and then I started and ran home as quick as I could.
> —Thomas J. Belyin, boatman[15]

> I stepped back a pace or two [from Mrs. Langdon's house] to bring myself out of the direct line; immediately another discharge took place . . . upon the discharge, a man fell on the sidewalk in front of us. There were but a few persons near him at the time; after he fell he remained on the ground half a minute, some supposing he was shamming being shot. On picking him up, a wound was discovered in his back, by the blood rushing . . . on examining [him], we found a wound in the lower part of his stomache.
> —Stephens W. Gaines, lawyer[16]

The summary of the wounded and mortally wounded grew longer in the newspapers in the days following the riot. One lead ball struck Mrs. Brennan, a housekeeper, in both thighs while she was passing through the Bowery on her way home from work. Student Stephen Kehoe, twenty-four, was shot in the eye and the ball lodged permanently in his neck. James Stewart, while stepping from a carriage on Fifth Avenue near Eighth Street, was hit by a lead ball in the neck; it nicked his jugular vein and he died within minutes. Thomas Aylwood, nineteen, was shot through the thigh, which fractured the bone; he later died from shock when the leg had to be amputated. Some bullets claimed victims more than two blocks away, and some people were hit while minding their own business in their own homes.

One publisher compiled hundreds of eyewitness accounts for a definitive report about the riot. One paragraph summarizes the carnage of that evening:

> *The horrors of that night can never be described. We looked over the scene that misty midnight. The military, resting from their work of death, in stern silence were grimly guarding the Opera House. Its interior was a rendezvous and a hospital for the wounded military and police. Here and there around the building, and at the corners of the streets were crowds of men talking in deep and earnest tones of indignation. There were little processions moving off with the dead or mutilated bodies of their friends and relations. A husband, uttering frenzied curses, followed his mortally wounded wife to the hospital. An aged mother found her only son, the sole support of her declining years, in the agonies of death. Many a wife sat watching at home, in terror and alarm for her absent husband. It was an evening of dread—and it became a night of horror, which on the morrow, when the awful tragedy became more widely known, settled down upon the city like a funeral pall.[17]*

By the end of 1849, it was reported that at least twenty-two people had died that evening, perhaps as many as thirty-one—some victims could not be accounted for, as they returned home to other counties to be treated and later died of infection or complications. At least thirty more people (including children) were maimed for life, and scores of others underwent long and painful recoveries. Fifty people were arrested for their part in the riot; police grabbed Judson just as he was raising a paving stone in the air. According to the *Evening Post*, the author "acted as the leader of the mob outside."[18]

Judson's part in the terrifying events of that evening of May 10 is best explained by some of his acquaintances and bystanders, also his then-brother-in-law, Francis Bennett, in court testimony presented on September 19, 1849, just a little over three months after the bloody incident occurred. Wardle Corbyn, a theatrical agent, remembered that Judson pulled up next to him in their wagons on Barclay Street and reached out to touch his shoulder. "Corbyn," he said, "you are the very man I want to see. Where does Ned Forrest live?" Wardle explained that he thought the actor lived on 23rd Street, Chelsea, but did not know the exact address. "You know," Judson said, "there is going to be a muss, and I want to see Forrest, to ascertain if he is right or wrong, for I consider myself as the leader of the Native American party in this matter. And if Forrest is right, I mean to see him through." Corbyn thought this was odd, and told Judson: "I should think you [have] had rows enough without interfering with this. I expect there will be some hard fighting, and I advise you to keep out of it." "That may be," Judson replied, "but I mean to see it out."[19]

Late that afternoon, when the Bennetts and Judson sat around the supper table, Judson asked his brother-in-law Francis—"Frank"—if he would accompany him on a walk. Frank was about five years younger than Judson and a tiny bit starstruck by his sister's husband. He thought it strange that Judson would put on a disguise just to go on an errand, but did not question him about it. And when Mrs. Bennett asked her son why they had to go do business with someone at suppertime, Frank ignored her just as Judson did.

After stopping to have several drinks at a pub a block away from the Opera House, and after insisting Frank take one of his two pistols to protect him from his enemies, Judson sauntered out into the dusky air of Broadway. Frank was shocked when Judson boasted that he also had a dagger with him that belonged to William, Frank's brother. "It will make such a show," the writer bragged.[20]

From Broadway, the pair made their way down to Eighth Street and headed toward Lafayette Street. When they got to the corner of Eighth and Lafayette, they heard someone exclaim, "The riot has commenced!" Judson pushed Bennett toward the center of the gathering mass of people, where he bellowed, "Are there any Americans here?" Someone responded, "I am a Northern Liberty boy!" Judson responded, "I am Ned Buntline! You are going to want a nucleus to this party!" He then complained to some of the gathered men that they would need to work in concert if they were to get anything done. And then the idea came to him: "Couldn't you get up the cry of fire?" he asked.[21]

Several men advised Judson that there were already ladders and men at the ready to put out any fires. The novelist thought for a moment, and then said if they could just get one going in the back of the theater, it would drive all the patrons and actors out through the front doors—presumably so the crowd could harass the British actor Macready and perhaps the "upper-crust" patrons who came to see him. More and more people started to gather around Judson, as whispers of "Ned Buntline" began to circulate. Some of the men and boys, excited, went to gather wood shavings. Others continued picking up stones and throwing them at the theater building. At about eight o'clock, Frank whispered to Judson that the captain of the Third Ward police was watching him; in response, the writer pulled out brother William's dagger and tried to get Frank to conceal it under his coat. At this, Frank's devotion turned. He told his brother-in-law, "I would not, even for twenty thousand dollars!"[22]

Frank managed to drag Judson away from the growing melee for a few minutes, but the writer decided to head back to the excitement. Dejected, Frank took his brother's dagger away from Judson so at least he would not be arrested with his family's weapon on hand. In return, though, Judson asked for his second pistol back. They agreed to meet at Thompson & Weller's Ice Cream Saloon on Broadway, a few minutes' walk away from the Opera House area. As he separated from his brother-in-law, Frank could hear Judson shouting words to the effect of, "Don't back down!" Bennett waited a long time at Thompson & Weller's; Judson never came.

Meanwhile, according to trial reports, the crowd outside the theater had gotten much bigger, and a group of about twenty young men had become especially active in "fomenting disturbance," and "conspicuous among whom was the defendant Judson, with whom many of the young men frequently conferred, and who appeared to be acting as their leader." Witnesses heard Judson say, "It is a shame that Americans should be served so!" and also start the following exchange with the youths after some discussion in low voices:

> *Judson: "Now, boys, whatever you have to do must be done quickly!"*
> *Young man: "Now, boys, for a shower!"*
> *Judson: "Hold, until you are all ready!"*

A volley of stones flew against the walls and windows of the Opera House, at which point the police started arresting some of the participants, which in turn ignited the hecklers inside, who were quickly arrested and put into the cells below the stage. But it was at this point that either Judson or one of the youths lobbed a large paving stone into one of the glass windows of the theater. It fell onto some audience members—effectively giving permission to the mob outside to hurl more stones and bricks at the doors and windows of the Opera House, smashing them in certain parts. It was at this time that the cry of "fire" from the back of the theater obliterated any way of safely getting patrons out of the building.[23]

In the dark, early-morning hours of May 11, 1849, Judson and dozens of others were arrested on suspicion of inciting this bloody riot. By noon, a friend had put up one thousand dollars' bail for his release, and he went home to Abingdon Place to sleep. A few days later, he wrote a piece for *Ned Buntline's Own* in which he condemned grand jury proceedings against him, claiming that he was mostly ministering to his sick wife the evening of the tenth and had just been an observer of the riot when he was arrested.[24] "If the wife of my bosom," Judson wrote, "who is now on a sickbed, dangerously ill, should die from this shock, there shall be more than one man held responsible for her murder!"[25]

It is true that Annie Judson was very ill. She was very heavy with pregnancy, and she was suffering from what may have been the effects of a venereal disease Edward had given her. Thomas Bennett allegedly told Judson's assistant:

Judson was sick about a month after marriage. His disease was a swelling on each side of his groin. It was what is called Pox. I knew it about two weeks after his marriage. I administered medicine for it. He took internally a medicine called "English diet-drink." I cannot say how much he took of his wife's medicine. His wife was sick shortly after Judson's sickness. He used sugar of lead for a wash—and hops—he was leeched also. I got the medicines at an Apothecary's. Judson's disease continued about two months.[26]

Their baby boy was born a few weeks later, and Thomas Bennett noted that the disease had lingering effects on the baby.[27]

Free on bail for the time being, Judson continued to write and publish fiercely. He also promoted the second sequel of *Mysteries and Miseries*, which first appeared in *Ned Buntline's Own* the first week of June 1849 and then as a stand-alone novelette, which sold out in bookstores faster than it could be stocked. But he also continued to party fiercely, even spending days on end in Philadelphia—where on July 3 he was severely beaten by a policeman outside Guy's Saloon. Ned Buntline had apparently written something in poor taste about the patrolman in *Buntline's Own*. On July 11, after dark, people reported loud noises coming from his yacht in "The Narrows," a body of water between Fort Hamilton and Staten Island; at some point later that evening, a man stumbled onto shore with gunshot wounds. It was not clear whether Judson was involved, but the ordeal did call attention to the yacht—which was repossessed due to nonpayment a few weeks later.[28]

Thomas Bennett and his daughter had had enough of Edward Zane Carroll Judson. The older Bennett had put up two thousand dollars' bond for Judson in the Crean libel case, and he now had every reason to suspect that his son-in-law's continued erratic behavior meant he was likely not to show up for trial in this matter, which was tentatively set for October 1849. It is not clear whether Bennett lured Judson somehow or the writer simply returned to Abingdon Square for his usual room, board, and wife; but Bennett managed to revoke his bail and New York City authorities rearrested him. After he spent thirty hours in jail, supporters raised bond for Judson again; and when freed, he took to his pen and paper:

New York, Aug. 14, 1849
THOMAS BENNETT—IMP OF HELL!

"Cowardly, thieving wretch" does not express one half the contempt, *the* indignation *of an outraged community for your last* hellish, malicious, inhuman act*!! You have thereby forfeited all claim to the respect, or* notice *of men, and deserve to be treated with more* contempt *than* the meanest thing that crawls the Earth, *which God in his mercy permits you to inhabit, but of which you shall soon* occupy but a small space*!! I mean your last act of surrendering* Ned Buntline, *your* son, *to the authorities by withdrawing bail! Meanness unparalleled!*[29]

This particular letter meandered on for several paragraphs and ended with a threat to put a bullet in Bennett's head. Judson wrote and sent Bennett several more missives like these. Bennett had Judson arrested for libel.

It is not clear if Judson was ever called to task for this alleged libel against his father-in-law or the one against Miss Crean, because on September 29, 1849, he was convicted of inciting the Astor Place Riot and sentenced to one year's confinement in Blackwell's Penitentiary, on what is today called Roosevelt Island in New York City. Anne Abigail Judson was granted an immediate divorce and full custody of their infant son.

Chapter Seven

Western Expansion
and the St. Louis Riot

The court granted Anne Abigail Bennett her divorce from Judson on September 29, 1849, on grounds of adultery. The decree stated that Bennett could marry again in the future "as though said defendant were actually dead," but that it would not be lawful for Judson to marry again "until the plaintiff is actually dead."[1] This was significant in the world of nineteenth-century American divorce—at least in the state of New York. Divorce at that time was not intended to allow couples to escape from identities assumed in marriage, as was the case with Anne Bennett, who had been "Mrs. E. Z. C. Judson"—merely an extension of her husband—unless the actions of one spouse were so criminal or dishonorable that a judge felt obliged to provide an escape from the moral contamination that might accompany continued cohabitation with a guilty spouse.[2] Clearly, the judge felt that Judson's behavior was so egregious that Bennett ought to feel free to start over without the taint of her first marriage. He even allowed for their son, Sydney, to carry his mother's maiden name as his surname—virtually unheard of in those days, even in cases of abandonment by the father.

Rumors of a pardon by the governor for Judson surfaced in March 1850, but in fact the writer served his year's sentence in Blackwell Island prison. Judson refused to eat for several days at first but soon wearied of this. He also refused to work in the rock quarry, which was part of his sentence, but he soon acquiesced to this too.[3] Judson demanded to be able to work on *Buntline's Own* from prison but was refused. He did, however, pass the time by writing stories (including *The Convict, Or, the Conspirator's Victim*, which was, not surprisingly, semiautobiographical) and reading many books and newspapers. Two of his printer friends began selling large portraits of Judson for a dollar each; it isn't clear whether they did this to raise money for the author or to simply capitalize on his recent notoriety.

Judson's supporters did not forget about him while he was incarcerated. The Order of United Americans (sometimes known then as Native Americans)—thousands strong in New York City alone—chartered a steamboat to retrieve him on October 1, 1850, when his sentence expired. They brought him back to the streets of New York City, where an estimated five hundred supporters met him with a "coach and four" carriage and paraded him down a few streets, followed by a marching band. "It is supposed," the *N.Y. Journal of Commerce* wrote sarcastically, "that after his decease he will be canonized."[4]

Despite the antics of his vocal supporters, Judson knew his welcome was worn out in New York—at least for the time being. He headed to Philadelphia, Pittsburgh, Newark, Cincinnati, and other cities, where he lectured on "Americanism." Judson mostly railed against Irish "popism" infiltrating the legislative branches of the United States, and made money doing it: Twenty-five cents per person is what it cost to see him rail against Catholics and President Millard Fillmore. At these loud lectures, Judson often wore a full suit covered with Masonic-type medals or—bizarrely—Indian garb, and had a band behind him playing popular patriotic songs. Judson drifted west, preaching American Party tenets to Mississippi Valley cities, which the party needed to gain enough popularity for an 1852 presidential platform.

In late 1851 Judson arrived in St. Louis with some cash in his pocket from the sale of a new story, albeit one based on his previous urban tales: *The Mysteries and Miseries of New Orleans*. He noted that all the news in the South seemed to be centered upon an adventurer named Narciso López—*Mysteries and Miseries of New Orleans* provided a fictional backdrop to a very real attempt by López to "free" Cuba from Spanish rule.

Born in Venezuela, López preached revolution in Cuba, ostensibly to free it from its empirical chains in Europe but also to annex the island as a new slave state like Texas. Here were two opportunities for Judson—one political, and one pecuniary: He would rally for Lopez's cause, which would unite proslavery Northerners and the South in their common desire for territorial expansion, and he could sell stocks for investment in a new Cuba at ten cents on the dollar, payable if López was successful. Judson took to wrapping himself in the newly designed Cuban flag that López was waving at all of his own rallies. Some newspapers subtly pointed out that Judson was straying from his literary capabilities to make a quick dollar on Southern sensitivities. The *Pittsburgh Commercial Journal*, for example, predicted that he, along with his flag and his uniform and his anecdotes, would be very successful in "acquiring quarter dollars." If he could just add, quipped the *Journal*, to his show "the man that wrote 'The Glorious News by the Schooner Merchant' and other interesting romances of the same character, the rush for seats would recall the triumphs of Barnum and Jenny Lind."[5]

Unfortunately for Judson, Spanish forces captured López in Havana during his attempt to start a revolution there in August 1851. They executed him a month later. "Ned Buntline" decided to make another go of things in St. Louis, the bustling Western city where not very many people had lost money on his Cuban scrip. He took a room at a boardinghouse where, according to one contemporary, he had an affair with the proprietress, a "Mrs. Ross."[6] He started a weekly newspaper called *The Novelist*, which he hoped would be a tool to gather supporters for the Know Nothing Party.

E. Z. C. Judson is often credited in history books as being a founder of the Know Nothing Party—more formally called the "American Party." As demonstrated by his actions in the Astor Place Riot, this party was the outgrowth of strong anti-immigrant feelings—especially toward Catholic immigrants, who were thought to be more loyal to the pope than the government of the United States. In the mid- to late 1840s, the party originated as a semisecret society. When asked about the organization, a member replied, "I know nothing." As a national party, it called for limitations on immigration, the exclusion of foreign-born Americans from voting or holding public office, and for a twenty-one-year residency requirement for citizenship. The party was also hostile to wealth, elites, and expertise, and was deeply suspicious of outsiders. Violence was associated with the party's activities.[7]

In truth, Judson was probably not an original founder of the American Party. There is no evidence (if only that he never claimed) that he attended its first convention, which met in Philadelphia in 1845. But he was certainly an early leader of it, and shaped and popularized the movement. Issues of *The Novelist* have yet to be discovered—it was discontinued after just a few months of publication. One historian said that the paper's "vagaries and highly melodramatic ideas of its editor were not suited to the practical commonsense people of that day," and failed to blossom.[8] Still, Judson attracted sizable crowds at his lectures in and around St. Louis, at which he stoked fears about German immigrants settling in the Midwest just as he had done with the Irish in New York. He would come on stage dressed in the uniform of a Cuban rebel and lecture on "Cuba and Her Martyrs" and add some remarks about the filthy rich in America. A quartet would play some popular patriotic songs while Judson changed into a costume meant to represent a Seminole chief. He would then deliver a speech about "Wrongs Done the Indians of America" and finally launch into the dangers of foreigners coming to the United States.[9]

As 1851 turned to 1852, Judson became aware that the Democratic Party in St. Louis was split into two factions: One supported an antislavery candidate for governor; the other supported a proslavery candidate. Notably, a large German faction supported the former. City elections were slated to be held in April, and Judson saw an opportunity to thwart the Democratic Party's attempt to pull antislavery Germans into its fold, and perhaps also gain a toehold in the region for the American Party. Almost every newspaper and political party in the region denounced what he did next, and the details of it were not reported until more than twenty years later, when Judson came to St. Louis with William F. Cody and was immediately arrested for jumping bail.

On the morning of April 5, 1852, the polls opened in St. Louis. At first, everything was quiet, and voters peaceably cast their ballots. Then word came that Germans, led by one Henry Boernstein, had attacked a carriage full of Whig voters and beaten up its driver. The mayor, a Whig himself, sped to the scene of the trouble but quickly left when an ominous crowd started forming around him and someone yelled, "I heard you abuse the Dutch in the ferryboat," and others yelled, "Hang him! Drown him!" He was not back at the office more than a few minutes when a constituent burst in and complained that Germans were keeping Whig ballots out of their polling wards. Shortly after, a couple more constituents came in to make the same complaint—but the mayor decided to stay out of the fray. This only served to anger the four hundred or so men out front, who were waiting to hear what the mayor would do about this affront. Then a man on a big horse rode forward; it was Judson. He yelled out to the first man who had complained to the mayor, "Come with me! I'll see that you get a chance to vote!" A local politician named Robert O'Blenis followed right behind Judson in a buggy loaded with a keg of whisky. Monaghan carefully reconstructed Judson's actions from reports in the *St. Louis Daily Globe*:

> *These two men led the way down Fourth Street toward the Soulard Market polls.*[10] *The crowd followed, men and boys packing the street, curb to curb—five thousand, it was estimated.*[11]
>
> *The Germans saw them coming. Veterans of street barricades in recent revolutions in Europe, they advanced toward the Americans. Buntline, on horseback, and a few fast pedestrians were far ahead of the City Hall crowd. The Germans waved their pistols. They threw rocks. Ned was knocked from his horse. . . . Buntline, bleeding and angry, whooped to the mob to come on: "Rush the lop-eared Dutch."*[12]

Judson and O'Blenis took over the polls, placed Whig ballots on the tables, arranged tumblers around the keg of liquor, and invited all who felt patriotic to come and vote. Drinking friends called on the writer for a speech, and someone brought his horse back. According to local lore, Judson remounted and rode back and forth in front of the polls reciting Revolutionary War speeches his father had taught him.

Meanwhile, fights broke out in the streets around the polls. Firearms, discharged from windows and doors of houses, wounded several people. One man was shot through the hand with buckshot; another had a bullet go through his leg; yet another received a load of buckshot in the face, and a fourth man had his leg broken by a bullet. Those without a gun used bats and stones.[13]

But Judson and O'Blenis's "victory" was short-lived. When they attempted to destroy Turner Hall, the German athletic club, they were repelled by German immigrants, who had the foresight to place guards with rifles at the four street corners and some on top of nearby houses. One of them fired off a shot, which caused Judson's mob to turn around. Someone pointed to the house of saloonkeeper Henry Niemeier and yelled that the shot had come from it. This action precipitated even more horror:

> *The mob surged up in front of the drawn shutters. A young man in a fireman's uniform, Joseph Stephens, pounded at the door with a club. A panel gave way. From the inside a gun appeared through the shattered door—a whiff of smoke and a dull report. Stephens turned, staggered down the steps, faltered across the street, and fell dead, his head on the curb.*[14]

Stephens's death incited Judson's mob beyond all reason or control, and it rushed the saloon. It upturned the stove, piled wood upon it; cooler heads ran upstairs when they heard shouting from above. A few men found the saloonkeeper in his bedroom with his wife, who had just given birth a few days before, and a man who was nursing a broken leg. These men grabbed the mattress Mrs. Niemeier was lying on and carried her and the baby down the stairs and out of the building, followed by Mr. Niemeier and the man with the bad leg. Their home and business did not survive; even though the fire department arrived quickly, someone from the mob cut the hose so the water could not get through. Later, at trial, several witnesses testified that O'Blenis said with shame, "When it comes to fighting I'm in, but when to burning houses I'm not there."[15]

By morning, all the rioting had fizzled out under the weight of its own energy. The Whigs won the elections, thanks to what the Democratic Party deemed "an unholy alliance" between them and the American

Party. But all the newspapers, no matter which candidate they might have endorsed, denounced the riot. The *St. Louis News* announced: "Radicalism in its worst has gained the victory," and the *St. Louis Republican* deemed it "disgraceful."[16]

There was no immediate mention of Ned Buntline, but newspapers from other cities soon began sending correspondents to St. Louis to investigate, and many soon cited him as the instigator of the riot. The *Baton Rouge Union Democrat* was particularly blunt: "The notorious Ned Buntline was at the head of the rioters, whose only object seemed to be to cut and abuse every German that came in their way." Several national papers printed a telegram that originated in St. Louis, which read suspiciously like Judson had sent it himself: "Ned Buntline had a horse killed under him—he acted like a man—fired several times and each ball took effect. Bob O'Blenis scattering the Dutch blood like dew."[17]

Both Judson and O'Blenis were arrested and led off to jail. Fireman James F. Milligan, who later gave a deposition in Anna Fuller Judson's pension battle, recalled that it was Judson who ordered men to set fire to Niemeier's saloon and home. Although the fireman was a member of the Know Nothing Party, he felt compelled to take action when he saw Judson do this. He aimed his rifle at Judson and shot him in one of his thighs and watched him fall from his horse. In all likelihood, this is the shot that felled Judson's horse and spurred the above telegram.[18]

In all, several homes and taverns were destroyed by looting, fire, or both. Ten people were severely wounded, and about twenty-five were slightly wounded. Joseph Stephens was buried on April 7, with his fireman's belt and hat on the coffin. The funeral procession was a half-mile long and carried a great banner with, as Monaghan notes, typical Buntline language: AMERICANS WE BEAR A BROTHER TO HIS GRAVE. FORGET NOT HOW HE HAS BEEN SLAIN.[19] Judson decamped to Carlyle, Illinois, a few dozen miles away.

In Illinois he married Margaret "Maggie" Watson on the 20th of April. Watson was about eighteen years younger than Judson, and the daughter of a Mormon farmer. How they met and married so quickly is anybody's guess, but the coupling gave Judson a place to stay while he waited out the court. Judson was arrested on May 29, 1852, and indicted for his role in instigating the St. Louis riot. Two acquaintances each put up five hundred dollars for bond, and the judge postponed his court appearance until July, then September, then to the following year. The writer passed the time writing for *The Novelist*, which had morphed into *Buntline's Novelist and Carlyle Prairie Flower*—an instrument he used to disseminate American Party support. It isn't clear whether Maggie accompanied him to Memphis, New Orleans, and other river cities, drumming up support for a Know Nothing candidate for the presidential election of 1854. The *New York Times* took notice:

> *We have often declared our dislike of all the popular harangues against the Catholics, into which a morbid Protestantism is so apt to run. They excite passions without convincing the reason—implant hatred instead of charity, and do far more hurt than good to the very interests they are designed to serve. Religion does not consist in hating the Catholics, nor is any man the better Christian for denouncing the Pope and detecting a Jesuit in every street.*[20]

The article explained that in spite of any perception of ugly speech, that speech must be protected as a First Amendment right. But it also noted it should not be hampered by the prospect of violence every time a speaker exercised this right, giving politicians a reason to shut down public discourse:

> *And any gang of ruffians, by starting or threatening a riot, can furnish him the only pretext he needs for such a course. "Ned Buntline" and his gang of "Know-nothing" natives can create a riot in the Bishop's Cathedral;—Isaiah Rynders will extemporize a mob at any obnoxious political meeting;—and upon the precedent established by the Mayor in the present case, the preacher or the speaker must be arrested and sent to jail. The principle asserted places all speech and all discussion at the mercy of a mob. This is not the freedom which our people have been taught to claim and prize, as among the choicest of their treasures.*[21]

But Judson was not concerned with his notoriety in the East. In January 1853 his case was called for trial in St. Louis and the court ordered his friends to forfeit their bail, since Judson neglected to show up. This no-show would plague him twenty years later when he performed with Buffalo Bill, but not nearly as much as the trouble he would start more immediately, when he met Lovanche Kelsey Swart, soon to be wife number four.

Chapter Eight

The Widow Swart

Trying to put distance between himself and another riot—and the prospect of being put in jail again—Judson fled St. Louis and went back to the place where he was most comfortable: New York City. As for Maggie Watson: No mention of her survives besides the pair's wedding announcement in the *Liberty Tribune*, in which the paper's editor acknowledged the receipt of "a large quantity of cake and other fixins', from the happy bride and bridegroom." A few years later, Judson wrote a story that he said was—truthfully or not—inspired by his time in St. Louis and across the river in Illinois. Called "The Widow's Wedding," it was about a young bride, "Josephine," and her groom, "Edward Belden." The groom was from St. Louis; the bride was from Quincy, close to Watson's hometown of McDonough, Illinois. In the story, Josephine makes her new husband extremely jealous so that he has no choice but to leave for adventures in New Orleans, Sacramento, and other points south and west. The lovers meet again some years later at a masquerade ball, where the depressed, barely functioning bride makes conversation with a man she does not immediately recognize:

> "Were you ever in California?" she asked.
>
> "I have just returned from California," he said, "where I have met with many strange adventures, which, were your ears as willing, I would relate, as Othello told to gentle Desdemona his hair-breadth escapes by land and sea."
>
> "Have you ever had such hair-breadth escapes?"
>
> The lady's agitation was still visible, though she endeavored evidently to conceal it.

"In truth I have, lady. I have laid on a couch suffering for over
a year from wounds received in an affray with a band of robbers—
have been published as dead—have been worth a hundred thousand
dollars—within an hour have seen the scorching flames shrivel my
whole fortune to ashes."

The story ends with Josephine and Edward falling in love with each other's words at the masked ball; they decide to marry while blinded to each other's identities. When their masks are lifted after the ceremony, after much "heaving" and "quivering," Josephine is elated to find that her groom is her long-lost Edward. In real life, Judson may not have realized that Maggie Watson was only thirteen years old at the time of their marriage. Presumably, it was annulled or ignored for age or religious reasons.[1]

In New York, needing money and a platform for his nativist ideas, Judson revived *Ned Buntline's Own*. He tried to track down his old friend Armamus Lafayette Swart, who had been the printing foreman of the paper three years before. The writer was surprised to discover that Swart had died suddenly in 1851.

Lovanche Kelsey Swart had already known E. Z. C. Judson for about ten years when she became romantically involved with him sometime in 1853, when she was twenty-six and he was about thirty-one.[2] By many accounts, Lovanche was beautiful, smart, articulate, and quick-witted.[3] When Armamus died, she was left alone to raise their toddler son. She moved back to New York to live with her sister and struggled to make ends meet as a seamstress. She was known, she said, as "the Widow Swart." Judson, she later recalled, did not have any place to live at this time and was continually moving from one place to another.[4] Within weeks, Judson asked Lovanche to marry him. She asked him about his divorce from Bennett—the scandal was still fresh in the minds of many New Yorkers. "At this time," Lovanche said, "he showed me a slip from a newspaper showing the death of this wife. And he assured me that she was dead." The obituary was "purported to be copied from a London newspaper," Lovanche noted, which made sense because it was commonly known that Bennett moved back to Britain when their divorce was granted.[5] She and Judson had a marriage ceremony of some sort on September 24, 1853, in Hoboken, New Jersey. The event took place at Palisade House, a small but upscale hotel. Judson told Lovanche that he owned it.[6]

The pair lived in New Jersey for a few months and then embarked on a lecture tour. Lovanche did not drink, nor did she approve of people who did, so she was pleased that her new husband had resumed his temperance speeches. Judson, in *Ned Buntline's Own*, started to take on the public discussion of slavery and race in general, ignorant about the reasons free blacks in cities were impoverished:

ETHIOPIAN BEGGARS—I have seen more than twenty old and young, blind and maimed negro beggars seated about the side-walks with labels on their breast, asking for charity, since I have been in town—in less than two weeks. During over two years residence and travel in the South and West in Slave states, I have never seen a negro beggar or a black uncomfortably clothed. The admirers of Uncle Tom's Cabin may stow that in their pipes and smoke it. There is more squalid wretchedness amongst the negroes in one block in this city than there is in the whole South![7]

At this time, Judson's attitude toward slavery cleaved closely to the Know Nothing Party's stance toward it, which was—simply speaking—not to take much of a stance toward it at all. His views would later evolve along with his fellow Northerners, which was to take an antislavery position after the 1857 *Dred Scott v. Stanford* decision, which denied citizenship to slaves and aroused abolitionist sentiment in the upper states. For the time being, though, Judson focused on attracting prohibitionists to the American Party. The nativists—opposed to alcohol because Germans and Irish were thought to be constantly drunk on beer and wine—thought the "drys" an easy target for membership.

By mid-1854 the Know Nothing Party had reached its zenith. It included more than one hundred elected congressmen, eight governors, a controlling share of a half-dozen state legislatures from Massachusetts to California, and thousands of local politicians. Its true numbers can never be known because of the secretive nature of the organization. In 1849, when the party consisted of Judson and other primary leaders Lewis Charles Levin and Augustine J. H. Duganne, members employed a "cloak-and-dagger" approach to their political activities; when asked about their organizations, members gave a canned answer: "I know nothing."[8] But by the time of Judson's return to New York in late 1852, the party openly rallied for support in the 1854 midterm elections, hoping to elect several members to congressional positions. The moral issues that Judson preached were still overshadowed by the issue of slavery. But the Democratic Party—firmly pro-slavery in the South and faltering in the North—seemed on the verge of its own demise, and nativists saw an opportunity. "Surely, in time," Monaghan wrote of their thinking, "peace-loving people who saw the threat of war over the Negro would find nativism a safety valve for the increasing pressure of abolition steam."[9]

In the meantime, Lovanche sent her little son, Frank, to live with her parents in Broome, New York. When they married, Judson had promised to raise Frank as though he were his own son; sending him to his grand-parents while she traveled with her husband was a small price to pay; at the time, Lovanche thought Judson might be elected to some office on the American Party ticket.

The pair crisscrossed upstate New York for a few months so that Judson could organize "secret military orders" with lofty names like the "Guard of Liberty"—though the newspapers reported on these regularly. Lovanche later said, "We went to all the Eastern states, had good times, and enjoyed life in all its pleasures."[10]

The "first cloud" appeared, she said, when they arrived in Boston in April 1854. Judson planned to deliver a series of speeches about Know Nothingism and start a Sunday newspaper. Established newspapers made fun of him, printing that Ned Buntline was in New England "for the purpose of solving the mooted question" about the American Party.[11] After all, no one could be sure how large or small the party really was. Because its members were supposed to be secret, Judson and his cohorts could claim victory any time someone who was remotely moderate in their views got elected.

The "first cloud" did not refer to Judson's political activity, though. In Boston, on June 13, 1854, Judson married eighteen-year-old Ione Judah, a beautiful actress appearing in Boston's Howard Athenaeum in the farce *Whitebait at Greenwich!* This bigamous marriage was almost certainly a reflection of a sexual relationship between the pair. Little is known about Ione, so it is perhaps unfair to categorize the union as something without some measure of true affection, however fleeting.

Judah was the youngest daughter of Emanuel and Marietta Judah, a famous theatrical couple made even more famous by the fact that Emanuel and some of Ione's siblings were drowned in a shipwreck off the southern coast of Florida in April 1840. Marietta remarried in 1851, to another actor and nurtured the careers of her daughters. She may have been horrified to read the announcement in any of the hundreds of newspapers that carried it:

> *NED BUNTLINE—This fellow,* alias *E. Z. C. Judson, of penitentiary notoriety, has lately been at his old tricks. The Charlestown (Mass.) Advertiser distinctly charges him with marrying a lady in Newark, N.J. in September last, and recently abandoning her at Fitchburg in Massachusetts, when, within a few days he clandestinely married again in Charlestown. When the first wife came to "see about it" on the 27th June, he had fled with his new wife to parts unknown.*[12]

One Pennsylvania newspaper put Judson in their "Marriages of Celebrities" column, intimating that Judah had placed him under some sort of spell: "Next was the somewhat equally notorious individual who has figured conspicuously under the sobriquet of Ned Buntline, but whose real name is Edward C. Judson. He is said to have been conquered by the melting eyes of a sweet Jewish maiden, who has led him into the captivity of the 'silken tie.'"[13]

It's not clear where Judson and Judah went for the rest of the month except for the fact that they lodged at the American House in Boston—Judson and Judah skipped out a week later, leaving the bill unpaid—but presumably the writer stayed clear of Lovanche.[14] In July, reports of his activities started to surface again, such as this one in the *Boston Herald*:

> *Ned Buntline & Co. are scaring the people in the country towns with stories that the Irish Catholics intend to celebrate the Fourth of July by poisoning and massacring the Americans, a la St. Bartholomew's day. We beg our country friends not to be alarmed by this ridiculous and malicious statement. It is our own opinion that a large number of Irish, as well as others, will be more likely to poison themselves with bad rum next Tuesday than to poison the food of Americans.*[15]

By August, the novelist and lecturer had made his way to Maine, where he hoped to pull more followers to the Know Nothing Party. The new mayor of Portland was Neal Dow, who had been elected on a prohibition ticket in 1851; the entire state went dry the same year. (Prohibitionists in New England had earned the term "Maine-iacs" because of that state's no-alcohol stance.) By the time Judson started making his lecture rounds in this most northeastern part of the country, several other states had "gone dry," or at least put the possibility on their ballots. It seemed to Judson that he could raise enough new membership in his nativist party to send a strong candidate to a convention of Know Nothings in Cincinnati in November.

Judson was scarcely in Maine but a few days before he raised hell. A carpenter later recalled what happened when Judson came to deliver a campaign speech in Bath, located about forty miles up the coast from Portland. It seemed that on the evening of July 6, 1854, the people of Bath had two choices for entertainment: a lecture on geology at Columbian Hall or an "anti-Catholic harangue by a travelling stump speaker" on the steps of the Old Universalist Church on Front Street. There was an Irish population in the town, owing to its need for shipbuilding labor, and bigoted sentiments ran high. Most people chose to listen to Judson's lecture, either out of sincere nativist feelings or sheer boredom on a humid summer night:

> *When Buntline reached Brunswick he missed the regular connection and so hired a team to drive through. The carriage was an*

old-fashioned two-wheel gig and he had been due to speak at two o'clock in the afternoon but as a matter of fact it was that hour when he left Brunswick.

He drove through as fast as possible and just as he reached the end of the Bay bridge in Niggertown, as it was roughly called, someone shot at him three times in rapid succession. One of the bullets went wild but the other two hit the seat of the gig and plowed through it within an inch of his body. There must have been more than one who fired, as repeating rifles were not known at that time and the three shots were all fired within a few seconds of each other.

Buntline put the whip to his horse and came into the city as quickly as possible. A crowd of not less than 3,000 men were in the square near the old Sagadahoc House and in front of the Gov. King place when he came in, and he told them what had just happened. I saw the gig, as did hundreds of others, and the bullet holes plainly showed.[16]

Others did see it, and they noticed that Judson wore a navy uniform of sorts, with all kinds of medals and badges on it. Mrs. James C. Ledyard remembered being courted by her future husband on the porch of her house and hearing the sound of thundering hooves and murmurs of a growing mob as Judson approached an area by the Old South Church.

News of his arrival ran through the crowd "like lightning," and "produced the wildest excitement," Ridley recalled. And it did not take long for the crowd to conclude that it was the Irish responsible for shooting at Judson's carriage, and this only served to inflame it:

In less time than it takes to tell the story it could plainly be seen that this crowd was determined on some kind of vengeance. Old Dr. Stallbridge, who at that time was one of the big guns of the city, got into a hack and ordered the driver to drive him right through the crowd. He shouted and by all other means tried to stop the riot, but it was too late. The crowd seemed to be perfectly infuriated. The doctor managed to get through the crowd and drove down to Candy Row, as it was called. Instead of letting well enough alone, he turned and came back.

Then the mob broke loose on him. They threw him out and tipped the hack upside down. Then they cut the harness from the horse and stove things to pieces generally.[17]

Somebody yelled, "Hurrah for the South meeting house!" and the mob then started for the South Church, which was a Catholic one near the courthouse. One resident old-timer recalled that the horde was led by a young man carrying an American flag. The mob marched up Centre and High Streets and arrived on South Hill, where it "made a furious onslaught" on the church. The rioters broke all its doors and windows, and then chopped the pews and furniture into kindling wood. In these early days of no gas or electric lights, the mob took lighting oil and saturated the pews and perimeter of the church. Judson—the "standard bearer"—ascended the belfry, where he stood waving the American flag over the heads of the mob. He barely escaped getting burnt by sliding on the lightning rod to the ground below. Reminiscent of the riot he started in St. Louis, firefighters could not get through to the structure in time to save any of it—the horde blocked them.

Meanwhile, the Irish of Bath, afraid for their lives, fled to Sewall Woods, about two miles away. They camped there for days until, one by one, they returned to town as hunger overtook them. In a few days, after their health and courage had been restored and the rest of the town had calmed down, some Irishmen swore out warrants and had some men involved in the church burning arrested. But their ringleader—Ned Buntline—was long gone.[18]

It wasn't long before Judson resurfaced, though. In Bangor, Maine, he lectured, wearing some sort of military uniform, on the subject "America for Americans," stirring up anti-Catholic sentiment to the point that a few dozen men broke into the home of a priest, tarred-and-feathered him, robbed him, and left him to die of exposure.[19] A couple of weeks after the death of the priest, on the evening of October 24, 1854, Judson arrived just outside Bowdoinham, about midway between the top and bottom of the state of Maine on the coast. According to Monaghan's account of the evening, the novelist bundled himself in a coonskin coat and buffalo robe to fight the cold and drove his gig hard to the outskirts of town in an attempt to make it to another town the next day for a lecture. There he met with an oxcart accompanied by five men walking and drinking; a quarrel ensued. Judson fired two shots and "whipped away." When he arrived at the Bay Bridge, he paid his toll and notified the gatekeeper that he had been held up by twenty-five or thirty Greeks and had to shoot his way through. One foreigner, Judson said, had grabbed his horse's bridle, forcing him to shout, "Stand by, Greek, and let me pass." The man did not, so, Judson claimed, he shot at him and he fell. "Another one jumped," he said; "I shot and think I missed him. Couldn't say whether he was dead or alive, should probably hear in the morning."[20]

The tollgate keeper told Judson that the road was dangerous after dark, and so the writer kept vigilant. His vehicle struck a pile of lumber and one wheel broke, so Judson took one roan horse and rode it across the Kennebec River to Bowdoinham and got transportation to his next city, about twenty-five miles away. What happened next is not disputed. He was arrested and taken back to Bath, the closest big town to Bowdoinham. The warrant for Judson's arrest was based on a complaint by Telemachus Freeman, a twenty-four-year-old black man who had escaped from slavery in Virginia and settled in Maine. Judson posted one thousand dollars' bail and decided he would represent himself when the matter came before the judge later that day.

What had really transpired is this: Freeman and some companions had been walking on the road. Judson had almost run them down, and yelled at them as he dashed past. About twenty yards down the road, Judson had stopped and asked the men if they wanted a ride. When they were close enough, Judson shot at Freeman twice; one of the bullets entered the fleshy part of Freeman's thigh, where it would reside permanently. Freeman's companions corroborated this story. However, the courtroom was packed with Know Nothings, and Judson provided a very convenient story after thoroughly discrediting Freeman's character: The road had been very dark, and he thought Freeman and his friends a pack of Irish. He shot in self-defense. The judge and jury believed him, and he was acquitted.[21]

Still, the court of public opinion had more than caught up with Judson. "The veriest pretender," wrote the *Washington Times*, "has but to start out on a crusade, and he finds thousands of clamorous followers flocking to his standard. Who would have deemed it possible that so degraded a wretch as Judson, better known as 'Ned Buntline,' could succeed in devising a scheme of agitation which should exceed in its wild fanaticisms even abolitionism itself?"[22] In Bangor the press made fun of him, writing that a "new order" had formed: It was called the Knights of the Star Spangled Banner, or "Guardians of the Tail Feathers of the American Eagle," and its purpose was a "devotion to the bottle and hostility to everything else."[23]

Unfortunately for Judson, by 1855 public discourse about slavery and abolitionism edged out that of immigrant threat. At statewide Know Nothing conventions that year, a slavery platform was introduced and the party split, North and South, just like the Democrats had done. *Cooper's Clarksburg Register* in Virginia and other Southern newspapers printed an exceptionally wonderful anthropomorphic version of Know Nothingism as it stood in mid-1855:

> *Many of our readers will be greatly pained to learn that on Thursday last, that promising young horse whose friends were certain would win the sweepstakes at the fall races of 1856, was irretrievably ruined in a race in Virginia and has been turned out to grass. It becomes our duty to give a slight sketch of his pedigree, performances, &c., &c. It is not certain where he was foaled, but he was bred near the Five Points, by his proprietor Ned Buntline, and is, of course, full brother to Abolition, Anti-Mason, Anti-Renter, and Higher Law, whose performances on the New York and neighboring courses astonished the lovers of the Constitution.*
>
> *Within the last two years this young horse has won a great many quarter and scrub races, and had raised the hopes of his friends that he would very probably win at the great four years race to come off on the first Tuesday of November '56. . . . It was with great difficulty that he was taken off the track and led to his stall, where at the last accounts he was dying, and is now most probably dead.*[24]

By August 1855 it was clear that Judson was not going to be able to come up with a stance on slavery that would be palatable or interesting enough to unite the Know Nothings on a single platform. And he made it clear that he, as an individual, was not willing to cleave to any ideas that others in this experimental party might come up with to attract more voters. Still in Maine, Judson sent a missive to regional newspapers to reiterate the principles with which he had helped found the American Party:

1. Americans are Americans by birthright only, by virtue of their sacred memory of their fathers and forefathers—only these Americans are capable of ruling their land.

2. That true Americans need to stand "firm as a surge-beaten rock" in opposition to the "overwhelming tide of foreign and pauper immigration rolling in from the old world—which has increased our taxes, decreased the price of labor, brought misery and suffering into over-crowded cities—filled to overflowing from our poor-houses and caused us to multiply them throughout the length and breadth of our land!"

3. Oppose the naturalization of foreigners and equalization with natural-born citizens before the age of twenty-one, and before they have proved themselves loyal to the American flag.

4. Oppose Catholicism and all that it espouses.

5. Believing that "all charity begins at home," favor other countries' support of their own paupers instead of "dumping them" here in America.

6. Remain "bitterly and fervently opposed" to those "designing knaves" who encourage suffrage for those born elsewhere, and take advantage of their "easily excited prejudices."

7. That we do not assume to interfere with the constitutional rights of any State, that we do not assume to interfere with slavery where it exists, but we sternly insist that the Missouri Compromise of 1820 was sacred and was only broken by faithlessness and treason, that the extension of slavery upon soil hitherto free, is a black and damning

shame upon our wisest statesmen, such as Clay, Webster, Bell, Houston, Benton, Adams and others, good men and great, who have grown grey in their country's service, or gone down honored and lamented to the grave.[25]

And there it was: Judson's public declaration that the American Party did not espouse the proliferation of slavery in America but would not take any stance against the practice. It was, as his seventh point continued, "an institution to be deplored," that slave labor "never is or can be so productive of either profit or happiness as free labor!" Furthermore, Judson said, practicing Catholicism in the privacy of one's home was just fine, as long as one did not get into politics.[26]

Judson threw his support behind the nomination of Millard Fillmore as the Know Nothing candidate on the presidential ticket of 1856. During the campaign, the Know Nothings adopted a more moderate platform that downplayed the party's opposition to immigration and advocated a rapprochement between the two sides of the slavery issue. The Republicans maintained a vehement antislavery stance, a position that garnered them the votes of most Northern states. The Democrats, however, citing the possible dissolution of the Union should antislavery sentiments prevail, managed to win several key Northern states, enabling James Buchanan to win the White House.[27]

Thus, Edward Judson's political career was over in November 1856. As the slavery debate intensified after the Dred Scott decision, Ned Buntline once again turned his energies from speeches and stumping and haranguing to fiction, in which he could offer those with nativist sympathies an imaginary country where white, Protestant men won the battle for freedom, dignity, hearts, and minds every single time there was a conflict, and even pacifist Quakers fought in the Revolutionary War because it was the right thing to do. Adding to Judson's probable melancholy was the fact that his beloved mother, Elizabeth, had died in Philadelphia just before the election.[28]

For the next year or so, Judson wandered back and forth between friends' homes in Maine, New York, and Ohio, seeking some sort of cause to espouse. He briefly experimented with Spiritualism, which had been sweeping the country ever since the Fox sisters of Hydesville, New York, made the budding movement famous in 1847. After their brief relationship, Ione Judah moved to parts unknown; her fate is unknown too. She definitely published poetry for newspapers and spiritual magazines. She may have been the Hagar I. Judah who appeared in Spiritualist circles in Buffalo not long after her marriage to Judson. "For the last three months or more," said the *Spiritual Telegraph*, "Miss Judah has been under the spiritual treatment of Mr. [Uriah] Clark; and through Spirit-aid alone, under the most astounding conditions, has been raised from the borders of death and despair."[29]

Throughout the mid-to late 1850s, Judson and Lovanche wrote letters to each other and occasionally "met up," though she recalled that "his habits were such that I had very little to do with him," and told him she would not until he reformed himself and embraced the temperance movement wholeheartedly—presumably in practice as well as speech. Reporters, though, still checked in with Lovanche from time to time, and the updates did not reflect well on Ned Buntline:

The Buffalo Republic *says that Mrs. E. C. Z. Judson, the gifted and beautiful wife of the notorious "Ned Buntline," was found lying dangerously ill, in a miserable hovel in that city the other day, utterly destitute and alone. Her villainous husband, "the Father of American Know-Nothings," having tired of her charms, has obeyed his brute instincts in cruelly neglecting and deserting her. She is a lady of excellent character, and was so unfortunate as to form an attachment for one of pleasing address, singular and mysterious attractiveness, of specious ability, but devoid of the finer feelings of the heart and honorable principles of a man. Her sympathy for Judson, whom almost every body abused, ripened into love for him. He played the deeply injured man so well, dissembled his true character so completely, counterfeited the gentleman so adroitly, and cloaked his passion so nearly by the guise of love, that he won "a lady (the New York* Tribune *says) of marvelous beauty and loveliness." Poor Mrs. Judson has paid the penalty of her attachment to the miserable wretch who claims to be the originator of Know-Nothingism—the patron especially of Louisville and Baltimore cutthroats—the leading spirit of lawlessness in the United States. The penalty is too great.*[30]

But as one special examiner from the government later pointed out, it may have been more of a two-way street: "It is certain," he said, "that this claimant [Lovanche] had some strong hold on [this] soldier. And she was either his legal wife, or else she had some hand that kept him in her power."[31]

CHAPTER NINE

Adirondacks, Eva, Sarah, and Kate

IN 1858 IT WAS CLEAR THAT EDWARD Z. C. JUDSON WAS HAVING A breakdown of sorts. In the cold of late February, he appeared in the streets of Syracuse, New York, with red ochre smeared all over his face and hands. He had borrowed an "Indian costume" from a Chippewa named Elliot, and paraded through the streets with dozens of young boys following him around. "It is a wonder they don't have him turn up at Sing Sing," the newspapers said, in reference to the prison, "with stripes on his breeches and bracelets on his ankles."[1] His American Party was dead—made irrelevant by the more pressing issue of slavery—and his temperance lectures were getting harder to sell as he frequently showed up intoxicated.

His publishers, at that time primarily the *New York Weekly Mercury*, were making money hand over fist with Judson's refreshed tales of nautical heroism, but his drunkenness and despondency over his failed political career was starting to show: He started to turn work in late, or sometimes not at all.

Judson was already familiar with the Lake Hamilton region of the Adirondacks before he moved up there full-time, in January 1859.[2] In 1856, perhaps after some time spent with Judah, the writer purchased fifty cleared acres on the installment plan from a local man. The property was situated on Round Lake—itself a middle body of water connecting the larger Blue Mountain and Utowana Lakes.[3] There was already a "dwelling house" on the property—just a log hut and a log hay barn.

The Adirondacks were—and are—composed of millions of acres of pristine wilderness in northeastern New York against the Vermont border. Monaghan likened the region in the mid-nineteenth century to that of central Africa or Alaska a hundred years later. It was a glorious haven for hunters, anglers, and loners—a perfect setting for Judson to clear his head and fill his personal coffers again.

Judson hired a guide, Chauncey Hathorn, who claimed to be the first white man to settle at Blue Mountain Lake.[4] With rod, gun, and camp outfit, Judson entered the dark forest at Lake Pleasant. Likely all of his fonder childhood memories of Wayne County and hunting and fishing with his father came flooding back to him. Camp life, as Monaghan called it, appealed to the writer:

> *With moccasins on his feet and cocked gun in hand, he enjoyed walking on the spongy black earth, watching for game along trails mottled with sunshine. He liked the damp fungus smell of cool deep forest, and the dry hot smell of sun-drenched hillsides where bears came to feast on fragrant berries. He amused himself calling the trees by name: maple, oak, witch hazel, spruce, pine, beech, silver and white birch. Deep in the forest he listened to the murmur of breezes passing overhead in the treetops. Guides showed him how to build a bark lean-to in the woods. He learned to make wet wood burn by using shredded birchbark for kindling.[5]*

Judson and Hathorn had become friends a couple of years earlier, when the writer came up for a brief hunting trip after the collapse of the Know Nothing Party. Hathorn had been staying at a log cabin in a clearing on Tallow Lake when the famous Ned Buntline arrived with some guides.[6] According to Hathorn's account, Judson liked the place and bought it. He named it "Eagle Nest"—the plural version evolved over time—and renamed the lake "Eagle Lake" because he had seen two eagles make their nest near the cabin. He was so enamored with his new existence that he immediately wrote a song about it, called "My Home":

> Where the silvery gleam of the rushing stream
> Is so brightly seen on the rock's dark green,
> Where the white pink grows by the wild red rose
> And the bluebird sings till the welkin rings.

Where the red deer leaps and the panther creeps,
And the eagles scream over cliff and stream;
Where the lilies bow their heads of snow,
And the hemlocks tall throw a shade o'er all;
Where the rolling surf laves the emerald turf,
Where the trout leaps high at the hovering fly,
Where the sportive fawn crops the soft green law,
And the crow's shrill cry bodes a tempest nigh—
There is my home—my wildwood home.

Some twenty-five years later, Judson's friend Fred E. Pond took the pen name "Will Wildwood" for his hunting and fishing magazine articles. It was Pond who collected anecdotes about his idol's prowess in the wilds of the Adirondacks, such as this one about his first full winter at his hunting cabin:

One day in January, my hounds, chained up in their warm dog-house, made a great fuss, and looking out on Eagle Lake in front of my log dwelling I saw a noble buck, a regal giant of the forest, attempting to cross its glittering surface. He was over half way across, slipping, falling and sliding on, when I went out. He did not seem to fear me, though he must have seen me. I believe the old fellow knew no white man would shoot him out of season, and was actually coming in for protection. For as I looked at him I heard a series of howls across the lake, and knew that a big gang of wolves was on the trail of the dear.

I hurried in and got my rifle, an Ogden double-barrel, made in Oswego, carrying 32 to the pound conical ball. By the time I had got it and my ammunition ready, and rushed down to a clump of cedars on the lake-side, the noble buck was within two hundred yards of the shore and doing his uttermost to get there, for the wolves were almost up to him.

Two or three tremendous leaps brought him within easy rifle range, one hundred yards, but the accursed wolves, at least twenty in number, were on him, and in a second he was down, with every jaw fasted in him that could find a place to bite.

Oh, if I had then had the glorious "Old Reliable" that now stands in one corner of my sanctum, I believe I could have killed every wolf in the gang before they knew what I was doing, while, they, half-starved, were gorging on their prey.[7]

Judson's description here is stark, yet detailed and vivid, as it would be for most of his descriptions of real-life adventures in the Adirondacks:

As it was, while they were plunging, growling and tearing the poor animal to pieces, I sent in shot after shot, as fast as I could load and fire.

It was not until nine of their number were dead or disabled that the wolves found out they were in an unhealthy neighborhood, and several of these limped away when they went at last, leaving a bloody trail on the glittering ice.

In that brief time that deer was so nearly devoured that you couldn't find a bone that was not broken or a bit of meat big enough for a bulldog's swallow. And some of the dead wolves had their hides torn so badly they were almost worthless by the numerous jaws of their mates in the blind, mad struggle for a feast.[8]

Judson's publishers were pleased and relieved at their contributor's output when he holed up in the mountains. To make sure he saved at least a part of his earnings, the writer made arrangements with friend Stephen Starbuck for the *Mercury* to bank with him a portion of those earnings each month.[9] "For the first six weeks after Winter set in I had a glorious time. Hermit life just suited me. I had plenty to eat and drink, good reading matter, and all of out-doors to myself when I wanted exercise. Writing sketches and stories filled up the intervals. . . . No temptation to deviate from the rules of health and morality appeared."[10] His stories of sea waifs and boat captains and pirates and Mormons and Revolutionary War spies made the *New York Mercury* fly out of newsboys' hands, and were so profitable for the paper that it hired famous artists to illustrate them—a hugely expensive undertaking for newspapers at that time. "The only man who can write a story of the Sea since [Frederick] Marryatt and [James Fenimore] Cooper," said one advertisement, "is the inimitable NED BUNTLINE, who is a thorough-bred seaman and writes such nautical tales as would stir the blood of the most supine." The writer would hunt and fish at least part of the day, and then lie down on a bearskin rug in his little cabin, writing away until the early hours of morning next to the fireplace.[11]

As winter turned to spring, Judson's loneliness—and sobriety—got the better of him, and he set out for a quick foray among crowds again. He made his way down to Lake George, where he set tongues wagging by his actions at Gales' hotel saloon: He strode up on his horse, sauntered in, and ordered a drink, and as the bartender fixed the order, Judson shot his revolver at a point in the wall a few inches above the poor bartender's head. "That's how William Tell did it!" he exclaimed. The bartender was either used to this type of behavior or perhaps did not think Judson would actually do it again, but when Judson ordered another drink, he shot at him again and said, "That would have taken a damn small apple off your head, young man!"[12]

From Lake George, Judson rode the New York Central Railroad down to Schenectady; the *Reflector* noted that he appeared to be in ebullient spirits, causing quite a commotion by buying out the orange and maple sugar dealers at the depot and scattering the treats among the youths lingering there. They cheered for the sweets while Judson treated them to patriotic speeches.[13] This quid pro quo with children at gathering places would become routine with Judson. From here, in mid-April, the writer made his way down to Troy, for what reason isn't clear, but his actions are well-documented:

The Troy Whig *says that Ned Buntline, whose indiscretions in Troy have been duly heralded by the local press, did something more serious and ludicrous than he is heretofore been charged with. He got married. "Ned" started down Sixth Street a single man. He espied a lager bier saloon, and in it a blooming Dutch maiden tending bar. Ned fell in love at first sight, and made an offer of his hand and heart. The girl accepted him; Ned went through the marriage ceremony himself, and immediately started off with his bride. We have these facts from an eyewitness, who says that E. Z. C. Judson was legally and indissolubly joined in wedlock to the pretty German.*[14]

The "blooming Dutch maiden" was Eva Marie Gardiner, the seventeen-year-old daughter of a farmer who lived in Minerva, New York. This was less of a "love at first sight" coupling than a transactional one, at least at first. A friend of the novelist who lived near him in the Adirondacks described how the pair came to live together:

In 1859, Buntline went to Minerva in quest of a woman to attend to his household duties. Miss Maria Gardner [sic], then employed as a domestic in the family of the late John Straight, near Olmsteadville [sic], was recommended as a suitable person. He interviewed the young lady. She was reluctant to go with Buntline to his secluded habitation, but his offer of five dollars per week and numerous presents soon overcame her objections and she became the matron of Eagle's Nest.[15]

Minerva is about forty miles west of Judson's home; he may have gone to Troy to get her after coming to an arrangement with her father.

Despite the image portrayed by the *Whig*, it most definitely was not a legal marriage. A friend of Judson recalled that Judson simply took Gardiner back to Eagle Nest. "Buntline, although rude and thoughtless under ordinary circumstances, was remarkably kind to his lady helpmeet and ere long a warm attachment sprung up between them, which culminated in Ned's offer of marriage." However, they were twenty-five miles from the nearest minister or justice of the peace, and because spring weather came late that year, the snow was deep and soft and the roads impassable. Eventually, Judson's friend Patrick McKenna was able to make his way to the little cabin and perform a simple ceremony for the pair. Nonetheless, there was at least one other legal wife out there, and the *Buffalo Daily Republic* stood up for its betrayed resident—whether it was Lovanche or Ione Judah or someone else entirely:

> *The* Whig *is mistaken in supposing that Ned Buntline married the woman taken by him to New York on Sunday. . . . [B]esides, the vagabond already has a wife living, and to those who have made her acquaintance Mrs. E. Z. C. Judson is known as one of the most gifted and most unfortunate of women. The lady, MRS. JUDSON, spoken of by the* Times, *has resided in this city for the last two or three years, most of which time she has been confined to her house and her bed by severe nervous and mental affliction. The* Times *does not say all, when it speaks of her as a gifted and unfortunate woman: she is not only gifted and unfortunate, but young, and very beautiful; with all of these accomplishments she has braved a world of trouble, persecution and affliction, and sacrificed everything but her virtue.*[16]

Gardiner's point-of-view of her situation is not recorded, but by outward appearances, she and Judson seemed like good companions. She helped him keep the hunting shack in working order, cooked, cleaned—no small feat, considering it was composed of split spruce logs and peat moss. Perhaps most importantly, she kept him at least moderately sober. His partnership with the much-younger woman allowed Judson to write even more: The editor of the *Mercury* trekked up to Eagle Nest to present him with a contract to send serials regularly, and not just hunting stories but also historical fiction "fitted to the masses"—things like *The Mysteries and Miseries of New York* but less sordid. "Clean outdoor romance" is what the editor wanted, and he was rewarded with more best-selling stories, like *The White Wizard, Or, The Great Prophet of the Seminole. White Wizard*, eventually fifty-two chapters, was set in South Florida, at that time still almost unknown to most Americans. Set against the backdrop of the Second Seminole War, the story ranged from the Ten Thousand Islands into the Big Cypress Swamp and the Everglades, and from St. Augustine to Havana to New York City. Its cast of characters included a future president, Zachary Taylor, and such major Indian leaders as Chekika, Coacoochee, and Osceola.

In spite of his efforts, drinking soon crept back into Judson's repertoire. One resident recalled that he often saw Judson driving a two-horse tandem rig into North Creek (a nearby settlement) and Olmstedville to buy supplies and get roaring drunk. In Glens Falls, Judson was known to nurse a ten-inch-tall barrel of whiskey for as long as it lasted.[17]

Tragedy befell the couple on or about March 4, 1860. Eva Marie had given birth to a baby boy, William Charles, but soon became very sick. Both mom and baby appear to have passed away when the baby was only ten days old. Any number of things could have caused their deaths, including the puerperal fever that was so common in the nineteenth century owing to lack of sanitary conditions in childbirth. By choice or because of his isolated conditions, Judson buried Eva Marie and Charles together in a "rude coffin" under the wet ground behind the cabin.[18]

According to a local historian, Judson gave orders for his hunting cabin to be burned down after Eva Marie and the baby died.[19] He built a new home—still rustic but a bit more inviting, according to one hunter:

> We dined on the trout and then visited Ned Buntline, on the shore of Eagle Lake. Col. E. Z. C. Judson has left the city, purchased many acres of wilderness, including a clearing and a log house; has built for himself a good dwelling, partly of hewn logs, partly of shingle clapboards, lathed and plastered, and two-storied; has surrounded it with grass and flowers, vegetables and young evergreens; has opened a post-office under Uncle Sam's patronage, and thus comfortably settled writes for the New York Mercury, oversees a good tenant farmer, runs a weekly express through the woods to Fort Edward, on the Whitehall and Saratoga Railroad, eighty miles distant.[20]

Judson, according to this account and those of other hunters, had a generous ice cellar, and kept his home stocked with books, medicines, herbs, and even leeches. Sometimes he demanded privacy and even shot at trespassers; other times he invited strangers in, cooking them trout or a freshly killed chicken from his yard.[21]

Keeping up a homestead of this nature would be backbreaking for even the hardiest of settlers. So it shocked few locals in Judson's corner of the Adirondacks when, sometime in July or August, he took another "wife," in the form of Sarah Jane Brooks, from the nearby hamlet of Horicon. She was fifteen years old. There is no record of this marriage, but Judson held a celebration of some kind at J. J. Wilson's Hotel, near her father's home.[22] Hunters returning from visits to the area reported her as "an active, intelligent housekeeper," much in the same way they described Eva Marie.[23] Within a month of coming to live with Judson, Brooks was pregnant, and within three months she was abandoned. Some months later, she married a local man, and the pair started a family of their own. The man raised her child with Judson as if he was his own.

In 1860, in spite of his hunting, baby-making, and boozy detours to post offices to deliver manuscripts, Judson was supplying some of his best work to the *Mercury*. Besides *White Wizard*, *The Knight of the Black Flag*, and *Luona Prescott, Or, The Curse Fulfilled: A Tale of the American Revolution*—tales of a bygone era—Judson started homing in on America's obsession with westward expansion and conflict with Native Americans.

By 1850 there was a tremendous influx of immigrants in the southwestern plains region of Texas. These people were either destined for California in search of gold or in search of land and a home on the frontier. Stories of their experiences had been filtering back to Easterners for years, notably those of Comanche hostilities toward whites who increasingly encroached upon their lands—lands that had once belonged to other tribes before whites forced Comanches onto the Southern Plains. The Lipan Apache tribe remained. The Lipan Apache–Comanche enmity dated back to the early eighteenth century, and warfare would continue between the two peoples until 1875.[24]

To preserve some semblance of peace on the frontier, the government of Texas activated nine companies of mounted Texas Rangers. The Rangers remained the primary defenders of the Texas plains until military posts were established, when they assumed a secondary role in protecting the frontiers. For Judson, this situation provided the perfect backdrop for an account of an imagined activity on the Texas plains for the *Mercury*. Historian John W. Schmidt posits that Judson's use of real-life Major Ben McCulloch of the Texas Rangers in his popular work *Stella Delorme—The Comanche's Dream* may be his strongest forerunner of the Western format that he would later perfect.

The setting for the novel was the Rio Grande area of Texas, and the cast of characters included the Lipan Apache; a Comanche brave, Lagona; the heroine, Stella Delorme; and Major Ben McCulloch. Buntline made the white maiden "Stella Delorme" a victim of numerous Indian raids perpetrated by either the Lipan or Comanche. However, on more than one occasion, she was rescued by McCulloch's Rangers. Buntline described this band of Rangers as "one of the most gallant that ever rode astride a horse." Moreover, when they were engaged in an Indian fight, "McCulloch's Rangers left bodies of warriors who will never tread the warpath again."[25]

As usual, Schmidt notes, Judson's account was inaccurate and sensationalized. "Ned Buntline" frequently had the Comanche brave Lagona come to the aid of Stella Delorme and rescue her from the Lipan. However, this situation was contrary to all existing evidence. At this time, the Lipan were generally allied with the Texans—more against the Comanche than in fondness for the white man. Regardless, this allusion to McCulloch's Rangers—which had been in press accounts in all the Eastern newspapers for more than a decade—thrilled readers and spurred Judson to write more about the real and imaginary violence on the frontier. "His characters," Schmidt writes, "were cast in the mold of Daniel Boone and set in the context of an untamed wilderness. The scene had shifted west of the Mississippi to the Plains region which was the mid-19th century stage for rugged individualism."[26]

Stella Delorme, published and circulated in New York, showed the Eastern audience that despite Indian raids by Lipan or Comanche or whomever, there was always a Ben McCulloch and his Rangers to come to the rescue. These men were taming the frontier against overwhelming odds . . . at least in the novels. "Buntline," Schmidt sums up, "was apparently unaware that such a format for promoting and exploiting the West would be copied several years later in books termed 'dime novels.'"[27]

It seems likely that with the death of a wife and baby and the news of another baby on the way with his new teen helpmeet, even the endless expanse of the Adirondack wilderness felt like four walls closing in on Judson. It also seems likely that with money coming in regularly from his work for the *Mercury*, he may have wanted to spend it. And even though the Know Nothing Party had flamed out, Judson must still have been interested in the feverish political debates going on in the city about the new Republican candidate for the presidency, Abraham Lincoln.

On November 8, 1860, in Ossining, New York, Judson married twenty-five-year-old Kate Myers. It's not clear how they met. The ceremony was performed by the Methodist minister who was also the chaplain for Sing Sing Prison in that city. According to Hochschild, Judson took his bride to Eagle's Nest immediately after the ceremony. Friend and guide Chauncey Hathorn met the pair on the south shore of Eagle Lake and then ferried Myers across the lake in a boat while Judson took their horses by the much-rougher route on the roads. "The lady at once began to question me in regard to her future home," Hathorn said of his time in the boat, "of which she had formed a somewhat romantic idea—apparently expecting to find a mansion in the wilderness. As mildly as possible I gave a clearer view of the cabin home, taking especial care to describe the beautiful scenery, and the woman gracefully accepted the situation."[28] Years later, Judson liked to tell how he got his bride to Eagle's Nest and then stole her shoes so that she could not run away.

As winter snow set in, so did Kate's discomfort with the cabin in which they lived, according to Monaghan. Her husband wrote at a fast clip—sometimes with very little sleep or food for days at a time—but he also became obsessed with a neighbor named Alvah Dunning. Dunning was a famous guide in the Adirondacks, and by all accounts was as "odd, opinionated, and self-willed as Ned himself."[29] The genesis of their feud is not known, but they seemed to take every opportunity to harass each other: Dunning shot holes in Judson's beloved skiff so that it sank the next time the writer took it out fishing; in return, Judson shot Dunning's beloved dog.

By the summer of 1862, Myers stopped making pretenses of finding happiness in her Eagle's Nest surroundings and moved back to her parents' with baby Carrollita. Judson was enamored of his new family, and kept a diary in which he documented how much he missed them, in the form of unsent letters:

> *The sun is out clear and bright now—at half past seven in the morning. The storm seems to be over. At noon I got extravagant. I thought of green peas and picked and boiled nearly a saucer full. They would have been good if you had been here to help me eat them. Nothing tastes good now. Baby isn't here to kiss papa's mouth and make him happy. It's a good thing I've got no rum on hand. I'd get drunk in sheer desperation. Oh, I am so lonesome—so lonesome! . . . It is almost nine o'clock—and I am going to bed to try to sleep. It is hard work, for then I think more than ever of you and the baby. Kate I love you and the dear baby better than life. I cannot live long away from you. I suppose now that you are with your friends you'll not think much of me alone in the woods miles away from any human being.*[30]

Judson's description of his natural surroundings puts modern-day greeting cards to shame, discussing morning glories, dahlias, hop vines, double rainbows, and crisp showers. Luminaries from Boston came to fish with him—like Jonas Chickering the piano maker—which he seemed to enjoy for a short while, but he would become irritated if they stayed past a day or two because it set him back in his writing.[31]

If Judson's diary entries are any indication, he was completely smitten with Kate, to the point of desperation, filling them with longing for her and willingness to give up all earthly possessions to be with her again. "Brown said," he wrote, referring to the guide who took Kate and the baby back downstate to Chappaqua, "that you said you wished you had not left me while you was going out. That looks as you did love me some!" He waxed further: "I shall have to come up once or twice during the fall and winter and if you want to spend next summer here, the house will be in order and the garden all made in the spring. But it shall be as you like. Be a good wife to me and a good mother to my baby, and you shall live where and as you choose." Judson told Kate he would put Eagle's Nest in her and their child's name, and bring more hired help to the home to make it more comfortable. He vowed to try to make her happy; and when she was not, he promised that he would "go where a kind bullet may give you a chance for another husband."[32]

CHAPTER TEN

Civil War

ONE MORNING BACK IN THE SPRING OF 1861, EDWARD TOLD WIFE KATE THAT he was traveling to Lake Pleasant, about thirty miles from Eagle's Nest, so he could stock up on groceries and get the mail. Kate, in her first trimester of pregnancy with their first child, was not surprised when her husband still had not returned after several days. Even in the deep woods of the mid-nineteenth century Adirondacks, there were enough tourists passing through Eagle's Nest for Kate to have heard about Edward's penchant for drinking in taverns dotting the wilderness down to the then-nearest post office. The trip down there usually took about two days, and it was difficult, especially during rainy weather when water stood high in cattail marshes at Cedar River and he had to take a long detour. "Ned liked to celebrate his arrival in the post office by getting drunk," Monaghan wrote. "After a day or two of relaxation, Judson would buy a bottle 'to sober up on' and start the trek home again."[1] And Kate must have had some inkling that her husband's presence might be erratic—two months after their marriage, he had been arrested and detained in Troy when he showed up in some kind of military outfit with a huge sword hanging at his side. The previous year he'd given an oyster dealer there a promissory note for cash, but the document turned out to be worthless at the bank.[2]

But this time was different. Instead of buying groceries in Lake Pleasant, Judson donned his hunting shirt and joined a company of militiamen at Fort Edward in nearby Glens Falls.[3] Judson's movements from here are not clear, but it seems the company rode to Albany; then, at some point, he caught a train on the New York Central Railroad and traveled to New York City. From there he made his way to Washington, DC, and on May 11, 1861, the writer met with Secretary of War Simon Cameron. A former senator from Pennsylvania—he succeeded James Buchanan in 1845—Cameron had made millions from railways, canals, and banking. A vocal opponent of slavery, Cameron switched to the Know Nothing Party in 1856, which is how he came to be acquainted with Judson. In 1857 he secured a nomination for the Senate by the People's Party, the Pennsylvania branch of what became the Republican Party, but no doubt Judson was able to cash in on their earlier friendship and schedule at least a short meeting.

At this meeting with Secretary Cameron, the dime novel author let it be known that he wished to join the Union cause in a formal way:

> *E. Z. C. Judson, well known as Ned Buntline, had an interview with Secretary Cameron on Saturday morning, and tendered to the government a regiment composed of fifteen hundred practical hunters and sharp-shooters from the Western part of New York State. The regiment is raised and ready for service.*[4]

He was not the only one to tender the services of other human beings at the outbreak of the war on April 12, 1861, after Confederate forces bombarded Fort Sumter in Charleston Bay. The wealthy and scandalous congressman Daniel Edgar Sickles, for example, successfully lobbied Cameron to let him lead what became New York's Excelsior Brigade. Thomas F. Meagher, journalist and Irish nationalist, was allowed to recruit and lead the Irish Brigade after joining the army.

But unlike Sickles, Meagher, and others, such as prizefighter William Wilson, Judson was not given a post as a "political general"—an office that Lincoln handed to some men during the beginning days of the conflict, even if they had no military training. Usually these assignments were more symbolic than strategic, designed to garner support for the North among certain voting blocs. For the most part, Lincoln parsed these posts to moderate Democrats and also respected foreign-born men who could raise large numbers of immigrant soldiers. Judson, with his recent Astor Place Riot notoriety, strong anti-immigrant rhetoric, and prominence in the Know Nothing Party, would not have fit these criteria. Secretary

Cameron fondly remembered his Know Nothing days and admired Judson, and perhaps did promise the writer some post in the future.

Three days later, on May 14, 1861—perhaps while drunk, perhaps while trying to persuade Cameron of his Northern loyalty, or both—the storyteller borrowed a horse and galloped over the Potomac on the Long Bridge that connected the capital city with Alexandria, Virginia. There he seized a rebel flag but was immediately captured by Virginia guards. They simply brought him back to Washington. Just ten days later, Virginia voters ratified the state convention's decision to secede from the Union. Colonel Elmer E. Ellsworth—a close friend of Lincoln and commander of the 11th New York Volunteers—became the first Union casualty of the Civil War when he and his troops entered Alexandria. Innkeeper and zealous slavery defender James Jackson fired on Ellsworth at point-blank range with a shotgun as the latter removed the offending flag from the roof of Marshall House.

Judson loved being where all the action was. He was a fixture at local pubs and theaters, almost always wearing the same red flannel shirt and white cap. One correspondent reported that Judson had been parading the streets in and around Washington, striking a menacing pose on his horse while brandishing a large sword. He challenged at least one person to a duel with pistols (the other gentleman declined) and was forced to leave one Baltimore play because his mere presence produced loud cheers for both the Union and the Confederacy. Judson's boardinghouse proprietor had the good sense not to fulfill his requests for Moët & Chandon Champagne when he brought men back to the house for nightcaps.[5]

On June 30, 1861, a letter written to Judson by his sister appeared in the Washington, DC, *Sunday Morning Chronicle*. Irene may have been better informed of Edward's whereabouts and plans for the future than his wife:

Pittsburg [sic], June 15, 1861,
My Darling Brother,
I received your letter last evening, and although too weak to write, I must exert myself to do so. I have been indisposed for weeks, caused principally from overexcitement and fatigue in preparing clothing,

&c., for the army; but your few words have revived me. My dear brother, how I have longed to hear from you. I saw by the papers that you were in Washington some time since, and your old friends here felt assured that your arm was once more raised in defense of our glorious old flag—dearer now than ever. Do you know, Edward, that the very light of its starry folds stirs my being to its inmost depth, and I almost grieve for my womanhood, that I too might rank among the faithful defenders of our native land. But I can only pray, and bide my time in patient waiting for that glorious triumph of the right which is sure to come.

She implored her brother to take the time to write her often, and that she hoped the Almighty would keep him safe and free from temptation and harm:

I feel that I shall never have cause to blush for any act of cowardice on your part. I fear your daring disposition; you always place yourself in danger, and I fear may meet the fate of the gallant Ellsworth. But if you fall in defense of your country, I trust it will be fighting to the last. Our race is almost extinct. So for my sake, do not run into unnecessary danger. I have, as you know, the best of husbands; but if long-continued war rages, I may lose him, and be all alone. Yet I would lose all that is dear to me on earth, rather than give up one tithe of our glorious Constitution. *No* compromise, *only at the cannon's mouth.* Crush rebellion, *now and forever.*[6]

Judson went back to the Adirondacks sometime late in June 1861, maybe even before his sister's letter appeared in the *Chronicle*. He might have been irritated that the government would not give him an official post in the army, but in reality, it did him a pecuniary favor by not giving him a commission. Two of Judson's books were selling out everywhere. His publicity in the more recent war spurred his publisher to reissue his novel *The Volunteer, Or, The Maid of Monterey—A Story of the Mexican War*, which was originally published in 1852, republished in 1860, and sold forty-seven thousand copies in another printing in 1862 before the first half of the year was out.[7] In 1861 he wrote *The Rattlesnake, Or, The Rebel Privateer*, which debuted in the *New York Mercury* as a multipage color insert just before Christmas. There are no estimates available for the number of copies sold, but this romantic tale of a Union woman who loses her fiancé's affections to the Confederate navy was reprinted by publisher F. A. Brady every year all the way through 1905 and then sporadically after that. Judson's primary publisher at this time, the *New York Mercury*, billed him as "Lieutenant" and promoted the stories as tales of "military spirit" and "vivid and truthful" stories of soldier life.

On January 10, 1862, Kate Myers gave birth to the couple's first child: Mary Carrollita "Carrie" Judson. She was a healthy little girl, and of course, named after her father. "Carrollita is the smartest little child of her age I ever knew," Judson told his sister later when the little one was two years old. "She is all like me & talks & thinks of nothing but her Papa."[8]

In spite of this happy occasion, Kate was miserable at Eagle's Nest. Edward spent days and nights locked away in his rickety office churning out story after story for the *Mercury*. She had no female company to help her with chores and a new baby or just to talk to, and the specter of Eva and baby Charles had to loom large for her. In the spring of 1862, when the snow melted and Mary Carrollita was five months old, the family traveled 130 miles down to Kate's parents' home in Ossining, Westchester.

Kate's time with Edward in more comfortable suburban surroundings was short–lived. Judson decided that one way or another he was going to join the Union forces, and so on September 25, 1862, he enlisted at Mt. Pleasant as a private with the 1st New York Mounted Rifles, Company K.[9] Thomas Place, a childhood pal who bumped into Judson when enlisting at the same time, was bewildered that he did not have to strip his clothes off below the waist like everybody else. This also bothered John Habberton, who also enlisted that day. "My impression is," he later recalled, "that the surgeons passed him when only partially stripped simply because he was known to them as Ned Buntline."[10]

In later testimony, most of Judson's fellow enlistees—even if they were irritated about his seeming preferential treatment—recalled thinking

Judson was very serious about defending the Union cause at the time he signed up for the service, and one young man even wrote home about it: "Among the recruits recently arrived for New York Mounted Rifles, I noticed the somewhat famous E. Z. C. Judson ("Ned Buntline"), who had enlisted as a private. Ned was in good spirits and health, and sober, and as full of patriotism as he used to be of whiskey." Indeed, a lieutenant in his company later joked that Judson would "fight a buzzsaw" if it said anything against the United States.[11] If he survived his term of enlistment, the letter went on to say, "His literary talent will, no doubt, be turned to the manufacture of thrilling army tales."[12]

Company K of the New York Mounted Rifles was dispatched to Suffolk, Virginia, under the command of Colonel Charles Cleveland Dodge. About twenty years younger than Judson, Dodge had successfully seized the Norfolk & Gosport Naval Yard the prior spring. When Judson joined in the fall of 1862, Dodge was in the midst of trying to choke off supply roads around the Great Dismal Swamp—a coveted transportation route for the Confederates in southeastern Virginia and northeastern North Carolina. Dodge liked Judson, later recalling that the writer visited him at his New York office several times a year after the conflict ended, and was impressed by Judson's claim that "pride and patriotism" forbade him from applying for a pension earlier than he did, hoping that his work could adequately support his family.[13] According to fellow soldier Lieutenant John Dolan, Dodge gave Judson special consideration in the regiment. Though the scribe joined as a private, Dodge promoted him to sergeant within a month of enlistment. "That the talent of said Judson as a special scout beyond our lines and as an advanced guard during many important expeditions in Eastern Virginia were continuous, hazardous and of great value," Dodge testified after the novelist's death in 1886.[14] Judson got a tent all to himself, and had a glossy black horse that he used to "go scouting" when he felt like it. "He used to write Col. Dodge up in the papers," Dolan recalled. "We used to laugh at Judson for the puffs he gave Dodge."[15]

Though Judson had spent plenty of time in the South by this time, this Everglades-like region must have seemed eerie to him and his fellow New Yorkers. In his inspired-by-true-events novel (1864) *Life in the*

Saddle, Or, The Cavalry Scout, Ned Buntline describes what he likely saw when he arrived in Virginia:

> *From the tops of the rocking cars the troopers looked at the dirt and log huts of the garrison. Loafing soldiers made insulting but jovial gestures at the newcomers. The town of Suffolk seemed to be nothing but an army cantonment—new, temporary, utilitarian as a construction camp. Work gangs of soldiers and of Negro laborers, or "contrabands" as they were called, marched along the wagon ruts among tree stumps. West of camp, the muddy Nansemond, like a moat, protected Suffolk from the enemy. A drawbridge led across to the pine forest between the lines. Company K was assigned a campground one mile out of town, back along the Norfolk railroad track.*[16]

Judson, according to one comrade in arms, was heavily armed when he arrived in Suffolk. He was wearing a belt around his body with two Colt revolvers and a bowie knife prominently displayed. In addition, he often wore a "buck skin suit"—with feathers adorning the sides of the pants—foreshadowing his time with "Buffalo Bill" Cody on stage.[17]

According to Monaghan, Judson's fellow soldiers found him highly entertaining, and no doubt he was, given his profession as a sensational storyteller. Older than most, if not all, of his regimental mates, he was tough, talkative, and full of mischief. "The soldiers liked him, called him 'Uncle Ned,' [and] soon learned that he saw a story in the dullest everyday event." It is also true that Judson had plenty of military experience from the Second Seminole War, at least in terms of doing reconnaissance in swampy areas. "He knew so much from long experience," Monaghan wrote, "that they could never be sure when true history ended and Ned's imagination began."[18] Judson's quick promotion to sergeant on October 24, 1862, was probably warranted. He was, after all, an expert marksman from his navy experience, from hunting at Eagle's Nest, and from waging bets at shooting galleries around Barnum's.[19]

Setting aside paradoxes of war and the good life, E. Z. C. Judson's first four months of Civil War service were exactly how he had hoped and envisioned, filled with patriotic duty and backdrops to use for his stories. In addition to having the independence of a scout, Judson was given the task of "regimental marker": He carried small flags to post at each flank of the regiment in line to assist the field officers in maintaining a straight line of battle.[20] During Judson's first few months with the Mounted Rifles, his fellow soldiers were not only entertained by him; the special duties and treatment conferred upon him by Dodge made them revere Judson a bit as well. Even his detractors conceded a few instances of bravery: Once he took over a gunboat that ran from the mouth of the Nansemond River up to Suffolk when its pilot was shot, and got it past rebel batteries to camp. Another man remembered that at Zuni, Lieutenant William Wheelan was killed on the skirmish line, and while the troops fell back, Judson went forward under fire and brought Wheelan's body off the field.[21]

Any goodwill felt by Company K toward their "special scout" dissipated when the weather turned cold and Confederates started to raid Union guard lines dotting the road from Petersburg, about six miles south of Suffolk. In late November, rebels appeared in Franklin, about twenty-five miles away from Suffolk. Over the next month, Colonel Dodge's regiment and rebel forces attacked each other in the "no man's land" between Suffolk and the Blackwater River. At this time, scouting and reconnaissance work was of great importance, because rebel troops took every offensive and defensive advantage of hiding in the densely wooded areas. "I should say that Judson's services were of no value," B. H. Engelke recollected in 1887; "on the contrary I should say they were detrimental. As a general thing he managed to go out with his canteen full of whiskey and the result was that he returned with a cock & bull story founded on imagination." Alexander Hunter thought similarly: "He would go outside the lines—get full of whisky & come back & report some cock & bull story & the regiment would be turned out at all hours of the night—and find nothing." Charles Combes concurred: "He frequently pretended to go outside the lines and discover [illegible] of the enemy & the regiment would go out & find nothing. His services as a scout did not amount to much and I think the Regiment would have done better without him."[22] Many in Company K also remembered that at some point around this time, Judson's horse fell on top of him and crushed one of his limbs, or that he was thrown from it. He later told wife Anna Fuller that the horse incident happened at Blackwater Bridge in 1862.

Then-captain John Elmer Mulford, commissioner for the exchange of prisoners, encountered Judson in Baltimore sometime in late 1862 or early 1863. He was astounded to see the novelist in Barnum's Hotel, wearing a second lieutenant's cavalry shoulder straps. "My attention," Mulford recalled, "was called to him by the people who kept the hotel, as he was boisterous and disorderly." Knowing Judson was not a commissioned officer, Mulford asked him, "What right have you to be wearing those shoulder straps?" Judson told him that he had recently been to Albany and had received a commission. Mulford knew a bogus story when he heard one, and demanded he produce proof that he was entitled to be in Baltimore, away from Company K. Of course Judson could not produce such proof, and Mulford proceeded to arrest him. Since there is only one court martial proceeding noted in Judson's voluminous files, this was probably the incident Lieutenant John Dolan had in mind when he recalled that Judson was once off under the guise of scouting when he was "pulled up by some other Regiment and brought to camp as a deserter—but they found it was all right."[23]

On January 8, 1863, Judson received a week's furlough to go to New York City to get treatment for an unspecified illness. On January 14, according to Lovanche, the two ran into each other on the street in New York City. She recalled that he was wearing a cavalry uniform. He asked for her address and if he could visit with her. She obliged, and he showed up at her home later that afternoon. "He looked pale, haggard and nearly worn out," she said, "only weighing about ninety-six pounds. He said he had come home to die and could not do so without a reconciliation." Lovanche doctored and nursed him; Judson proposed a second marriage because the first was not legal in New York. According to Lovanche, Judson went to get Reverend Isaac H. Tuttle, pastor of St. Luke's Episcopal church on Hudson Street. The reverend "legally, morally and religiously" married the pair at Lovanche's Christopher Street home in front of witnesses. Judson apparently felt much better very quickly, because the ceremony took place that very evening of January 14.[24]

Lovanche continued to nurse Judson back to health until the middle of February. The army had charged him with desertion two weeks prior and reduced his rank back down to private. According to Monaghan, Lovanche realized that at some point he had slipped away to visit his other wife, Kate, in Ossining.[25] According to some sources, she was so angry that she reported Judson to the authorities as a deserter, and the provost guard jailed him at Fort Hamilton.[26] From prison, the novelist wrote to General Dix and pleaded with him:

> *General. While on my way voluntarily to return to my Regiment, after having overstayed my furlough through unavoidable circumstances (sickness) I have been arrested and held here as I understand as a deserter. General I have served the United States nearly half my life and never before have been under arrest or had a charge preferred against me. In this case I have not been one moment out of the uniform of my Regiment, or by word or action exhibited a design to leave the service which I voluntarily entered, and my service in my Regiment—promoted in my first battle with it—& three times mentioned in General orders for good conduct in the face of the enemy, ensures my attachment to it. If I have erred, I most respectfully request that I may be permitted to go or be sent to my regiment where those who know me & my services can try & judge upon my conduct & its causes.*
>
> *Pardon me General for intruding upon your valuable time but every hour of the mental & physical agony I am enduring in the new & degrading associations I find myself with is unfitting me for duty & literally killing me soul & body. Set me then [illegible] General from your justice & generosity—the relief I pray for.*
>
> *Respectfully,*
> *Edward C. Z. Judson*
> *Sergt., & Regimental Marker of the 1st New York Mounted Rifles*

Lovanche and Kate might have come to some kind of bizarre understanding about their shared groom. According to a letter Lovanche wrote to historian Pond—a letter which no longer exists—some months after Judson was transferred back to Suffolk, she moved up to Chappaqua, where she just happened to run into the pregnant Kate Myers. The two women, according to Monaghan, even lived in the same house for more than a week, "becoming more jealous with the passage of each day." Mutual regard for Ned held them together, Monaghan continues, although it seems likely this was more about sharing finances than esteem.[27]

Meanwhile, in Suffolk, Judson was court martialed and found guilty of being absent without leave. He was sentenced to two months' confinement in the regimental guardhouse along with a ten-dollar reduction in monthly pay.[28] The writer was certainly not the only one to be charged with desertion during the war; in fact, desertion rates spiked to their highest on the Union side during this winter and spring of 1863. But for Judson, this red mark on his fervently patriotic reputation was unpalatable. He asked his editors at the *New York Sunday Mercury*, William Cauldwell and Horace Whitney, to write President Lincoln to see if he could pardon him. They acquiesced, and the plea said, in part:

> *Dear Sir,*
> *We write on behalf of one who has done good service in the field but also, when absent in this city, on a [illegible] furlough, through the mistaken friendship of friends who insisted upon his drinking with them, overstayed the allotted time, and this by a malicious superior officer was characterized as desertion . . . notwithstanding that his health was much impaired through exposure in military operations in the Nansemond. . . . All reports go to show that he made an excellent soldier, and was generally complimented for his bravery and daring. And it is hard for him after doing so well and so much as he has done, to have his life literally wasted away, to gratify the spleen of a superior officer activated by a spirit of revenge upon he who enlisted as a private is in many respects his mental superior.*

Moreover, Cauldwell and Whitney wrote, Judson should be discharged because his health was "almost completely broken by the experience he has endured," and that his spirit was "absent by the injustice" he believed done to him. For these reasons, they explained, Judson would no longer be useful to the military, and should be given a chance to go home to his wife and child.[29]

The letter did not work; it was simply forwarded to General Dix, who did nothing with the request. In confinement, the novelist claimed illness and was placed in Hampton Hospital, Suffolk, Virginia. Fellow soldiers recalled he had his own dorm here too. In all likelihood, Judson suffered from malaria or another tropical disease from living near the marshy, muggy surroundings of the Great Dismal Swamp. Colonel Dodge's impression was that Judson contracted some sort of "rheumatic trouble" from his scouting the bogs. Regimental comrade John Habberton thought he suffered from malaria or some similar tropical disease around the time of his return to Suffolk. Judson mentions his illness and what was probably the result of his fall in a letter he wrote to sister Irene on July 12, 1863:

> *Dear Sister,*
> *When I received your long delayed letter I was in the hospital at Suffolk & unable to write, suffering all at once from an arm disabled near the close of Longstreet's siege of Suffolk, a crushed foot & a bad fever.*
>
> *I am now better, was even able on the 4th of July by official request to give my brother invalids & cripples a patriotic speech which they seemed to enjoy. I have been here for nearly or quite a month & shall probably never again do my duty right. The surgeons wish me to go into the Invalid Corps but under my circumstances I would rather be discharged.*

Besides his saying so to his sister, there is some evidence to suggest that Judson fought during the Siege of Suffolk in mid-April, when muster rolls note he was released from confinement. On April 11, 1863, Confederate general James Longstreet moved his troops across the Nansemond in an effort to both forage for supplies and protect Richmond, as well as to capture the Union garrison at Suffolk (he failed at this last goal).[30] Judson could very well have participated until April 21, when he entered the hospital. In addition to the likelihood of being genuinely ill, the writer was exasperated with the whole experience of the war in general and, like so many others, ready to go home:

> *My farm in Northern New York suffers for want of supervision—I have got a good wife & a baby girl 18 months old that wants to see her papa, whom she has never seen since she could walk & talk & [I] am sick of niggerism, favoritism & politics in the army & [want] out of it.*
>
> *One of your Pittsburgh girls, a daughter of J. K. Morehead, is a nurse in this hospital. She wears specs & looks old maidish but may be a blossom in the wilderness for all I know, for I have never spoken to her.*
>
> *I suppose [General George Gordon] Meade's success on a sea shore has retired you non city folks from all present alarm without [Brigadier General John Hunt] Morgan below has given you a scare. Were it not for Northern Copperheads this accursed man would now be in a way of prison in 6 or 8 weeks. They may prolong it years while we who are in the field die by thousands in battle & in hospitals. Here we lose from 20 to 30 a week by fever.*
>
> *Give my respects to Alexander and consider me ever yours,*
> *Edward Z. C. Judson*
>
> *P.S.: You grumbled at my tentative likeness. It was very correct—you know we are of Dutch descent, Sis.*[31]

During his service, Judson had witnessed the popularity of Beadle's adventure paperbacks among the soldiers. He also recognized that a market existed for the type of literature he had written a decade earlier. Writing "trash for the masses" now became his goal, and though Judson continued writing for the *Mercury*, he also revived a *Ned Buntline's Own* series in April 1865. In the series he wrote a fact/fiction account of Abraham Lincoln's assassination entitled *The Parricides*. This novel caught the attention of the editors of Hilton's National Publishing House, which offered him a lucrative contract a few months after the end of the Civil War.

The exact date varies in his military file, but sometime during the summer of 1863, Judson was transferred to the 12th Company, First Battalion, Invalid Corps, which subsequently became Company A, 22nd Veterans Reserve Corps, which lodged in Scranton, Pennsylvania. He wrote wife Kate to tell her of his new circumstances, and to perhaps encourage her to be glad of his possible return home soon:

> *Hyde Park near Scranton*
> *August 9th, 1863*
> *Dear Wife,*
> *I received your letter with $5 enclosed a half hour ago just as I was starting for this place on duty. I have a leisure moment & write to tell you that I will soon be a lieutenant in this corps. I will send you a picture of me in my new uniform in a day or two. We have a great deal to do. A copperhead villain tried to kill me today. I took him prisoner & he is now in irons in the guard house awaiting trial. I was too much for him, tho' I am an invalid.*

He urged Kate not to worry about toddler Carrollita's temper, because when he got home, the little one would mind them. "In a few weeks," he wrote, "you will be with me. When that time comes we will need <u>never</u> to part again till death parts us."[32]

He wrote Irene and told her he had been given a commission in the Corps (he had not) and to complain about chasing "cursed deserters" all the time. "The duty here," he said, "is harder than I ever had it in the front and thrice as unpleasant."[33]

Military records show that Judson did not obtain any leave to visit with family, but perhaps he could not. In mid-November he sent word to Irene through a commanding officer that he suffered from fractured ribs and a head injury. "It would be well for you to come as soon as possible. He is very anxious for you to be sent for, as he has an idea he will not live through it."[34] She apparently did not reply, because a few weeks later, Judson followed up with another letter about the matter:

> *Dear Sister,*
> *Lieutenant Browning wrote to you sometime since when I was very badly injured by a gang of the "Buckshots" as the draft and adminis-tration opposers call themselves. For several days I was not expected to live & it will be months before I am fit for duty, if I ever am again. Three broken ribs, a gash in the face with a knife, slashing open my right cheek to the bone—& a skull broken with a club or sling shot and severely injured breast & spine make up the benefits rec'd at their hands.*[35]

The Buckshots—later known as the "Molly Maguires"—referred to miners living in Pennsylvania's coal region, which included, among others, Luzerne County, in which Scranton was located. The Buckshots consisted of mostly Democratic, wretchedly poor Irish coal miners who, when faced with the Civil War Military Draft in March 1863 and the possibility of leaving their families without even one wage earner, fomented resistance and occasional violence against conscription officers and those aiding them. This rebellious group also saw an opportunity to raise their wages by forcing engineers to stop working and hold Pennsylvania's vast coal reserves hostage. Judson's voluminous files make no mention of wounds received at the hands of the Buckshots, or that he was even near the coalfields. But it is entirely possible that Judson volunteered to be among the 150 or so guards that accompanied the 10th New Jersey—a five-hundred-strong regiment called in to quell the violence in Beaver Meadow, Audenreid, Mauch Chunk (present-day Jim Thorpe), and a few other coal towns—and was wounded in some skirmish that did not reach the attention of newspapers or the pen and paper of Reserve Corps medical officers.

During Judson's "season of inactivity," he wrote songs and tales of the war for the *Mercury*, including *Sadia, A Heroine of the Rebellion*, advertised as being based on facts and real people from the conflict, as was *The Pilot: A Secession Story*. Ned Buntline was finally discharged from all military duty on August 23, 1864. His book *Cavalry Scout* became immensely popular and subsequently appeared as a series in the *Mercury*; many aspects of this novel would later appear in Judson's formulation of Buffalo Bill stories. When Judson returned to New York, he displayed his picture in a colonel's uniform that he had taken in Baltimore and told everyone he had served as "Colonel—Chief of Scouts." He used the title "Colonel" throughout the remainder of his writing career.

Image of Judson taken sometime after his Civil War service, probably during a temperance tour. Note the patriotic scarf. OHIO HISTORY CONNECTION

Judson's certificate of membership to the Good Templars of New York. The novelist was fond of secret societies and fraternities, many of which espoused abstinence from alcohol and promoted the brotherhood of upright, Protestant white men. ADIRONDACK EXPERIENCE

Cover of *Buffalo Bill's Best Shot*, Judson's second dime novel featuring Buffalo Bill. ADIRONDACK EXPERIENCE

LOG CABIN LIBRARY · (Pocket Edition) 10 CENTS

DASHING CHARLIE
THE TEXAN WHIRLWIND

BY
NED BUNTLINE

No. 32
July 20, '98
STREET & SMITH, Publishers,
81 Fulton Street,
NEW YORK.

Cover of *Dashing Charlie: The Texan Whirlwind*. Charlie's character was that of a Texas Ranger and Indian fighter. Judson produced a play featuring the "real" Charlie and a character named Arizona Frank, backed by a group of Comanche or Modoc actors. It failed to take hold like "Buffalo Bill" had. Judson wrote no more of this character, but Prentiss Ingraham wrote nine novels that were very popular. ADIRONDACK EXPERIENCE

An image of Judson's grand Eagle's Nest residence in Stamford, New York, as it looked when he resided there. The flag in front could allegedly be seen from miles away.

FROM MUNSELL'S "HISTORY OF DELAWARE COUNTY, 1797–1880"

Even late in life, Judson proudly wore quasi-military uniforms, usually of his own design. The cane here might
be a gold-tipped one given to him by Cody.
ADIRONDACK EXPERIENCE

From left to right: Anna Fuller Judson, Edward Z. C. "Eddie" Judson, Jr., E. Z. C. Judson, and Sarah Fuller, Anna's mother. Circa 1883. STAMFORD VILLAGE LIBRARY

According to two historians, descendants of E. Z. C. Judson (aka Ned Buntline) and a local girl were in the Adirondacks as late as the mid-1940s. This photo, taken in 1916, shows a son of Judson who was raised under another family name. *Hint:* He is in the left third of the image, and his likeness to his father is unmistakable. ANONYMOUS

CHAPTER ELEVEN

Chappaqua and California

AFTER HIS DISCHARGE, JUDSON RETURNED TO KATE AND TWO CHILdren, Mary Carrollita and Irene Elizabeth. He also kept in touch with Lovanche, writing her some five hundred letters between 1864 and 1865. In fact, during the war, the novelist—for reasons unclear, but perhaps to hide his money from Kate or his drinking from his publishers—had Lovanche bring some of his manuscripts to Street & Smith, whose specialty was the newfangled "dime novel." Lovanche kept all this correspondence, and later begged a reporter to look at the way Judson signed one: "Arrange with Mrs. Judson, who is better prepared to do business and take care of money than I am."[1] Judson even sent her a valentine of some sort in February 1865 and asked her to move back in with him. But Lovanche held her ground and refused to have anything to do with him unless he stopped drinking. He even camped out on her front doorsteps in Albany for two hours one night, she said; and when she would not let him in, he went down to the Hudson docks and jumped into the water to attempt suicide—though he was quickly fished out by passersby. Finally, she later recalled, she "despaired" of him ever getting sober and moved her dressmaking business to New Orleans. It was at this time, she said, that she heard that Judson had left for California.[2]

Of course Judson was married to Kate Myers during this time. In 1892, some years after Judson's death, Myers gave her own version of Judson's relationship with Lovanche—although this did not necessarily strengthen her case for her own marriage's validity. He was, she maintained, never married to the widow until sometime during the Civil War. "For a number of years before the war," she maintained, "Lovanche kept a house of prostitution near a market near the corner of Hudson and Grove

Streets, New York City. At least the soldier told me it was a 'bed house.'"
Myers recalled that there was a sign above the house that read, "Cloak
and Mantel Making," and that it might have been on Christopher Street.
"I was never there but once, and then nine or ten men came in, that was
a day or two after he married her," Myers said. She remembered this day
quite clearly, noting that it was her birthday, which also happened to be
Valentine's Day.

Myers offered an explanation of why Judson married Lovanche:
"When the Legislature met she used to go to Albany and open a house
there. She had all the prominent politicians and patrons of her house and
that was the secret of her influence over Judson."[3] Furthermore, she said,
Judson could not help but marry Lovanche, because she drugged him in
her house of ill repute and then sent for a preacher. In fact, he told Myers,
she drugged him so much that he could not leave the house, and this was
the reason the army arrested him for desertion during the Civil War.

Myers then offered an explanation as to why she had gone to see
Lovanche at her alleged home of prostitution. According to Myers, the
widow came to her house in Westchester on February 14, 1863, and
showed her a marriage certificate for her and Judson. She told Myers her
marriage was a "mock" one, and that Judson was living at her home in
the city. "I told her," Myers continued, "that I would face him, and went
with her to her house in New York. [I] took my child, the only one we
had then, and remained at her house until 9 o'clock and Judson failed to
appear, but these men came in one after another—9 or 10 of them—and
after them came so many I left." The house, she added, was elegantly furnished, and Lovanche seemed to "occupy the whole house"—a Victorian
way of saying that she was a madam or a prostitute.[4] As awful as Civil
War service might have been for Judson, it certainly provided him with
an escape from his marital mess at home.

In the mid- and late 1860s, while living in Chappaqua with Kate,
Judson frequently talked about going west but in reality would not do so
for another few years. After the war's end, he still had commitments to the
Mercury and, of course, to Kate, who had refused to go back to Eagle's Nest
after two harsh winters there. The pair and their children—ultimately, three

girls and a boy—lived in Chappaqua, Westchester County, near Kate's parents, where they were neighbors of Horace Greeley, founder of the *New-York Tribune* and cofounder of the Republican Party.

By all accounts, Judson resumed writing furiously during his time in Chappaqua. As always, he capitalized on his personal experience. In 1864, for example, he wrote a semiautobiographical novel called *Life in the Saddle, Or, The Cavalry Scout*, based loosely on his service with the New York Mounted Rifles. He contributed regularly to the *Mercury*, and in April 1865 he had revived *Ned Buntline's Own*, adding a banner head with a picture of himself in a Civil War soldier's uniform. His story about Lincoln's assassination, *The Parricides*, allowed Hilton's Ten Cent Books to compete with Beadle for the dime-novel market. Hilton's offered to absorb *Buntline's Own*, relieve Ned of any middleman issues with printers, and issue and distribute a *Ned Buntline's Own* series through their organization.[5]

This deal sounded good, Judson thought. He could still have his name and stories out there under *Buntline's Own* with some of the profit, none of the risk, and still write for the *Mercury*. In addition, *Street & Smith's New York Weekly* featured stories written by Judson under one of his pseudonyms: "Edward Minturn," "Clew Garnet," "Sherwood Stanley," and even "Julia Edwards." In all probability, notes Monaghan, the writer was up to an old trick of selling a monopoly on all the writings of "Ned Buntline" and then writing under other names for other publishers. He was rumored to be making about twenty thousand dollars a year at this time, and boasted that he sometimes wrote six stories per week.[6]

If enthusiasm was any gauge of his output and earnings, the twenty thousand dollars is probably accurate. One Chappaqua resident remembered Judson's daily routine while there. Judson had built a platform on the branches of a large oak tree located on the outskirts of Greeley's property. Every morning he would shinny up, pen in teeth, paper and ink in pocket, and remain there all day, sitting cross-legged and writing on a smooth board. From time to time, he would drop a bucket on the end of a rope down from his perch into a nearby spring and pull up a "king's share of sparkling, cool, water to quench his thirst."[7]

Ned prided himself on the devil-may-care speed with which he dashed off his stories, scarcely stopping to eat or sleep. "I once wrote a book of 610 pages in sixty-two hours," he told an interviewer:

> *I never lay out plots in advance. I shouldn't know how to do it, for how can I know what my people may take it into their heads to do? First, I invent a title. When I hit a good one I consider the story about half finished. It is the thing of prime importance. After I begin I push ahead as fast as I can write, never blotting out anything I have once written and never making a correction or modification. . . . If a book does not suit me when I have finished it, I simply throw it in the fire and begin again without any reference to the discarded text.*[8]

His reading customers did not seem to mind the haste. They bought his *Mercury* stories as fast as he could churn them out, and put him in the same bestselling company as pulp fictionists Sylvanus Cobb, Margaret Blount, and Prentiss Ingraham, who would one day pick up the "Buffalo Bill" phenomenon created by Judson. "These novels are," the *Mercury* bragged, "beyond all question the most popular and saleable in the market." And Judson's "ten-cent stories" published by Hudson's as well as others in Boston and New York were also top-sellers.

During the late 1940s, when Harold Hochschild was researching his book *Township 34*, he learned that Edward and Kate's son Alexander had died, but that his sisters were still living. Hochschild interviewed Carrie (Carrollita), Irene, and Edwardina, who told him that family life in Chappaqua was often turbulent, in spite of Judson's earnings. This was not, however, because Judson beat his wife or was cruel to his children, as one might expect with someone who had a domineering personality mixed with a penchant for alcohol. It was, according to the children, because Judson was downright scared of Kate. She was, as one historian said, "one of the few persons he ever met, male or female, who could intimidate him." Hochschild reported that a knife-wielding Kate once locked her husband in a closet, where he huddled shamefacedly while visitors called. More than once she drove him out of the house.[9]

One thing Judson and Kate argued over was the girls' education. The practical Kate, according to Hochschild, "wanted them taught household skills; [whereas] Ned demanded that they be educated in languages, history, literature, and elocution." Irene recalled that her father taught her to recite in public, and that when Kate drove him from the house, he had tried several times—always unsuccessfully—to kidnap his talented daughter. Robert D. Pepper posits that Judson did this to turn Irene into another Charlotte ("Little Lotta") Crabtree, the child star who had captured America's mid-century imagination in a manner not duplicated until the advent of Shirley Temple. Judson may even have known the Crabtree family, since Lotta's father owned a Manhattan bookstore in the late 1840s, when the swashbuckling writer first came to that city.[10]

Another thing Judson and Kate argued over was Judson's erstwhile sobriety. One neighbor in Chappaqua recalled that he would go several months completely dry, but then he would "fall off the water wagon" and "go on a tear." He even earned the moniker "Reverend" while in Chappaqua because of the temperance sermons he delivered while abstaining from alcohol. But when Judson did succumb to booze, according to the neighbor, he would carry his guns and shoot at the slightest provocation—although he never did hurt anyone, the man added to his account.[11] During these bouts of intoxication, Judson sometimes put his characters in the wrong narrative, and more than once he failed to sober up in time to meet a publishing deadline. In one instance, according to Monaghan, a ghostwriter took over the script and, with some malice, killed Ned's hero and gloated over the great novelist's predicament. But, so the story goes, Judson read the copy before writing his next installment and cleverly made his hero's ghost take an active part in the story to its end.[12]

Kate did not appreciate her husband coming so close to the edge of insolvency, and was tired of hearing reports of him looking like a homeless man on the streets of New York City when he went off on a "tear." By the time fourth child Edwardina arrived in July 1867, she had managed to establish a relationship with Judson's publishers at the *Mercury* and also Street & Smith so that payment for his writings would go to her and not to him.[13] While the tenets of alcoholism dictate that a person who wishes to drink will find a way with or without money, it seems that, for at least the time being, Judson went cold turkey. And adhering to his lifelong pattern of finding opportunity in the face of adversity, Judson decided to make temperance more profitable.

As early as 1865, Judson had experimented with lecture touring. A man with a recognizable name could earn very good money doing so. After the War Between the States, Major General O. O. Howard of the Freedman's Bureau earned one hundred dollars per lecture delivered in New England, as did abolitionist Anna Dickinson—a woman! Ralph Waldo Emerson was earning an incredible three hundred dollars per lecture. Two months before the war formally ended, the *Lawrence (Kansas) Tribune* advertised that "Edward Judson is about starting on a lecturing tour, with the 'The Romance and Reality of War' as a subject. Ned has been in the service, was wounded, and has recently been honorably discharged. He is now about to turn his experiences into account, in the lecture in question."[14] Judson's writing and carousing had kept him from pursuing a tour in earnest, but by late 1867, he was ready.

On September 27, 1867, Judson joined a Brooklyn lodge of the Independent Order of Good Templars (a temperance group); closer to home, the Westchester lodge of the Sons of Temperance anointed him Deputy Grand Worthy Patriarch.[15] That fall and the following winter, residents of parts of New York and Pennsylvania could pay fifty to seventy-five cents to hear Judson lecture on the evils of alcohol. Some turned out because of sheer curiosity about the author, especially in larger, more sophisticated port cities. During the first few months of his lecture tour, Judson appeared unsophisticated—uncomfortable, even. One Brooklyn reporter called him "stiff," and "uneasy," that his gray eyes were "restless and nervous" and that he appeared unclean because of his long hair and unshaven face. The novelist spoke with a twang usually reserved for clergymen, the reporter noted, and seemed "afraid to trust himself fully."[16]

Judson overcame any nervousness he might have felt speaking in public without the "courage" of alcohol. Some were disappointed at the absence of the humorous and bombastic Ned Buntline of years past, but Judson delivered "capable" and "acceptable" speeches about his past struggles with alcohol—sometimes discussing his first taste of it as a midshipman in the navy, and how one drink of wine or whisky became two, which became the consumption of a bottle, which led to the drinking of jugs of it.[17]

Judson's lectures in support of complete prohibition made sense to a lot of his audiences. Many believed that the social ills of the cities in a postwar America—homelessness, high crime rates, joblessness—could be directly attributed to alcohol. Moreover, the populations most closely associated with drunkenness were immigrant ones, primarily (but not exclusively) German and Irish. In turn, these immigrant populations tended to compose the low-wage labor force of a rising number of factories in postbellum America. By advocating prohibition in America, Judson not only provided a redemption narrative for himself but also provided fodder for his belief that immigration was the root cause of all lawlessness in the country.

On April 13, 1868, the *New York Times* announced that Judson would be leaving for California by the week's end. Neighbor Horace Greeley gave one of the many speeches wishing him Godspeed, and Judson gave his own farewell address.[18] Judson's plan to widen his temperance lectures to the western United States was a smart one: Membership numbers in the Sons of Temperance had already peaked ten years before the Civil War, and the organization had emerged from the conflict much smaller and with little national structure. As sympathy for prohibition shifted from the Northeast to the southern and western states, the Sons of Temperance remained an important force, and its membership an important constituency, in local prohibition efforts. Clearly, Judson saw an opportunity to unite local movements in the western part of the country and become the leader of this body politic. This effort could replace the opportunity he had lost with the demise of the Know Nothing Party. Kate Myers's feelings about his leaving are not recorded.[19]

On April 15, 1868, the writer and lecturer—now sporting a long beard—boarded the steamship *Oregonian* in New York Harbor and sailed for California. A little less than a month later, he arrived on the Pacific coast of California by way of Panama. He embarked on a rigorous tour of the northern part of the state, starting in San Francisco and wending his way through bustling mining and agricultural hubs like Healdsburg,

Petaluma, Marysville, Carson, Silver City, Auburn, Lincoln, Folsom, and Sacramento. He made it to each town on time and sometimes delivered two or three lectures per day.

To be sure, temperance and reform newspapers were very enthusiastic about his appearances, which sometimes pulled as many as one thousand people to some halls. Wearing a military uniform of some sort, he talked both humorously and gravely about the ills of alcohol, and audiences laughed and cried at the appropriate times. Bigger newspapers in bigger towns were a little more critical—the *San Francisco Chronicle* summed up the thoughts of other regional outlets when it acknowledged that Judson was in the same league as the best temperance speakers, but that it would be a "tight race between them for the palm of balderdash," and that to hear Judson was enough to make one "die of weariness."[20] Some, like the *Golden City*, merely took note of the unique personality in their midst:

> *But for the wild, irregular manner in which he passed the golden years of his early manhood, this same E. Z. C. Judson would have achieved as high a name in American literature as the best of them. Perhaps the experiences gained in this "wild irregular manner" are what constitute the individuality of Buntline, and make him what he is.*[21]

After two months of travel through the Sacramento River region and a detour through the majestic valley of Yosemite, Judson landed back in San Francisco, where he had first made a pledge to form California divisions of Sons and Daughters of Temperance in every town he visited.[22] His record of conversions to temperance was not impressive. In faraway Sierra County in eastern California, he reported founding Table Rock Division No. 37 of the Sons at Howland Flat. In nearby Martinez, east of San Francisco Bay, he organized Hope Division No. 17, but could show the signatures of only fourteen charter members. The writer mistakenly attributed the ghost towns he saw in the interior of the state as having fallen because their citizens drank; conversely, he attributed sobriety to those who seem to have done very well, ignoring simple facts like market capitalism and inheritance. In short, California immigrants differed from

Easterners who had come from nearby parochial communities, and they were not confused or dismayed by mushrooming industrial cities.[23]

By Christmas of 1868, Judson seems to have realized that organizing California into a state of temperance was going to be an uphill battle that he did not wish to spend years trying to win. It was a huge state, with disparate communities—many of which were not in favor of abstinence. Needing money, Judson proffered his services as a comedian and storyteller, appearing on stage mostly in Marysville, where he stayed with friends for a few months. Here he wrote a serial for the *Daily Alta* about the adventures of a ship's captain and his slave in California, but it failed to attract the usual attention from other newspapers and demand for reprints and sequels.[24] He did, however, write some stories for the esteemed *Golden Era* newspaper, which just a few years earlier had showcased works by his erstwhile friend, Mark Twain.

As was usually the case when Judson had lived in one place long enough, reports of him drinking started to filter through communities. In Vallejo he turned up to deliver a "wild story of right and wrong, given in full Indian costume and paint." The paper had advertised the evening as being appropriate for ladies and children, but it did not turn out that way:

Ned Buntline, the notorious, was here last Saturday night. To style his blathering a "lecture" would be burlesquing the English language. Buntline may be a hero and a man respected in his own land, if so, we advise him to travel home instanter. The Order of I. O. G. T. [International Order of Good Templars] made a bad hand of it when they started that polluted and nonsensical piece of humanity around the State to preach temperance and morality to Californians. A man must practice what he preaches, and the people saw in his countenance that his sermons and his actions were not alike. His modesty was like the points in his "lecture"—had none. His Indian costume consists of a pair of dirty drawers and undershirt, a meager head-dress, something thrown over one shoulder, and in this rig he calls a "Comanche costume" he appears before the people and makes a speech. Ned Buntline you won't do![25]

The exact date isn't recorded, but sometime in 1869 Judson was in Sierra Valley, near the California-Nevada border, and showed up at a lodge belonging to the local "E. Campus Vitus" (ECV), a fraternal organization that served as an alternative for miners who thought the Masons and Odd Fellows were too formal for their liking. "Clampers" wore red shirts symbolizing miners' long johns underwear and cut pieces of tin cans to pin to their vests. In these early days of the society, ECV lodges were known to be primarily drinking clubs. "The night I was there," recalled one member decades later, "Ned Buntline attended and we sure had a time, as he was smart—having traveled a great deal. He was the writer at that time of most of the dime novels. They asked him a lot of questions and he had an answer for every one."[26]

Most likely, this lodge was just one of Judson's many stops on the way out of California in the spring of 1869. He allegedly started a faro bank in White Pine, Nevada—a bustling mining area at the time—and drank rather openly, though he vehemently denied all this in the papers.[27] In Utah he provided newspapers with sweet poetry about his travels through the state:

> Through the gorges grand and gloomy
> Oe'r the deserts wide and drear,
> Pushing on so swift and madly
> Comes the weary traveler here.[28]

Judson's experiment with California was over, but his dalliance with temperance was not: In September 1869 he turned up in Chicago as a delegate to the National Temperance Convention. The *San Francisco Chronicle*, which had so carefully followed its recent resident celebrity and given him every benefit of the doubt while in the Golden State, did not take kindly to this "writer of sensational trash and a degraded and murderous villain" misrepresenting California:

> *He coolly asserted that "seven-tenths of the adult population of California, male and female, went down to their graves through drink." Of course the hoary hero of ten thousand drunks said this "with malice*

aforethought." His temperance farce was too flimsy to deceive anybody out here but a small number of temperance advocates who took the "reformed" drunkard and libertine by the hand and encouraged his hypocritical proceedings. The Colonel's lies arouse no enthusiasm; they simply evoke our contempt.[29]

What the world could not know at this time was that Judson, while en route to Chicago six weeks earlier, had met the man he would make a star for the ages. The writer had no idea what this chance meeting would spark.

CHAPTER TWELVE

Three Wives and Buffalo Bill

JUDSON DISCOVERED THE FUTURE "BUFFALO BILL" BY ACCIDENT. AS THE novelist made his way back East toward Chicago during the summer of 1869, he needed to pay his lodging bills and thus lectured every time he found an opportunity. As was always the case with Ned Buntline, he adapted his speeches and writings to the towns in which he found himself. So, in late June, while in Salt Lake City and Ogden, Utah, he lectured about temperance and complimented some tenets of the Church of Jesus Christ of Latter-day Saints. It appears that he might have come across as an opportunist, for the *Deseret News* tired of him even more quickly than the *San Francisco Chronicle*:

> *Col. Judson, alias "Ned Buntline," whose lecturing experiment in this city proved such a signal failure some two or three weeks since, has been lecturing in Cheyenne, his subject being "A year in California and Nevada and the Curse of Chinese Immigration, as it affects the labor and position of the white man." A lecture on the "Mormons" is announced. If this gentleman, when lecturing on the "Mormons" talks as nicely of them as he did to them while here, his lecture will not be very likely to draw above once, for he will tell so many good things about the industry, temperance and other virtues of the people of Utah that he will almost be suspected of being a "Mormon" partisan. We shall look with some degree of interest for the report of his lecture on this subject, and hope to find in one public writer and lecturer honesty enough to tell of the good traits of character he saw exhibited by the people of Utah during his very short stay amongst them.*[1]

From Cheyenne, Judson took the Union Pacific Railroad straight across Wyoming's southern border and, after a stop at Fort Sedgwick, Colorado, landed in North Platte, Nebraska, on or about July 20, 1869.

In *The Great Rascal*, Monaghan makes an educated guess at what Judson must have seen when he got off the train in this busy hub:

> *A crowd of loafing soldiers and civilians, as well as a few blanketed Indians, stood outside the railroad station watching the train. Hack carriages, army wagons, and an ambulance or two waited to take passengers to the hotel or down to Fort McPherson, eighteen miles away. Ned was obviously perplexed. Should he ride to the fort in the hack with a motley assortment of plug-hatted salesmen, gamblers, and calico-clad soldiers' wives—the kind of people who haunted the outskirts of every army post?*[2]

With or without the company of strangers, Judson got to Fort McPherson on or about July 16, 1869. His reason for going to this outpost is still disputed today. "Quite a myth has grown up around the meeting of Buffalo Bill with Ned Buntline," Don Russell said in his landmark book, *The Lives and Legends of Buffalo Bill*. "This is not surprising, as nothing in the Buffalo Bill legend has been more exaggerated than Ned Buntline's part in it."[3] Russell refers to the story perpetuated by Monaghan and others since it was first told by Luther North, brother of Major Frank J. North of the US Army's 5th Cavalry, in which Judson headed to Fort McPherson, looking for heroes of a conflict known as the Battle of Summit Springs.[4]

On July 11, the US Army's 5th Cavalry had attacked a village of Cheyenne Dog Soldiers. The Cheyenne had two white captives, and during the fight, one of them was killed by one of the Cheyenne. Major Frank J. North of the US Army's white soldiers and his band of Pawnee scouts tricked and then killed Tall Bull, leader of the Cheyenne. What better hero for Judson to write about?[5]

Major North had no interest in becoming Judson's hero. In fact, he did not care for writers in general. "If you want a man to fill that bill," he told Judson, "he's over there under the wagon."[6] The writer, so the story goes, stumbled into the area among recuperating soldiers trying to sleep in the fly-infested heat. He poked beneath a wagon, perhaps looking for shade, and found a "young giant" with sleepy eyes and straw in his long hair. After some discussion, Judson realized that William Cody could become a "frontier hero" to write about.

This, Russell maintained, was not true. "Ned Buntline did not come West seeking a hero; instead, he was returning from California after an unsuccessful tour as a temperance lecturer." While it is true Judson did not set out for the western states looking for a particular hero, the fact is, the writer was always looking for a hero.

William Frederick Cody was already well known in frontier circles at the time he and Judson met. He was twenty-three years old and had served first as a Union scout in campaigns against the Kiowa and Comanche; then, in 1863, he enlisted with the 7th Kansas Cavalry, which saw action in Missouri and Tennessee. After the war he married Louisa Frederici in St. Louis and continued to work for the army as a scout and dispatch carrier, operating out of Fort Ellsworth, Kansas. In 1867 Cody took up the trade that gave him his nickname, hunting buffalo to feed the construction crews of the Kansas Pacific Railroad.

According to his own count, Cody killed 4,280 head of buffalo in seventeen months. He is supposed to have won the name "Buffalo Bill" in an eight-hour shooting match with a hunter named William Comstock, presumably to determine which of the two Buffalo Bills deserved the title. In 1868 Cody returned to his work for the army. He was chief of scouts for the 5th Cavalry and took part in sixteen battles, including the Cheyenne defeat at Summit Springs. Cody even took credit for killing Tall Bull, though there is evidence to suggest that another man did it.

Whatever the case, Cody knew all the details of the fight at Summit Springs and all its participants, which must have been tantalizing for Judson. Ten years after they first met, Cody recalled his first encounter with the writer, when the scout was ordered to accompany soldiers under Major W. H. Brown to subdue Indians who had killed some white men:

Major Brown said to me:

"By the way, Cody, we are going to have quite an important character with us as a guest on this scout. It's old Ned Buntline, the novelist."

> *Just then I noticed a gentleman, who was rather stoutly built, and who wore a blue military coat, on the left breast of which were pinned about twenty gold medals and badges of secret societies. He walked a little lame as he approached us, and I at once concluded that he was Ned Buntline.*
>
> *"He has a good mark to shoot on the left breast," said I to Major Brown, "but he looks like a soldier." As he came up, Major Brown said:*
>
> *"Cody, allow me to introduce you to Colonel E. B. O. Judson [sic], otherwise known as Ned Buntline."*
>
> *"Colonel Judson, I am glad to meet you," said I; "the Major tells me that you are to accompany us on the scout."*
>
> *"Yes, my boy, so I am," said he; "I was to deliver a temperance lecture to-night, but no lectures for me when there is a prospect for a fight. The Major has kindly offered me a horse, but I don't know how I'll stand the ride, for I haven't done any riding lately; but when I was a young man I spent several years among the fur companies of the Northwest, and was a good rider and an excellent shot."[7]*

Of course, Judson had never spent any time in the Northwest, but if Cody's recollection was correct, it fits right into the writer's pattern of puffing up his credentials when telling the truth would have been just as impactful. With delight he accepted Cody's invitation to ride with him to scout for Indians, something Judson claimed he had done as a teenager, when fighting the Seminole in Florida. More recently he had allegedly used similar techniques to ferret Confederates from their nests in the woods of Virginia.

New friends Cody and Judson, according to the former, soon pulled out for the South Platte River along with Cody's soldier friends. Cody noticed that Judson limped when he walked, and that one of his legs seemed shorter than the other; he understood from the writer that it was from a wound suffered in the recent war.[8]

The river was very wide and high due to recent mountain rains, and when they crossed it, they had to swim their horses in some places. Judson, noted the scout, was the first man across. The group, led by Cody, managed to track the Indians' trail, but it was cold, owing to a two-day head start, so the majority of the party went back to Fort McPherson while Cody and Judson went to nearby Fort Sedgwick. "During this short scout," Cody recalled, "Buntline had asked me a great many questions, and he was determined to go out on the next expedition with me, providing he could obtain permission from the commanding officer."[9] Judson did not get permission, or otherwise decided not to go. But in the short amount of time they were together, he found the scout to be engaging, talkative, and believable. Most importantly, he found Cody to be the perfect embodiment of righteousness, adventure, and gallantry— the perfect hero for a new serial.

From North Platte, Judson made his way due east and arrived in Omaha on or about August 10. He gave yet another temperance lecture— no doubt to earn his passage farther east. A businessman there, who had known Judson in New York years before, attended the lecture, prepared to see a "dissipated" man. He was pleasantly surprised: "The lecture here was well attended, able, eloquent and interesting. If anyone in the whole country can speak personally of the evils, injury, disgrace, shame and misery caused by the habit of intemperance, that man is 'Ned Buntline,' and if such as he can reform, after living years of vice and dissipation, none need despair."[10] Judson made more stops on his straight-line route through Iowa and Illinois until finally landing in Chicago on August 31.

The fledgling Prohibition Party gave Judson a hero's welcome, anointing him a vice president of the entire organization, as well as a delegate from California. The writer vowed to cheering thousands of devoutly sober men and women that California, Nevada, and Oregon would carry the Prohibition Party ticket the following spring. He joined with other party leaders in crafting a plan for nominating a candidate for the 1872 presidential election.[11] The remarks Judson made about the majority of California's residents being perpetually drunk speedily made their way west, and the papers there roundly denounced them, and Judson. "His career as a temperance lecturer in California was a failure," said the *Oakland Daily Transcript*, for example. "Although heralded with great flourish of cold water bugles, and his lectures largely advertised, he drew very small houses, and few of those who went to hear him once ever attempted to kill a spare hour in the same murderous style again."[12]

In late September 1869, Judson finally headed home to New York. He had not seen Kate and his children for a year and a half—little Edwardina was only fourteen months old when he left for California. He quickly set up temperance lectures in New York City and Newark, New Jersey, with a soprano in tow to sing a song he wrote about the virtues of abstaining from drink.

By late 1869 temperance was a perfunctory meal ticket for Judson, but it gave him an opportunity to "feel out" the sophisticated audiences of a postwar New York City. An astute West Village reporter watched him give a speech there and wondered if the novelist was amused at the way sensationalism had evolved, since he was one of the largest generators of it: "Ned, however, drew his characters from the realms of fiction. They were men and women of his own fertile imagination," he reminded his readers. "But the new sensational school takes living, prominent individuals, putting such words into their mouths, and dressing them out in such garbs that their most intimate friends can scarcely recognize the picture, and the parties themselves are utterly dumbfounded."[13] To be sure, the reporter was—at least in part—talking about gossip, but he touched upon something that Judson himself was already experimenting with: writing the "real stories" of "real characters."

On December 7, 1869, Judson—as Ned Buntline—published his first story about William F. Cody in *Street & Smith's New York Weekly*. It was entitled *Buffalo Bill, The King of the Border-Men*, and it was printed in installments between the waning weeks of 1869 and March 1870. It featured the exploits of hero Buffalo Bill and his erstwhile sidekick, Wild Bill Hickok, and villains like Jake M'Kandlas (a misspelling of McCanles), a pro-slaver and Missouri bushwhacker. Buffalo Bill's character was a frontier champion who grew up to avenge the murder of his father by M'Kandlas and along the way rescued Lottie, his fictional sister, who was kidnapped by another M'Kandlas gang member. Other villains challenged the pair, and after seemingly nonstop action scenes set against any number of geographical backgrounds, the climax occurred at the Battle of Pea Ridge. Naturally, Cody and Hickok smote all villains by the end of the story, and the heroes left their readers breathless for the next novel.

The 1870 US Census shows Judson residing in both Chappaqua with Kate and the lower east side of Manhattan, with a housekeeper. He was making solid income again with *Buffalo Bill* and an immensely popular serial for the *New York Weekly* entitled *The Shadowed Altar: Betrothed, Wedded, Divorced.* In it, the thinly-fictionalized Colonel Edgar Mansfield rescues fair lady Anna from a carriage accident planned by a gambler who wished to rescue her himself. Anna immediately falls in love with this veteran of the late war, who explains that he resigned from the infantry when he became sick. "Love is the result," the papers advertised for the serial, "matrimony follows; and the leading villains, drawn from life, plot against their happiness, aided in their vile schemes by the MOST BRILLIANT WOMAN of New York society. By a train of circumstances, which seem only too reasonable, JEALOUSY IS AROUSED, and a DIVORCE FOLLOWS."[14]

Intentional or not, there is no question that this story reflects some aspects of Judson's marital position in 1871. The author spent much of his time in his city apartment, away from Kate and the children, although for a while he sent rent money for the Chappaqua house and fifteen dollars extra per month from his Street & Smith earnings. At some point this year, though, he found a home for Kate and the children in Mamaroneck, New York—about twenty miles from Chappaqua—and moved them there.[15] Unbeknownst to Kate, Judson had met a young woman from his home town of Stamford and was corresponding with an Indiana court to see how he could obtain a divorce.

Meanwhile, a playwright named Frank Maeder had written a play based on Judson's *Buffalo Bill* serial. Its successful run in New York in 1871 had made Buffalo Bill's name familiar not only to readership in large and small cities alike but also to those who actually encountered Cody in the flesh. For example, when Grand Duke Alexis of Russia toured the United States in early 1872, he was thrilled when General Philip Henry Sheridan produced the now-world-famous "Buffalo Bill" Cody as his hunting guide.

Early in 1872, publisher James Gordon Bennett Jr., who had been a member of the Sheridan hunting party, invited Cody to come to New York. Bennett had to have been aware of the animosity between his father and Judson decades earlier, but he had taken over editorship of the *Herald* from his dying father, and clearly he, like Judson, saw the entertainment potential of the rugged scout and probably did not think much about their parallel aims. Sheridan, pleased with the outcome of the grand duke's hunt, smoothed the way by giving Cody a leave with pay. Thus, in mid-February 1872, William "Buffalo Bill" Cody came to New York City for the first time.

In New York, writes Joy Kasson, Cody discovered the significance of his own theatricality when E. Z. C. Judson took him to a performance of the Buffalo Bill play at the Bowery Theater. When the theater manager learned that the real Buffalo Bill was present in the audience, he invited Cody to the stage to take a bow and later tried to interest him in acting. Judson showed Cody around the city and arranged interviews for him with reporters. After taking Cody on a quick side trip to see relatives in Philadelphia, Judson began work on another Buffalo Bill dime novel.[16]

Although Cody went back to a scouting assignment with the 3rd Cavalry, he continued to receive letters from Judson urging him to try his luck on the stage. Finally, in December 1872, he convinced Cody to meet him in Chicago to collaborate. On December 16, at Nixon's Amphitheater, the pair debuted their first play: *The Scouts of the Prairie, and Red Deviltry as It Is*, starring Cody, John Baker "Texas Jack" Omohundro, and ballerina Giuseppina Morlacchi as "Dove Eye," an Indian maiden, and Judson himself as a trapper.

The foursome were exhausted on the night of their first performance. Monaghan carefully reconstructs what happened in the few days leading up to the launch of *Scouts*. Judson had promised theater owner Jim Nixon that he would provide two "real scouts" and twenty real Indians. Nixon thought this would be a great draw for Chicagoans, and they would pay plenty to see these Wild West men. He made a deal with Judson; then, to Judson's chagrin, Cody arrived with only Omohundro and "no redskins." Nixon was furious. Scrambling, Judson tried to persuade Nixon that twenty professional (white) actors might be hired to take the Indians' parts. Mulling this over, Nixon asked to see Judson's script. Judson said that he had not written it. This was a huge problem for the owner, given that it was Thursday and the opening was scheduled for Monday.

Undaunted, Judson hurried his scouts to a hotel room and ordered pen and paper. He wrote *Scouts of the Prairie* in four hours, Judson later boasted, and they only rehearsed it twice, but not without a lot of trepidation on the part of his costars, Cody recalled:

The parts were then copied off separately by the clerks, and handing us our respective portions Buntline said: "Now, boys, go to work, and do your level best to have this dead-letter perfect for the rehearsal, which takes place tomorrow morning at ten o'clock, prompt. I want to show Nixon that we'll be ready on time."

I looked at my part and then at Jack; and Jack looked at his part and then at me. Then we looked at each other, and then at Buntline. We did not know what to make of the man.

"How long will it take to commit your part to memory, Bill?" asked Jack.

"About six months, as near as I can calculate. How long will it take you?" answered I.

"It will take me about that length of time to learn the first line," said Jack. Nevertheless we went to our room and commenced studying. I thought it was the hardest work I had ever done.

"This is dry business," finally remarked Jack.

"That's just what it is," I answered; "jerk the bell, Jack." The bell-boy soon appeared. We ordered refreshments; after partaking thereof we resumed our task. We studied hard for an hour or two, but finally gave it up as a bad job, although we had succeeded in committing a small portion to memory. Buntline now came into the room and said: "Boys, how are you getting along?"

"I guess we'll have to go back on this studying business as it isn't our forte," said I.

"Don't weaken now Bill; you'll come out on the top of the heap yet. Let me hear you recite your part," said Buntline. I began "spouting" what I had learned, but was interrupted by Buntline: "Tut! tut! you're not saying it right. You must stop at the cue."

"Cue! What the mischief do you mean by the cue? I never saw any cue except in a billiard room," said I. Buntline thereupon explained it

to me, as well as to Jack, who was ignorant as myself concerning the "cue" business.[17]

On the evening of December 16, 1872, all seats were filled for *Scouts*. Before the footlights, waiting for the curtain to rise, Omohundro, Judson, and Cody stood, not saying a word. The opening line belonged to Cody, but he suffered from stage fright, so Judson tossed him a cue: "Why, you've been off buffalo-hunting with Milligan, haven't you?" Judson fed the stage-struck scout encouraging questions throughout the act, and then signaled the manager to turn loose the actors dressed as Native Americans.

Nearly three hours later, the curtains closed to thunderous applause. "On the whole," the *Chicago Times* concluded, "it is not probable that Chicago will ever look upon the like again. Such a combination of incongruous drama, execrable acting, renowned performers, mixed audience, intolerable stench, scalping, blood and thunder, is not likely to be vouchsafed to a city for a second time,—even in Chicago."[18] The reporter was wrong. Nixon added several more performances for that week, all of which sold out. Judson offered ladies who attended a printed, photographic portrait of Ned Buntline, Buffalo Bill, and Texas Jack.

The successful engagement closed and the troupe moved to St. Louis, where some local politicians remembered that Judson had jumped bail twenty years prior for his part in the St. Louis riots. Also, the death of actor Edwin Forrest on December 12 filtered throughout the newspapers and reminded people of Ned Buntline's part in the Astor Place riots. And so Cody and Omohundro were surprised but also found it humorous when a deputy marshal arrested Judson in their St. Louis hotel on Christmas Eve 1869. "If we were out on the plains," said Omohundro, "we might have something to say; but here in the city it is no use. We must take what comes." Judson did not have sufficient funds for bail, but a friend, treasurer of the Kansas Pacific Railway and president of a bank, bonded him out in time for him to limp grimly into the first act of *Scouts* that night at the St. Louis Opera House. The troupe finally left St. Louis, somehow managing to spend every dime they earned and perhaps Nixon's share too.[19]

On April 3, 1873, a critic with the *Chicago Tribune* gave his thoughts about the play he had seen in New York City three nights before. "The 'Scouts of the Prairie,' he wrote, "now performing at Niblo's, for the express purpose of introducing to the public 'Buffalo Bill,' 'Texas Jack,' and 'Ned Buntline,' is the most ridiculous, though not in the least ludicrous, drama ever presented at that theatre." Worse, the reviewer wrote, the immense amount of gunfire on the stage was pointless, because not one of these "three redoubtable persons" was killed in the first act. "'Buntline' is declared to be the author, and he must be," said the critic. "I doubt if any other man could write such execrable stuff."[20]

Many other newspaper critics concurred with this writer's assessment. "The play, itself, is atrociously bad," said the *New York Times*, and the London *Era* called it a "horrible mass of rubbish." Cody, said another paper, was good-looking, tall, and ramrod straight, but ridiculous as an actor.[21] He often forgot his lines and even got embarrassed at times being the center of attention. During one Cody scene, a young newsboy seated in the back—unable to contain himself—shot up and yelled, "He's not stage-y!"[22]

But many critics knew that what they were seeing was something that would change the world of American entertainment. "The drama," wrote the *Daily Herald*, "of which we understand Ned Buntline is the author, is about everything in general and nothing in particular. . . . Everything was so wonderfully bad that it was almost good."

And for many patrons of *Scouts*, the script was of secondary importance. They had come to see the fine specimens of manhood the handsome scouts represented. The audience was composed of working-class men looking for a way to whoop and holler and blow off the stress of fourteen-hour days of hard labor. But there were also plenty of attendees from middle- and upper-class segments of society. One Boston critic felt the drama, written in the author's "highly-spiced style," appealed not only to the least expensive, often children-filled galleries but also to those in the parquet and high-priced seats.[23]

All these critics probably had a difficult time squeezing their way into the theater to see *Scouts* the evening of March 31, 1873. The venue on Prince Street and Broadway, its full name Niblo's Garden, was newly built after a fire had destroyed it the year before. The theater was meant to hold about thirty-five hundred people, but hundreds more paid ushers to look the other way in return for twenty-five cents. Patrons of *Scouts* poured in from the streets, jostling against glass lanterns and trampling the gravel pathway to the entrance.

When the velvet curtains creaked and curtains lifted, theatergoers tentatively cheered and sat patiently through a short comedy. After this bit was finished, the audience hushed as a five-foot, ten-inch-tall specimen of man strode onto center stage, firing both pistol and rifle. He was dressed in buckskin—a tan suede tunic fringed all around the bottom, and matching pants with fringe running up and down the sides of the pant leg. His glossy, dark-brown shoulder-length tresses were topped by a wide-brimmed Stetson hat, and he wore beaded moccasins. The audience gasped and then stood and cheered with a deafening roar as it realized the advertising was true: This gentleman was not actor J. B. Studley *playing* the part of "Buffalo Bill," as he had for several weeks. Rather, this was Cody himself, here in New York from Nebraska!

For the next three hours, the crowd went wild as Cody and John Omohundro—"Texas Jack," the real frontier scout from the Indian Wars—jumped and yelled around the stage with twenty or so white men plastered with red makeup and feathered costumes. Virtually the entire play featured triple warfare between the scouts, the Indians, and a party of renegade whites, one of whom—a trapper named "Cale Durg"— managed to stay drunk for several fictional days without sipping a drop of anything. There were bombastic speeches about the dew, the clouds, and the baseness of white men, and of course a romance between Indian maiden Dove Eye and Buffalo Bill. At the end of the first hour of the production, the actor playing Durg rushed onto center stage, unarmed, into the midst of his mortal enemies, the twenty Indians! The natives immediately captured the trapper, lashed him to a tree, and kindled a fire meant to torture him. The audience collectively leaned forward, waiting to see what happened to brave but unlucky Durg![24]

Durg, it turns out, had something to say at this critical time in his fictional life on the stage. The actors playing Indians lay down their weapons and looked down at the floor solemnly. Stagehands doused the steam and lycopodium powder used to build the fake fire. They turned down the gaslights, and aimed the limelight onto the red-haired, gray-eyed trapper, who, although shorter and stockier than his costars, was more confident than they. He strode to the edge of the stage and stared directly at the audience, which was taken aback by his sudden inclusion of them into his fictional world. His actual sermons during this play were not recorded, but later versions were, and they included phrases like these: "The temperance movement," he would have bellowed, "means mercy to humanity and justice to God! Let two thousand newly made graves teach New Yorkers a lesson of apathy!" The crowd gamely clapped, collectively wondering what "Cale Durg" would say next. Was this Cale Durg? Or was he meant to be another character altogether? "The law of our great city," the man on the stage continued, "is now the bowie knife, the pistol, and the bludgeon! Aided by the noble influence of woman, we are doing what we can, but there were hundreds of deaths by violence in this city last year, most by men under the influence of liquor! *The time has come for every Christian man to come out for Prohibition!*"[25]

This lecture against alcohol went on for another twenty minutes. For every man who applauded and hollered, "Go on, brother!" there was a man who yelled "Now cheese it!" or "Stop that chin music!" in an effort to get him to stop talking.[26] When the sermon finally ended, the "redskins" returned to the task at hand of killing Durg, only to be interrupted by Buffalo Bill and Texas Jack, who bounded in from the wings with smoking pistols. Unfortunately (or fortunately, said some critics), trapper Cale Durg succumbed to the bullet of a "red man" called Wolf Slayer at the end of act two.[27]

Despite the savaging by some critics, *Scouts of the Prairie* never played to less than a full house during its two-year run across New York and Pennsylvania. Every action scene was met with thundering applause, and every love scene between Buffalo Bill and Hazel Eye and Texas Jack and Dove Eye was met with "Oooooohs" of approval. The *Rochester Democrat and Chronicle* conceded: "Ned Buntline and his 'Scouts of the Prairie' have been 'catching it' pretty severely from the Philadelphia critics; but as 'Buffalo Bill' and 'Texas Jack' maintain their potency in attracting large audiences, the much-abused author pockets the criticisms with the dollars and—grins."[28]

Judson wrote only five more novelettes that featured the exploits of Buffalo Bill. The last of them appeared in 1885 and possibly was the last dime novel Judson published under the name Ned Buntline. Judson and Cody's stage partnership ended in June 1873, when, after their last appearance together in or around Poughkeepsie, Omohundro and Cody decided they could manage *Scouts of the Prairie* on their own. None of the three principals ever gave specific reasons for their split, at least not publicly, but it seems likely that Omohundro and Cody realized that Judson's character was replaceable, while their personal appearances were not.[29]

If Judson was unhappy about this turn of events, he did not show it. The writer-turned-showman simply wrote a new play based on a dime novel he had written the year before called *Dashing Charlie, The Texas Whirlwind*.[30] He hired a booking agent, two white actors, and about twenty Comanche and Modoc actors from Phineas T. Barnum and created a new version of *Scouts of the Prairie*—which looked a lot like the first version, except it was usually presented in clearings next to railroad tracks. Judson presented his wild tales of the border along the Hudson River routes before breaking off at Kingston and heading west through Pennsylvania and then Ohio.

Judson knew where to find his audience, which was usually in medium-size towns to avoid the Cody-Omohundro version playing in the largest towns. He was a brilliant publicist, floating rumors in the morning so that more customers would flock to the show in the evening. In Paterson, New Jersey, for example a huge mob turned out in hopes of seeing a fight between two indigenous men for the favors of a young woman:

> *Long before the doors were open, the sidewalk was obstructed by a thick crowd of half-grown men and boys, who scrambled towards the entrance, and extended as far as the middle of the street, looking for all the world like a swarm of exaggerated bees climbing over each other at the entrance of a monstrous hive.*[31]

In spite of the show's popularity in more rural areas, Judson did not make money. It could not have helped that he was intoxicated a great deal of the time and thus could not perform. Nor could some of his fellow actors, whom he plied with alcohol so he would not have to drink alone. On the way to perform a show in Yonkers, he even shot a boat engineer in the leg while intoxicated. And, it turns out, he was supporting three wives: Lovanche, Kate, and a new one, Anna Fuller.

But the biggest reason Judson's fledgling Wild West show did not succeed was because of the magnetism of the *real* William F. Cody. The explosive popularity of the *true* Buffalo Bill could not be surpassed—and never would be again. Judson's discovery of Cody and his immediate exploitation of him created a Western hero unparalleled in his era.

Chapter Thirteen

Hazel Eye

On July 15, 1870, Frank Swart turned twenty. This son of Lovanche and her late husband, Armamus, was a steam pipe fitter and lived with his grandparents about forty miles south of Albany. It was a source of disappointment for Lovanche that Judson was not able to be a father figure to her son, as he had promised when they first married. But it wasn't enough of a disappointment to keep her from once again cohabitating with the novelist, and in August 1870 she moved with him to an apartment at 13 East Seventh Street—notable because it was right next door to McSorley's Ale House, still the oldest "Irish tavern" in New York City and already famous for being a meeting place for politicians and celebrities.[1]

In terms of fame and fortune—between his first meeting with Cody and their stage tour—Judson was doing very well. He followed his first "Buffalo Bill" novel with the adventures of another frontier scout and hunter, entitled *Little Buckshot—The White Whirlwind of the Prairies*. The main character was described as a living hero—one of the best scouts and Indian fighters on the Plains. Judson identified "Little Buckshot" as Conrad Wentworth, a scout and guide for the US 2nd Cavalry. He said: "Like our famed Buffalo Bill, he (Wentworth) is a live reality, not a fanciful character." And like the Buffalo Bill series, this was another story based on rugged individualism and survival in the West.[2] Characters living in Buffalo Bill's world also got their own novels: Dove Eye, the Lodge Queen; Dashing Charlie, the Texas Whirlwind; Texas Jack, the White King of the Pawnees; and Will Cody, the Pony Express Rider.

During this time, in which Judson was writing, traveling, and lecturing, he furnished the apartment and generally paid the bills for Lovanche.

But in May or June 1871, she said, his financial support began to dwindle. He told her he was having trouble getting paid by his newspapers, and he eventually stopped coming to the home and stopped corresponding from wherever he was. Lovanche was now forty-four, and her hands were arthritic from years of sewing finery. But she was practical, so when she put up her sign for dressmaking again in order to make ends meet, she was surprised when Judson stopped by unannounced and ordered her to take the sign down. He paid some bills, left some money, and left again to lecture, or so he told her. "After a while," she said, "I became convinced that he was bestowing his affections and means in another direction. I learned that they had expended three hundred dollars for a watch, chain and jewelry for some lady friend, and he ceased visiting me and his home."

Finally, Lovanche had had enough. In May 1871 she had papers drawn up for divorce, citing abandonment. Judson avoided service of these papers until June, when a messenger finally caught up with him. He did not respond to her until September, when he—perhaps realizing he could no longer afford to keep her as a partner—offered to divorce her on her own terms. They decided on an amount he would pay; in return, Lovanche would "renounce all present and future claims on E. C. Z. Judson" for support, and promise not to "molest or sue said Judson or in any way give him trouble or annoyance" for these monies.[3]

But it seems the novelist could not quit Lovanche. He kept coming around to their home on 7th Street, one to three times a week, bringing both household necessities and money but also gifts like flowers and even a canary. When he wrote her letters and notes, he addressed her as "Mrs. Lovanche L. Judson." Things "ran along," according to Lovanche, until her mother sent her a copy of the *Stamford Mirror* of October 10, 1871. It contained the marriage notice of Judson with Anna Fuller as having occurred on October 3. It seems Lovanche's mother had gotten word that Judson might be considering marriage with a young woman in Delaware and wrote to a minister there about it. He wrote back on October 23:

Mrs. Rhoda Kelsey,
Madam: Your letter making inquiry about Mr. Judson is before me.
He is not only engaged but married to Miss Anna Fuller of this place.

They were married about a week ago. I was absent on my vacation when they were married. The Rev. Mr. Irving, United Presbyterian minister, married them. Irving is a teacher in the Stamford Academy. I did all I could to put Mr. Fuller's people on their guard against Mr. Judson, as I had intimations that he had other wives living. If your daughter is his legal wife, some of her friends should put the law in force against him, on the charge of bigamy. He has never passed himself off here as a bachelor; claims that one of his wives was never a legal wife, but only a mistress, and that another one was not true to him and he has a divorce from her, or at least he told Miss Fuller he would get one, and by promise he showed her papers of some sort to that effect, before their marriage. Yours, etc.,

L. E. Richards, Pastor of Presbyterian Church, Stamford, N.Y.[4]

Within an hour of Lovanche's receiving the newspaper clipping and her mother's letter, Judson came into their apartment. Lovanche described the scene as surreal: There was no fight, no angry words passed between them. Instead, both she and Judson expressed "shame and humility, mingled with pitiful tenderness, on both sides."[5] This odd acknowledgment of shame on the part of Lovanche might indicate that she had found romance in the arms of another at some point—a charge lobbed at her after Judson's death. Whatever the reason, the two decided to split permanently, and they drew up new papers of divorce, witnessed by Lovanche's sister. For the next two years, Judson faithfully made payments of support to Lovanche.[6]

Meanwhile, Judson occasionally slept at his home in Chappaqua, even after he had moved Kate and their children to Mamaroneck. A neighbor remembered that he kept his belongings there until 1873—also, a menagerie of cats. When the animals were fighting particularly loud at night, Judson would throw his boots at them and then have a villager bring back his shoes the next day.[7] This neighbor also remembered when Judson brought Cody up to the village, and at least the writer was drunk. The two went out for a buggy drive, and as he was wont to do when he was drinking, Judson brought his gun with him. About three-quarters up the road from Judson's home near Greeley, the neighbor recalled, neighbor

Steve Tompkins was plowing his field. Tompkins was peculiar, having a reputation for shaving only once a week, and that was on Sunday night at sundown. He would sit down under an old apple tree with a piece of soap in one hand and his razor in the other. Rubbing the soap over his face, he would sort of "wet" the razor on the palms of his hand and hack away. This was too much of an opportunity for Judson. He wagered Cody that he could put a bullet through the man's stovepipe hat without "touching a hair of his head." He then supposedly fired his revolver, but Tompkins kept plowing.

"Whoa," said Judson, pulling up on his reins and clambering down off the buggy with Cody. They walked over to Tompkins, who was about one hundred yards away. "Hey, lemme see your hat," yelled Judson. Tompkins, according to the neighbor, yanked up on his oxen and turned around, spat a stream of tobacco juice into the gutter, and stared at him.

"Hay, what say," Tompkins asked.

"Lemme see your [expletive, expletive] hat," repeated Judson.

Tompkins took off his stovepipe, and the novelist grabbed it. "See," he showed Cody, "right through the band." Cody saw a good-sized hole through the hat where the bullet had gone, just above the hairline.

"Say," Cody asked the farmer, "didn't you hear a noise about a minute or two ago?"

"Well," replied Tompkins, "I did hear a bee buzzin' around my head."[8]

Cody later conceded that Judson might not be true to his temperance speeches. "Ordinarily he took excellent care of himself," he said, "but once in a while he would indulge in a little tear—but did not keep it up as a regular thing."[9]

Cody spoke little about his time with Judson outside of Chicago and New York City, but it is clear that he considered Anna Fuller of Delaware County to be the novelist's legal wife. "He was a very good husband and was very much devoted to his wife and children. He had two children—but one died and one is now living, a boy, I think."[10]

In fact, Judson had married Miss Fuller on October 3, 1871—before Cody and Judson commenced work on their Chicago production. Kate Myers later swore that she and Judson still saw each other throughout 1872, and that she never had divorce papers served upon her. In fact, she testified, she did not know Judson had married again until his death notice appeared in the *New York World* in July 1886 and said he was leaving "all his property 'to my wife Annie Judson and to educate my boy Edward.'" This may be true, because Judson obtained a divorce from Myers by posting his intentions to do so in an Indiana newspaper—a common if wholly unfair way to separate in the nineteenth century. He then obtained the actual divorce decree through the Scott County, Indiana, court on November 27, 1871—a full month after his marriage to Anna.[11]

But even in 1871, Myers was most certainly aware that for all intents and purposes, Judson had abandoned her and their children. A fifth child, a son, was born to Myers on September 1, 1871; she named him Effington.[12] In the 1880 Census, Myers is listed as the sole head of the household, with the last name Judson, the name all five of her children carry at this time too. Adding to the confusion about Effington's paternity is the fact that Myers later testified that she had lived with second husband John Aitcheson since 1873, and that they were married by "verbal contract." But Aitcheson was still married and living with his first wife until 1885. Myers may have wanted to give her fifth child the benefit of a surname that was not notorious, but it is also possible that she had a relationship with Aitcheson long before the death of his wife and her spurious divorce from Judson.[13]

Anna Fuller was the daughter of John W. Fuller, a farmer in Stamford, New York. She recalled that she first met the novelist in 1869, perhaps at a temperance lecture in Delaware County. The family held property that included thousands of acres that shared a boundary line with land deeded to Judson's cousin by their shared grandfather, Samuel Judson. The Fullers and the Judsons had known each other for as long as anyone could remember. Samuel Judson Sr.—the writer's great-grandfather—helped found Stamford in 1789. Willard Fuller, Anna's grandfather, settled in Stamford around 1813 and farmed the fertile acreage of the Delaware River mouth next to Samuel Judson Jr. The families were often named guardians of each other's minor children, or godparents. Mary Fuller, Anna's older sister, was named trustee for Judson's grandfather's estate— an interesting choice given that both Judson himself and a cousin were available for this role.

Fuller and Judson were married on October 3, 1871, in her father's house by a Presbyterian minister. He was fifty; she was eighteen. Thus, during the time Judson was writing Buffalo Bill stories and crisscrossing the eastern seaboard—before he and Cody parted ways—he kept Kate in Mamaroneck, Lovanche in the city, and Anna with him on the road. According to Monaghan, Judson referred to his lovely young wife as "Hazel Eye" in some of his writings. It may be that he modeled "Hazel-Eye, The Girl Trapper"—a character in one of his stories and also in *Scouts of the Prairie*—after Anna.

The still-hyperenergetic Judson must have felt he could carry all these different worlds on his shoulders, and by outward appearances he did. In the fall of 1869, he had signed a contract to write exclusively for the *New York Weekly*, and they paid him handsomely for his Cody serial. Under the terms of his contract, he received between ten thousand and twenty thousand dollars a year for his serials, including his "Buffalo Bill" stories and *The Shadowed Altar*. His salary was extremely high in comparison to other serial writers. *Frank Leslie's Weekly* paid popular novelist Mayne Reid eight thousand dollars for his serials, while the *New York Weekly* paid a frequent female contributor, Mary Jane Holmes, four thousand to six thousand dollars.[14]

In addition, Judson had successfully created a new world for William F. Cody. "Before Cody met Buntline," writes historian John Schmidt, "his life on the plains was neither more skillful nor daring than many of his companions. Buntline established a pattern for him to follow, as he had for his heroes in earlier adventure stories." However, notes Schmidt, he (and his successors) made the divergence between fact and fiction even greater. Where earlier heroes had been represented as slaying several opponents, Cody now began slaying hundreds. Buntline created the character—Cody gave the character credibility by not denying the exploits. "His living presence, or simply being, was a powerful inducement to a faithful following that such things—and such people—could really happen. All of the many writers who later followed the Buffalo Bill trail simply emulated the legend Buntline had founded."[15]

Just before and after his split with Cody and the petering out of his Indian tour, Judson returned to Stamford with Anna and began building a name for himself as the town patriarch he never was. His grandfather, Samuel Judson, left a bequest to the Stamford Seminary for the purchase of a library, provided townspeople could match his bequest of fifteen hundred dollars. Judson joined the board of trustees overseeing this bequest, and was able to use some of his influence to purchase books from New York City at a reduced price—something he had done for the Blackwell Prison library while he was there.[16] He founded the Judson Literary Association, for which he was an occasional speaker, and worked to have stately monuments erected in town and at the Stamford Cemetery honoring respected forefathers of the town, including some from his family.

But Judson's biggest undertaking by far was building a new home: a new Eagle's Nest. After living with Fuller's father for a while, the novelist convinced John Fuller that a grand home built on some of his fallow property would be a testament to the family's status and a place where he could start a family with his daughter. Fuller agreed; after all, Judson was a celebrity and earning more than anyone in Stamford had ever seen. Also, he was well aware of Ned Buntline's reputation with women, and figured that building such a home would anchor him firmly to Anna and the town of his birth. Furthermore, his son-in-law spoke often about leaving travel behind permanently—his leg bothered him, and he wished to write even more works, which must have given the senior Fuller confidence about his income. Lastly, Judson invited his in-laws to live with him and his bride in this new home once it was built.[17]

In late 1871 Judson hired an architect and commenced building a home on the 120 acres Mr. Fuller had given him. Fuller also gave him cash to put into the structure (after Judson's death, he was quick to point out that he had received no accounting for this investment). It was, by all descriptions, incredible. It was built in the Second Empire style still popular among the well-heeled after the Civil War, with its ubiquitous mansard roofs and heavy ornament. The residence was built and furnished at an expense of nearly twenty-five thousand dollars, and, as Fred

Pond described it, its surroundings indicated the culture and sporting proclivities of the owner:

> *A tract of twenty acres close at hand was kept as a game preserve, and his favorite room, the armory or curiosity shop, as he was wont to call it, contained a rare collection of guns, pistols, sabers and other implements of warfare and the chase. His library sanctum, as he remarked, were one, and in this cosy retreat his prolific pen produced the numerous thrilling tales which brought him wider fame and fortune.*[18]

The family moved in when Judson finished touring with Cody and his own set of actors, around late 1873.

For obvious reasons, the new Eagle's Nest and Stamford's prodigal son, fresh off his Wild West tours, attracted a lot of attention, including that of the widow Swart. He had made regular support payments to her since his marriage to Anna in 1871 but stopped in September of 1873. Instead he brought her a few gifts and called on her several times throughout October. In fact, he gave her reason to think they might yet again reconcile, appearing hat in hand in the parlor of her new boardinghouse. In the presence of her landlady and several other boarders, he made a great show of apologizing to her for his behavior and fell to his knees, begging forgiveness. Would she consider marrying him again, he asked? "As usual on such occasions, and there had been many of them," she said, "my feelings got the better of my judgment, and I freely and fully forgave him and became reconciled." He stayed overnight; the next day he said he had to leave for a few hours and would return. He did not.

Unbelievably, Lovanche continued to meet up with him until late December 1873, when she joined him at Taylor's Hotel in Jersey City. It is not clear whether she followed Judson or not, but once she was there, he introduced her to his wife, Anna Fuller. "When I left, Judson went with me as far as the ferry and offered to go home with me, but I told him to [go] back to his last wife, and call on me the next day. He called [the] next day, and between that time and the 21st of January, 1874, we had several interviews looking to a final settlement." When he did not agree upon anything, Lovanche took her case to court. In February 1874 a New York Supreme Court judge issued an order for Judson to pay her fifteen dollars per week alimony and her lawyer fees.[19]

The novelist ignored the court order, so in May 1876 Lovanche borrowed some money and traveled to see him in Stamford. It must have shocked her to see Eagle's Nest and all its trappings while Judson pleaded poverty and said he did not have any of the nearly two thousand dollars in back alimony he owed her. She demanded that he at least cover her travel expenses; he gave her fifty dollars and a promissory note she could take to Street & Smith publishers in the city to obtain the rest of his obligation. They refused to pay her—not because he told them not to, as she initially thought, but because he had already used up any credit he had with them for his work, even though he still kept the *Weekly* well stocked with stories. She telegraphed Judson, who came down to the city for a few days and met with her lawyer—but again he gave her nothing, save for twenty dollars he managed to scrounge up.[20]

Pitifully, Lovanche claimed she had started physically declining around the time of Judson's marriage to Anna. Her exact ailments are not recorded, but she spent six months at St. Luke's Hospital in New York City as a patient and then was discharged as "incurable." The doctors told her she was unfit to work, or "endure any privation," without suffering severely.[21]

In August 1876 a New York City judge sent an order to Delaware County ordering the sheriff there to arrest Judson for nonsupport. When the sheriff arrived at Eagle's Nest, though, the writer and his family were gone. Judson and Anna were at the Beaverkill—the first of an annual fishing event in the next county down from Delaware featuring hatchery-stocked trout; native species had been declining for years. Anna also liked fishing. For the first time in his life, Monaghan notes, Judson had a wife who could match his driving energy—no surprise, given their respective ages. The novelist became enthusiastic about "female fishermen" and wrote an article for the *American Angler* describing several famous fisherwomen, particularly those who were great fly casters. He also recommended that more women enter the sport. All summer long, with a camp outfit in a light wagon, Judson and Anna jogged along soft dirt roads, visiting trout streams in the Catskills and also the Poconos of Pennsylvania. Judson always carried an

American flag with him and, like he did at home, displayed it at whatever inn the couple happened to stay. During this trip, Anna became pregnant with their first child.[22]

During their summer vacation, Judson learned that his old partner, Buffalo Bill Cody, had used the Battle of the Little Bighorn to promote his own fortunes. Cody had not forgotten Ned Buntline's lesson about keeping himself remembered as a scout, not an actor. On receipt of the news of General George Armstrong Custer's death, Cody closed his show to join the soldiers. Soon the papers announced that he had taken "the first scalp for Custer." Also this summer of 1876, "Wild Bill" Hickok was shot in the back of his head in Deadwood, Dakota Territory—he had given up show business to join the gold rush. No doubt Judson wondered if Hickok ever regretted doing only one season of theatrical touring with Cody after the latter parted ways with Judson. Hickok refused to remember lines inherited from Ned Buntline, such as: "Fear not, fair maid; by heavens, you are safe at last with Wild Bill, who is ever ready to risk life and die if need be in the defense of weak and helpless womanhood."[23] He had a stage carpenter deliver a message to Cody: "That long-haired gentleman, who walked out a few minutes ago, requested me to tell you that you could go thunder with your old show."[24]

If the Judsons' summer of 1876 was a renaissance for both of them, the winter that followed was equally miserable for both. The temperature in Stamford was particularly cold, with the thermometer rarely rising above zero until March. Anna was heavy with pregnancy, and Judson broke three ribs when he slipped on some snow on their front porch. He complained of soreness from old wounds, like a bullet that had supposedly been embedded in his spine since June 1863—almost certainly a simple case of sciatica.[25] Still, the writer's output was enough to pay for new baby items when daughter Irene was born in April—he now had two daughters named for his sister. For the holiday season he wrote, "In the Toil; or, The Lottery Gambler's Victim," a story about fictional New York family man Charles Brennon, whose purchase of a winning lottery ticket immediately put him on the path to ruin by way of gambling and then drinking too much liquor.[26]

The novelist's spirits lifted when summer came to Stamford in 1877 and he could plan the town's Fourth of July celebrations—emulating his father a bit. He apparently felt that the festivities the year before—the centennial—had been somewhat overshadowed by "the curtain-dropping climax of Custer's Last Stand" and presumably the press surrounding Cody's co-opting of the event, as well as Hickok's death. Judson planned speeches, games, and luncheons for the Fourth, when he also planned to announce that he was now a "red-hot Republican" and available to stump for the party's causes.[27]

The idea of another winter in Stamford scared the writer, owing to his various aches and pains and the challenges of keeping a working farm going during the snowy season. In mid-November Judson packed up his current family and set out for Florida to spend the winter. The press marveled at his fancy "conveyance," an expensive carriage and thorough-bred horses. Among his vacation items, the *Pittsburgh Daily Post* noted, was a beloved Sharp's rifle, seventy-five pounds of ammunition, and a full assortment of fishing tackle.[28]

For Judson, this was not just a trip to avoid cold weather—it was a way to revive the adventurous spirit he had had before his joints started to creak in recent years. The family rode an average of thirty miles a day and had no problems until they reached Rosendale, New York, where Judson had to "bounce a drunken man" out of the road with his carriage pole. He lost no sleep over this, he said in the *Stamford Mirror*, because in addition to being drunk, the man cursed a lot when the writer hit him. But for the most part, the family pleasantly wended its way down the eastern seaboard, sending dispatches to the *Stamford Mirror* about the grand inns they stayed at along the way and various sites of Civil War battles—certainly Gettysburg, Pennsylvania. He then drove down to Maryland, glorying in the fact that he was following the road used by General Robert E. Lee in his retreat.

Judson had intended to take his family to the southernmost part of the country and show them where he had fought the Seminole while in the navy. They made it as far as Warrenton, Virginia; the novelist enjoyed the "delightful society" there and his ability to hunt game easily in the warmer climate. He wrote home about meeting former Confederate leader Colonel John Singleton "Gray Ghost" Mosby and William H. F. Payne, former commander of the famed rebel "Black Horse Cavalry." Judson socialized with Robert S. Granger, a retired general from the Union army, and wrote, "It is a delight to talk with the old hero of our early days in Florida and Mexico, for we both saw hard as well as jolly times in those wars."[29] Judson may have meant to give his in-laws some peace of mind when he wrote this next passage for the *Mirror*: "I've met Stuart, Ashley, and Hampton's cavalry many a time in deadly fray," he lied, "but I tell you what, old friend, were I not protected by the golden shield of matrimony, a charge of flashing glances from the dark eyed daughters of the sunny south would conquer one who never surrendered to the heroes named above. But I must stop this, or I'll get my hair pulled."[30]

The Judsons followed spring across Maryland and Pennsylvania, and in April they returned home to Stamford. The writer and adventurer hoisted the American flag above Eagle's Nest to let people know that Hazel Eye and Ned Buntline had returned.

CHAPTER FOURTEEN

Ever the Fourth of July

IN 1879 JUDSON FEATURED JOHN WALLACE "CAPTAIN JACK" CRAWFORD in a dime novel, *The Terrible Dread, Or, The Seven Scouts*. Three years later, Jack again appeared as the hero in Judson's "Merciless Ben, The Hair Lifter," published in the *New York Weekly*. Crawford was a protégé and friend of Cody's—he replaced Cody as chief of scouts of the 5th Cavalry—but he was an accomplished man in his own right. Crawford made a famous horseback ride with urgent dispatches from the Battle of Slim Buttes to Fort Laramie, a distance of 350 miles in four days. This battle took place on September 9 and 10, 1876, and was the first victory the US Army had over the Sioux after the Little Big Horn. Crawford was a bona-fide adventurer, but he was equally famous for putting events down in verse, such as the murder of "Wild Bill" Hickok by Jack McCall in Deadwood:

> Sleep on brave heart, in peaceful slumber,
> Bravest scout in all the West;
> Lightning eyes and voice of thunder,
> Closed and hushed in quiet rest.
> Peace and rest at last is given,
> May we meet again in heaven.
> Rest in peace.

Crawford despised the dime-novel format, later stating that his name had "never yet figured in one of those trashy concerns with my consent." Judson wrote two stories featuring the captain and Prentiss Ingraham wrote one, but after these, Crawford never appeared as the central character like

Buffalo Bill, who became the hero of more than five hundred original dime novels.[1]

In spite of Crawford's disdain for the format that had made Judson a wealthy man, the writer and the adventurer–"cowboy poet" stayed close friends. They attempted to use each other's celebrity to make more money: Judson became the Stamford agent for the "Lode and Placer Prospecting and Mining Association," which promised "Energy, Pluck, Perseverance, and a Squar' Deal" from Crawford in return for ten dollars per share. (This does not appear to have panned out for either man.)[2]

It was Crawford who memorialized one of the greatest sorrows of Judsons' life: the death of his four-year-old daughter Irene on January 11, 1881. The cause of her death is not recorded, but the *Windham (New York) Journal* described her illness as having come on rather suddenly and lasting only two days.[3] "Three words speak the agony which volumes could not describe," Judson confided in Crawford, "the loss which all the gold in your mines could not replace, the shadow which hangs darkest in all my long, eventful life—*Irene is dead!*" Crawford responded with a touching poem entitled "Irene is Dead," in hopes that he might offer some comfort:

> Bow not thy aged head in grief,
> For Irene knows no pain,
> And all is love, and joy, and peace,
> Where you shall meet again.[4]

Had Irene lived, Judson might have achieved his greatest accomplishment: the complete re-creation of his childhood family, molded to his own rosy ideal. In spite of her crushing grief, Anna brought a full-term baby boy into the world on May 19, 1881. They named him Edward Zane Carroll Judson Jr.

Had nature not intervened in Judson's happiness, Lovanche Swart Judson would have done so. On Tuesday, April 19, 1881, the erstwhile Mrs. Buntline appeared once again in Stamford, armed with at least one marriage certificate and several legal documents from New York City judges, demanding alimony from Judson. She also brought a sheaf of letters written to her by Judson, in which he referred to her as his lawful wife. Again, Judson denied her claim, and went so far as to tell a reporter, "Good God, how can this woman be my wife? Why, I had five wives before she presented herself."[5]

Lovanche, having no place to spend the night, appealed to Stamford's overseer of the poor to get lodging and enough money for train fare to go back to New York and file more paperwork.[6] At first, some of the Stamford villagers doubted the tale of Judson's complicated marital record with Lovanche, but soon many of them started to gossip, asserting that she and not Anna, now very pregnant, was the legitimate "Mrs. Judson." Newspaper reporters came up from Kingston to get more details. One reported:

Mrs. Judson appears to be about fifty-five years old, and is crippled and an invalid. One who knew of her years ago says she was most beautiful then, but she has no traces of beauty now. She seems to have seen much of the world, is quick-witted, and has a most effective tongue. By most persons she would be considered to be more than ordinarily intelligent.[7]

According to an eyewitness, Lovanche chased Judson around the streets of Stamford and sent notes to him, ostensibly from her lawyer. The novelist did his best to avoid her, but finally—exasperated—he told her that he had nothing to give her and to "go ahead or go to the devil." He suddenly found that he had business to attend to in New York City and got on the next train down there. Soon word came from Kingston that he had stopped there long enough to give its newspaper office the following explanation:

Editor Freeman:
The attempt to blackmail me by false statements and forgeries alluded to in your paper of today has been repeatedly tried but has failed in this as in other attempts of the same woman. She is not, never was my wife, nor has any legal claim upon me. I shall hold my slanderers to a strict account in this matter.
Yours, respectfully,
E. Z. C. Judson
Rondout, 14th April, 1881.

Judson told the editor that he would return to the office on the way home the following week and give even more detail about Lovanche's machinations; he failed to appear.[8]

The arrival of Judson's son filled him with hope that once again the ghosts of his past and the sadness of losing a daughter would stop haunting him and he could be left in peace to write and be a gentleman farmer. The writer, dismayed by the declining numbers of trout in local streams and rivers, purchased fifteen thousand California mountain trout eggs from the Seth Green State Hatchery at Rochester and worked with local experts to replenish nearby Schoharie Creek, which fed miles of local tributaries. He invited the entire town to picnic in the orchard he planted on Eagle's Nest property, and invited neighboring farmers to pasture their cows there too.

From the moment he married Anna Fuller in Delaware County until his death in 1886, E. Z. C. Judson commandeered Fourth of July celebrations. "There are four things in this world that I especially love," he told members of a Stamford band. "One is a nice woman; the next is a good horse; third, sweet music; and fourth the Flag of our Native Land."[9] In the days leading up to Independence Day, the writer and his wife welcomed townspeople onto his property, served lemonade, gave speeches all around the county, and directed bands to play patriotic pieces. On the Fourth of July in 1880, the villagers made the mistake of not including the bombastic Judson in their plans for the holiday. He retaliated by sponsoring the activities of the town's best band, purchasing their uniforms and instruments, and proclaiming that he would celebrate George Washington's birthday in a manner that would make Stamford's Fourth look like "a Sunday afternoon."[10] When daughter Irene died some weeks before Washington's February birthday in 1881, it "melted the hearts of his neighbors," and they turned out in force for Judson's great dinner, toasts, speeches, and fireworks at Eagle's Nest.[11] From then on, Stamford placed its Fourth of July celebrations in the hands of its celebrity resident—Levi Judson would have been both proud and envious of his son.

There were other Judsons in Stamford. The novelist's uncle, Samuel, died in 1870, leaving a good-sized fortune, which he distributed among various cousins, nieces, and nephews, including Irene—the writer's sister—and trusted friends, like county magistrates Francis R. Gilbert and William Gleason. He left a considerable amount of money to relatives, with instructions to purchase farms and live on them, and a small fortune for the Stamford Library purchase and charities in New York City, such as the Pease's House of Industry, which provided support for the area's predominantly Irish Catholic working class. Samuel bequeathed one thousand dollars to his executors in trust, to be spent by them as they deemed best for the "education of colored persons in the Southern States," and hundreds of dollars to several denominations of Christian churches in Stamford.[12]

Notably absent from Samuel Judson's will was any gift to his nephew, E. Z. C. Judson—something the novelist would have realized when he attended his uncle's funeral in late August 1870 and heard the will read a week later. It may well be that he thought the writer did not need any extra income, given his public display of wealth. But it could not have gone unnoticed by his relatives that Judson married Anna Fuller just thirteen months after his uncle left significant amounts of money to her family as well as other members of his own: For example, he left one thousand dollars to her mother, fifteen hundred dollars to a Fuller cousin, a gold watch to Anna's father, two hundred dollars each to Anna and sister Julia and three hundred dollars to their mother, and so forth. With his nuptials to Anna, Judson inherited lands his family had once deeded over to the Fullers, and presumably some of the cash they put into the building of Eagle's Nest came from his own grandfather.[13] Noah Pratt Judson, his first cousin, farmed acreage that shared a boundary line with Eagle's Nest; Monaghan was probably correct in his assessment that Noah could be "counted on to stand at his division line, malign his wealthy cousin, and warn the onlookers against trespassing."[14]

When Edward Jr.—"Eddie"—was about six months old, the Judsons once again headed to Virginia for the winter, hoping to avoid the aches and pains that had plagued the novelist in increasing frequency. When they returned home in March 1882, they brought with them boxes and baskets full of toys for Eddie—most too complicated for the nineteen-month-old child. "I mean that his childhood shall be happy as mine was not," Judson proudly told friends. The family replicated their trip the following summer, after which he announced himself an Independent Republican who would stump for Democrat Grover Cleveland.

It made sense that Judson would try to step back into the national political arena. By 1884 he had run out of boards on which to sit on behalf of his uncle's bequests, and he had little interest in lobbying for agricultural improvements on behalf of the county. The months leading up to the presidential election of 1884 proved very exciting—with no major substantive issues separating the candidates, the election turned on the candidates themselves. Republican James G. Blaine was attacked for his close relations with the railroad interests, from which, it was claimed, he received financial benefits. Blaine's opponents published what were called the "Mulligan Letters," which purported to show that Blaine received bribes. Cleveland, on the other hand, was attacked as being immoral for fathering a son out of wedlock. The Republicans would chant "Ma, Ma, Where's my Pa?" at Cleveland's speaking events. Cleveland was able to defuse the issue by telling the truth, and he ultimately received the support of many reformers, including several leading Republicans.

Judson never expressed his reasons for supporting Cleveland instead of Blaine. One of his good friends, writer Henry Ward Beecher, was vocally against Blaine, so perhaps Judson decided to follow suit. It's somewhat ironic, given that Cleveland stood with his party in opposition to temperance—something for which Judson still earned money lecturing. While Cleveland ran on a platform of anti-corruption, this would have been of little concern to Judson. It may well be that Judson felt some sympathy toward the South, having spent time there in recent years and having interviewed former Confederate soldiers. This might have been a factor in his lack of support for Blaine, who had wished to keep more stringent Reconstruction policies in place.

But the most obvious reason for Judson's vocal support of Democrat Cleveland—rather, his vocal antithesis toward Republican Blaine—is his certain irritation that Blaine was downplaying his Know Nothing work in the 1850s. To be sure, the Know Nothings were really a product of the late 1840s to mid-1850s, and the party faded once the Republicans established themselves out of the ruins of the old Whig Party in 1857. Both the Whigs and Republicans were eventually rejected by many Know Nothings, who had no interest in abolitionism. Neither did Judson, in particular, even though it became the cornerstone of the moderate Republicans during Lincoln's administration. In 1884 Judson seemed to line up more with the Mugwumps, who represented Republicans who were disgusted with the spoils system and wished to see a return to rule by old Protestant families who were not enriched by a new industrial society.

Still, Judson's hostility toward Blaine was probably simpler: Judson's Know Nothing Party was a bona-fide party, and if Blaine downplayed its importance or its tenets, then he downplayed Judson. Blaine's supporters claimed that his anti-foreign sentiments were a thing of the past—that membership in that party had long ceased to hold any meaning. "It was a good many years ago" was one refrain. "It was before war and before the Republican Party was fairly organized" was another. But the novelist took every opportunity to emphasize how zealous Blaine was at that time, and that those ideals could not be tempered with time. The *New York World* put out a lengthy interview with Judson regarding Blaine's membership in the Know Nothings. After establishing that Judson had been the "young, active, vigorous and somewhat fiery" head and speaker of Know Nothings in Maine thirty years prior, the reporter asked if perhaps Blaine was not quite so involved. Judson vigorously denied this:

> *There can be no doubt of it, and those of us there who were active and instrumental in building up that movement in Maine and elsewhere never had any misgivings as to where Mr. Blaine stood. He was with us heart and soul, and there must be at least fifty persons in Portland who could, if they would, prove what I say.*
>
> *Why, when I reached Maine he was among the first of the many people whom I met. He was then young, bright and ambitious for*

a seat in the Legislature, and, as the record of his whole life proves, ready to serve any cause that could aid him. Our movement had swept Maine, the other New England States, and was believed would surely sweep the nation. That Mr. Blaine then joined our order I knew then, know now, and I wish to make the statement with all emphasis and wish to give the words all the weight they will bear. . . . After a lapse of 30 years or more, and with all record probably lost, Mr. Blaine evidently thinks he is safe in denying all connection with these movements; but the memory of some men is still good, and mine, unfortunately for Mr. Blaine, is so unimpaired that I am able to state beyond peradventure or cavil that he was a Know-nothing [sic] then and undoubtedly would be now had the movement continued to be popular.[15]

In a twist that could only be thought of by the mercurial writer, Judson then said he could not vote for a man such as Blaine, because he was a liar.

In 1884 Judson's political thoughts were of much less consequence on the national stage than they had been in his earlier years, but they still carried some weight, especially in New York. Newspapers still sought out his opinions, if only to have a reason to trudge up and see the magnificent Eagle's Nest residence or have the very entertaining writer visit their offices, limping along proudly with his gold-tipped cane—a gift from Cody. At times Judson wore out his welcome at the *Stamford Mirror* office—he and editor Simon B. Champion were frequently at odds—so he would invite correspondents from the *Kingston Daily Freeman* or the *New York World* to discuss things of more import to him than the price of butter. For example, when Johnson Chesnut Whittaker, one of West Point's first black cadets, was accused of staging his own beating and mutilation to get out of taking a philosophy test, the *Freeman* sought out Judson's opinion:

I believe in sustaining the aristocracy as in former years, void of profanity, and in training cadets to the work of gentlemen of rank. In the case of the mutilated cadet it may be that Whittaker himself performed the act to enlist the sympathy of the American people. I am a true American, and believe in protecting the rights of the negro, but I do not wish to be in a class with him or occupy the same table.[16]

And when he wasn't busy writing for both Street & Smith and the Beadle firm, "Ned Buntline" was happy to give his thoughts on New York politics and environmental concerns of his home state.

In July 1884 Judson invited President Chester Arthur to come visit him at Eagle's Nest. The leader did tour the Catskills in August and September but did not stay at Judson's home—though it may be that a pressing crisis with Judson's daughter prevented him from chasing the president down. An ugly scandal story appeared in the New York *Morning Journal*:

COURTED BY MOONLIGHT:

NED BUNTLINE'S DAUGHTER AND HER FAITHLESS SUITOR
Grief and Terror of a Lonely Girl Deserted Just Before Her Wedding
ROMANCE IN THE GROVES OF WESTCHESTER

Below this heading readers learned that Edwardina Judson, youngest daughter of Kate Myers and the novelist, had "too far trusted" a young man named John McCormick, a local boy who had promised her marriage the previous April. Edwardina, just eighteen years old, might have learned something from her mother's marital ordeal: When McCormick refused to set a wedding date, Edwardina wasted no time filing a complaint with the sheriff. Seduction laws were still a very powerful force at this time, and the would-be groom found himself answering to a grand jury hearing in White Plains. When the jury found in favor of the young woman, McCormick finally consented to marry her, and they were wed immediately at the courthouse.[17] "The prominence of her father," the paper gossiped, "makes the case of interest to all." Monaghan notes that this may have been enough scandal to ruin Judson's political influence in the 1884 campaign, but in all probability his influence was limited to denigrating Blaine.[18]

Edwardina's situation, though, did provide an opportunity for Lovanche to call attention to her own plight yet again. Cleverly—if transparently—she wrote the following to the *Morning Journal*:

TO THE EDITOR OF THE MORNING JOURNAL.

My attention was called this evening to an article in this morning's issue of your paper under the heading "Courted by Moonlight," that proved an "tonishing" [sic] and "unthought-of-revelation" to me, as I was not aware that I do or ever did live in "New Castle" Westchester county, or that I have or ever had a daughter named "Edwardina J. Judson" or "any other name."

But I am and have been the wife of E. Z. C. Judson (better known as "Ned Buntline," "the well-known author," with "many-sided entertainments"), for over thirty years, having been legally married to him on the 24th of September, '53, at "Palisade House," West Hoboken, N. J., as can readily be proved to the satisfaction of any person who is sufficiently interested to investigate by calling on me at my residence.

Mrs. E. Z. C. Judson
No. 277 East Eighty-First street, New York City
September 3d, 1884.[19]

When the election was over and Grover Cleveland was elected president, Judson returned his attention to a new contract to write a series of stories for the Sunday section of the *New York World*. Sunday papers were something new, as dime novels had been a quarter of a century earlier. For other papers, Judson wrote stories about the Civil and Seminole Wars, fishing trips, and snakes he had known—one so big it carried off a trout Ned tossed on the bank.[20]

On Tuesday, September 25, 1884, the *Stamford Mirror* printed a letter from the *Troy Times* that asked if "Ned Buntline" was alive or dead. The *Mirror* responded that their celebrity resident was "alive and well," and that he'd recently sent his "better half" and child by railroad to Warrenton for the winter, where he planned to meet them after finishing a story for the *New York Weekly*. But it was too ambitious a plan; he never made it. He made it as far as New York City, where he spent some time with Bill Cody, but he went back to Stamford when Anna became very sick; it's not clear whether she and Eddie made it very far on their trip south before returning home.[21] Also, it had become increasingly difficult for Judson to leave his beloved Eagle's Nest for anything except short trips into town. He had gained a considerable amount of weight and developed some kind of pulmonary problem that could have been asthma, a function of weight pressing on his lungs and heart, or both. Still, he faithfully entertained literary figures and reporters and enjoyed showing off his beautiful "Hazel Eye" and his young son, on whom he doted: "I get for him all the toys any boy needs," he liked to say with an adoring glance at four-year-old Eddie, always dressed in some sort of elfin military uniform. "During my childhood I never had a kite or a ball, a trumpet or a marble. I never knew how to play," he said, though he usually followed up with remembrances of wonderful fishing and hunting exploits from his youth.[22]

W. A. Croffut of the *Detroit Free Press* came to see the legendary Ned Buntline in July 1885. "All my ideas of 'roughing it,'" he said, "vanished as we exchanged salutations and I climbed in to be carried away to the house on the hillside." Judson, he said, greeted him in some sort of army fatigue uniform, with a blue coat with brass buttons, and upon his blue vest twinkling decorations: the badge of the Sons of America, the head of Washington set on a gold shield with two American flags crossed above it, the original badge of the order of United Americans that he originated, a golden hand crushing an enameled serpent, a Grand Army badge, and a Masonic pin. He noted that Judson's gray hair was cut short and his beard was gone, but he did have a full white mustache. Croffut found himself endeared by Judson's attempt to instill patriotic fervor within his child: "Come on Eddy!" the writer shouted, "Come on, my son! It is sunset; let's pull down the flag."

After dinner, Croffut—like many others who had come to interview Judson—asked him how many stories he had written over his lifetime. "I made a little calculation the other day," Judson replied, "and I am alarmed to find that I have written between 300 and 400 novels, which, if published in book form, would each make a book of about 400 pages each. Of course most of them have escaped being brought out in covers, but my published books make quite a library." Croffut intimated that he would like to get his recipe. Judson laughed, and remarked that many had tried. "Women send their stories to me to correct their style and method. I send them back. One woman came and told me that if I would teach her how to write she would give me half the profits!" Several broken-down or incompetent ministers had approached him for help. Judson told one particularly persistent supplicant that brains were required, and off he went, dejected. "Of course I was joking," Judson added. "It doesn't require a large amount of intellect to write a successful novel. Some of the poorest stuff I have written has had the largest circulation and brought me the most money."[23]

When the reporter asked Judson about the various ailments he seemed to have, the novelist's explanations switched from plausible—even probable—to downright fiction: He told the naive cub reporter that he suffered from no fewer than thirteen bullet wounds (seven from battle), neuralgia in one leg from a Confederate bullet lodged in it, and a bullet hole through one lung and "the touch of a Seminole spear" in the other. He did have very visible scars on his forehead and on his back, which he attributed to saber cuts.[24]

Edward Zane Carroll Judson's last winter dragged painfully—slow, cold, and dreary. In March he became very ill and seemed to think the end might be near. One sleepless night he wrote a poem, and he let a neighbor copy it for the *Mirror*:

> Counting pulse-beats, faint and slow,
> Counting seconds as they go—
> Oh, how weary and how dreary!—
> Throbbing heart—full of pain—
> Eyesight dim and aching brain—
> Thus passes time to me.
> Drifting on the ebbing tide,
> Slow but sure I onward glide—
> Dim the vista seen before,
> Useless now to look behind—
> Drifting on before the wind,

Toward the unknown shore.
Counting time by ticking clock,
Waiting for the final shock—
Waiting for the dark forever—
Oh, how slow the moments go.
None but I, meseems, can know
How close the tideless river.[25]

In spite of his progressing blindness and fatigue, Judson continued to write for New York papers and author some sporting sketches. His last column for *Turf, Field and Farm* was filled with wistfulness that he would never pick up a fishing rod again, or walk through his beautiful orchard:

Propped up in my invalid chair by the window of my sick-chamber, where I have battled for life for ten long weary weeks, I look out on the opening leaves, bright apple blossoms, and the flashing waters of my private trout brook, while for the first time at this date for years I see no sign of snow on hillside or mountain. To-morrow a hundred rods will bend over bright waters within a radium of four or five miles of me, yet I must look sadly on my pet "Orvis" in the corner, and let the split bamboo rest.

He lamented that he could not enjoy the fruits of his labors restocking nearby waterways with California trout:

It is hard when sympathizing visitors, and they are many, tell me the streams never before gave better promise of sport in this section.

Stocked liberally by John N. Bennett and John Griffin, aided by myself, the west branch of the Delaware and the many brooks near by are literally alive with speckled beauty. The two first-named gentlemen have died within a year, and here am I, on my "beams' ends," looking sadly, yet not hopelessly, on dark waters ahead.

Strange, is it not? We, who have done so much to fill the waters, past the reward of labor and expenditure! Telle est vie.

Judson ended his letter with appreciation for the schoolboys who brought him trout they'd caught to cheer him up.[26]

Anna tended to her husband day and night. The *New York Waverly* sent the writer an invalid chair, in hopes he could write them a serial, which he tentatively entitled, "Incognita." He wrote the *Waverly* and thanked them profusely for the chair and said, "I will repay you in good work on 'Incognita.'"

Unfortunately, it was a promise he could not keep. He died less than a month later.

CHAPTER FIFTEEN

Ned Buntline's America

As soon as Lovanche read about Judson's funeral, which took place July 18, 1886, she packed her bags and made her way to Stamford from Prattsville, Greene County, where she lived with relatives. "It is supposed," said a reporter, "that a 'warm wave' will strike Stamford about the time she reaches there," referring to the inevitable conflict that would arise between her and Anna—and any other wives or family who might come forward.[1] The principal claimants who "shook out" among many who poked around were Lovanche K. S. Judson, Katherine Myers Judson, Anna Fuller Judson, and, by extension to Anna, Edward "Eddie" Zane Carroll Judson Jr.

Literally hundreds of pages in the pension file of E. Z. C. Judson are devoted to trying to sort out who was married to whom, and when, and how much weight to give each marriage. With the exception of his marriage to Severina, all Judson's marriages could be contested. Judson's bigamous behavior was beyond the pale, even by the most extreme nineteenth-century American standards, whereby thousands of men and women negotiated their marital status in practical, personal ways, outside of courtrooms. As one scholar writes:

> *Identifying deserted, deserting, and otherwise separated husbands and wives is a difficult task. For some husbands or wives, there were few advantages to revealing they had been abandoned. Being deserted reduced social status; abandoned wives might qualify for charitable assistance, but single women and widows had higher social standing and more options, both economically and for remarriage. Personal shame led many others to hide their pasts, while others may have had no interest in remarriage.*[2]

At the time of Judson's death, Severina Marin and Eva Maria Gardiner were long dead, along with their infant boys. What happened to Sarah Williams after her marriage to Judson has yet to be discovered. Annie Bennett's son with Judson—Sydney Algernon Bennett—stopped investigating on her behalf after his initial letter to the Delaware judge. He probably realized the field was already crowded with contenders. The courts would likely have dismissed him and his mother outright: There were no consistent child support laws when he was born, and his grandparents and then stepfather ably raised him.

Margaret Ann Watson quickly remarried after Judson left Illinois soon after the St. Louis riot; Ione Judah's exact whereabouts after her marriage to the novelist are unknown. This left Lovanche, Kate, and Anna to spar over Judson's pension.

An equal number of pages in the novelist's pension file is devoted to Judson's health, because before the US government could consider paying any pension amount to a widow or child, it had to consider whether a veteran's failing health was directly caused by something that happened to him during his military service. Just weeks before his death, Anna Fuller Judson sought a doctor's report for her husband. She knew the end might be near, and needed to establish the cause or causes of his misery in order to apply for an invalid pension on his behalf. She hoped no one would take note of this application, because Judson had always declared that he was too patriotic to collect a pension. As late as 1885, Judson had done an interview in which he discussed the issue, and his answer was reprinted in dozens of newspapers. The reporter asked Judson why he did not apply for a pension when his leg was stiffened by a bullet lodged there. Judson replied, "I don't want to be a government pauper. I suppose I am entitled to four pensions," he said, erroneously, "and a pension under the proper conditions is honorable enough, but I have seen so many loafers and shirks get pensions for disabilities incurred before they went to war that it just disgusts me with the notion."[3]

But Anna knew if his invalid application were not approved before he died, there would be nothing for her to collect. She applied on his behalf on July 12 and hoped he would live long enough for the application to be approved.

He did not. In hopes of possibly collecting something anyway—pension laws were changing all the time—Anna enlisted Delaware County judge Frank N. Gilbert to take deposition from her husband's doctor, detailing all the ailments that purportedly had led to his death. Ezekiel W. Gallup, MD, said that he had treated Judson since the end of the war. His report said that when he first started treating the writer, he was "suffering severely" from the effect of wounds in the breast and the thigh, and that he had two large chest wounds—one to the right of the sternum and one to the left. A few months later, the doctor clarified his assessment: The heart disease from which Judson died was a result of chest wounds he said he received while serving in the army. The scars, he said, seemed to contract a lot, which indicated to him that the wounds had been large, and that they cleaved to the rib cage, causing pressure on the heart. The deceased patient, said Gallup, had been greatly impaired due to hardships, including a fall from a horse and a gunshot wound in the thigh.[4]

A US pension special examiner found Dr. Gallup's report unusual and, in many instances, contradictory—for example, in some places he said the writer had suffered from wounds for years; in others he said his illness had come on suddenly and, no, he kept no records. The examiner asked to meet with Gallup to question him in more detail. On May 9, 1887, he told Anna Fuller Judson that he had denied an invalid pension for Judson, taking pains to be polite but intimating that perhaps she and the doctor had tried too hard for a particular outcome:

> *The doctor bears a good reputation for truth and appeared to aim at the truth while at the same time trying to make his testimony as favorable to the claim as he could conscientiously. The doctor's testimony shows soldier to have died of Organic Disease of the heart, partly produced or in part the result of Asthmatic trouble and therein in a speculative way endeavors to connect some scars he had on his breast as a result of heart disease. It will be further seen that he made a physical examination of the soldier 5 years previous to his death and found no functional derangements excepting Asthma. And it was not until a year previous to his death that he discovered the heart disease.*

. . . As soldier died of heart disease and the discovery is so far removed from his service that I am also of the opinion that there is no merit in the Widow's claim.[5]

On July 9, 1888, Anna Fuller Judson married Eben Locke Mason. With this, her claim for the pension of her first husband ended. Pension rules stated that remarriage was grounds for denial, though it is likely her claim would have ultimately been rejected anyway had she pursued it. The government's denial of pension support for Eddie is perhaps the most succinct version of Ned Buntline's matrimonial tangles:

The marriage though legal in form was null and void in the eye of the law, in the fact that Catherine M. Judson was at that time Oct. 3, 1871 his undivorced wife and continued so until Nov. 27, 1871 when a decree of divorce was granted as before indicated. There having been no marriage ceremony performed subsequent to Nov. 27, 1871 between Edward Z. C. Judson and Anna F. Fuller therefore as I understand the law the fact remains the same. I therefore submit the case for rejection.[6]

Lovanche doggedly pursued her own claim until her demise in 1916, but for the most part the claim's death knell came in 1892 with a rejection by a special examiner. Ned Buntline's family affairs were twisted, but they were no match for the bureaucracy of the US government, which was intent on streamlining payments to its aging veterans and their families: "Yet after all this man had so many wives that it will be hard to get at the exact facts and there are a great many contingencies. . . . Surely this is more romantic than one of his sensational novels."

Judson's beloved Eddie died on August 11, 1894. The cause of death was labeled Bright's disease—which, in children, usually meant diabetes. Anna, who by this time had moved to Philadelphia and had a five-year-old son with Mason, was naturally despondent. She also struggled with her second husband's depression, which in 1891 resulted in his attempted suicide by slashing his throat with a straight razor; Anna found him on the floor of their bathroom in a pool of blood.[7] When he died in 1901,

Anna moved back to Eagle's Nest, where her parents and some siblings still resided. Here she found more heartache: Noah Pratt Judson, her former cousin-in-law, successfully sued her for misappropriating funds from his father's trust meant for the care of her mother.[8] Anna Fuller Judson Mason died of flu in 1917.

Lovanche Kelsey Swart Judson passed away in 1916 at the Greene County Almshouse, where she had lived since 1888. Son Frank anglicized his last name from Swart to Black and made his living as a printer.

Katherine Myers Judson Aitcheson died on July 12, 1911, in Ossining, New York. She and husband John appeared to have had a very fluid marital relationship. They don't appear to have lived together very often if census material is any indication, and she vacillated between using the surnames Aitcheson and Judson in various census and legal materials. Her three daughters started their own families and survived through at least the first half of the twentieth century; sons Alexander and Effingham also started families and died in 1923 and 1933, respectively.

Sister Irene Ann McClintock did not have any children of her own, but she did raise a stepdaughter with husband Alexander. The pair had lived frugally, and Alexander's lumber business was steady. She was left very well off when he died in 1873. It is not clear who made the request, but Irene gave testimony at her local district court about her brother's health condition before and after the Civil War. He was, she said, robust and vigorous in health, and there was no trouble with his breath and he was "never troubled with asthma" until he entered the War Between the States. She clarified that, as well, he was unwounded and in good health when he came home from the Florida wars. But after the Civil War, she said, he suffered from asthma that he must have contracted while there.[9] Irene passed away in 1906.

In the mid-1940s, when researching his Buntline biography *The Great Rascal*, Jay Monaghan heard rumors in the Adirondacks that offspring of a clandestine union between Judson and a servant girl still lived in the area. There are still, in fact, some living there today.[10]

In the end, none of the wives or children received so much as a penny for the soldiering efforts of their husband and father, Edward Zane Carroll Judson. His family life was too complicated, as was documentation of his service. As for his personal property, most of the furniture and furnishings in Eagle's Nest were his, but Anna had to sell most of the expensive items to make ends meet.

Judson's family could not profit from his writings, explains Clay Reynolds, because the rights to any given piece were assigned wholesale to the publisher. The editors could reprint any story at will and could do so for years, sometimes marketing it under a different title (a "house title") or even under the name of a different author. Thus Judson received no royalties for any of the characters he created, including Buffalo Bill, Texas Jack, Dashing Charlie, and any number of others. Even as late as 1885, when Judson published his final Buffalo Bill saga, there was little protection. "He was, as all knew, careless and reckless in his habits," noted friend Fred E. Pond. "He never saved a book, a sketch, a scrap or a story of his own composition as long as I was his companion and correspondent." At least one friend thought he deserved a pension. "He was extremely patriotic," said William "Buffalo Bill" Cody, "and had great love of his country—and from what I know of him I would say that he deserved well of our nation as much so as any who took up arms in its defense."[11]

In the early 1880s, in association with actor Nate Salsbury, Buffalo Bill organized a "mammoth aggregation" called the Wild West. They set out on a new career of glory, as author and reporter Leon Mead described:

> *The Wild West was planned to illustrate life on the plains; the Indian encampment; the cowboys and vaqueros in their daily work, and sports; the herds of buffalo and elk; the lassoing of animals; the manner of robbing mail coaches; feats of agility; horsemanship, marksmanship, archery; the reproduction of typical scenes and events of the frontier of that day. While in no wise partaking of the nature of a circus, the performance was at once new, exciting, instructive.[12]*

Some years later, after Judson died, Mead caught up with Buffalo Bill in his tent when the Wild West performed in New York. He worked up the nerve to ask Cody if he felt at all grateful to Judson for what the latter had done with his pen in making him a popular hero.

Cody's answer was not positive. In fact, he told Mead, Judson had done him quite a bit of harm by putting him in a false light as a ruthless, wholesale murderer of Indians, and had made wild statements about him that were injurious and untrue. "Did you make any protests to the authors and the publishers while these serial stories were running?" Mead asked.

"No," said Cody, "because I didn't realize what injustice they were doing me, how cheap they were making me, at least in the estimation of people worth knowing."[13] He insisted that he had "won his spurs" without Buntline's aid, as well as a distinction to be proud of, in the service of Generals Sherman, Miles, Crook, Custer, Carr, and any number of other military leaders. Western historian Don Russell drives this point home in his landmark biography of Cody, *The Lives and Legends of Buffalo Bill*:

> *Quite a myth has grown up about the meeting of Buffalo Bill with Ned Buntline. This is not surprising, as nothing in the Buffalo Bill legend has been more exaggerated than Ned Buntline's part in it. . . . The Trans-Mississippi West was already a familiar subject to dime-novel readers, and Buntline, for all his prolificacy, made no large contribution to the Western type. He did not write a series of stories about Buffalo Bill; he wrote one story only, then dropped the subject for some three years. His total output of Buffalo Bill dime novels was four. The story he wrote in 1869 was not about the postwar frontier, but about border fighting in the Civil War. His discovery of a Western hero was, then, quite coincidental.*[14]

In fact, Russell continues, there is no valid reason to doubt that Cody had been "Buffalo Bill" since his buffalo-hunting days for the railroad contractors. The theory, he said, that Ned Buntline invented not only the name "Buffalo Bill" but also the entire Buffalo Bill legend could be formulated only by those who had neither read Ned Buntline's work nor investigated Cody's pre-Buntline career. The theory is based, he continues, on the myth that Cody was "just another scout" who would never have been heard of had not Buntline discovered him and written books about him.

In reality, Judson never claimed to have invented the moniker "Buffalo Bill" for Cody. But Russell's determination leaves out two basic facts: that it was Judson who convinced Cody to come east and perform in a play that he had written, and that it was Judson's first novels of Cody that elevated his real-life army work into the exploits that every American wanted to believe were happening west of the Mississippi River. Someone besides Ned Buntline may have eventually discovered Cody and made him a folk hero—certainly others had already written about Kit Carson, Daniel Boone, and John "Johnny Appleseed" Chapman. And certainly Cody might have been mentioned in pioneer annals of the West—at least as a character in American history. As Mead explains, if fancifully:

> *But to be an idol of the people, to be lionized by aristocrats and high society—that was something else again: and it may be safely asserted that he never would have been that idol or that lion had he not been given such wide publicity by Ned Buntline—and in just Ned Buntline's wizard way of getting out of a hero all there was in him with much of the mystic and glamorous that was not in him.*[15]

To the average Easterner of the mid-nineteenth century, says historian Schmidt, the "Wild West" offered a marked contrast to routine city life. The Cody-Buntline association provided the Eastern public with a picture of the West in its primitive state—a region where tenets of survival of the fittest and self-reliance became principal axioms of social behavior. Buntline depicted Cody as portraying all these virtues and more. Through the efforts of a novelist seeking fortune from his yarns, Buntline met the requirements of American mythology and became the first of many mythmakers of Buffalo Bill.

Using a wider lens, says Clay Reynolds, Edward Zane Carroll Judson bridged the gap between post–Revolutionary War tales of exploration, fighting with native people, and conquering the rugged lands of the Ohio River Valley and the closing of the frontier in the 1880s. Henry Nash Smith, for example, couldn't have written *Virgin Land* without having read Ned Buntline, at least in part. American historian Vernon Louis Parrington's assessment of the impact of the frontier on the American imagination also had to have been filtered through the dime novel, bringing with it all the impurities and corruptions the form deliberately added. One can read cliché after cliché in Judson's novels, but they were not clichés when he wrote them. They were wholly original—but became clichés through repetition, imitation, and even transformation.

In 1858, E. Z. C. Judson came to Grand Rapids, Michigan. He had heard about the terrific run of sturgeon to be fished there and wanted to test his mettle. He made friends with Bob Robinson, one of the best canoe men in town, and they started out to do the rapids. According to a local historian—just a boy at the time—Judson watched the Indians standing astride the top edges of their canoes and, wishing for all the same thrills, tried the same. They drew up to the chute where the water came with a rush over the dam, tumbling about in swirls of foam. Judson had been warned not to strike a fish any place except close to the head, but when he saw a huge sturgeon, he got "buck fever" and struck near the tail. The electric shock that came along the spear pole and the rush of the waves sent him headfirst into the cold water. "But he was a dead game sport," the local recalled; "he clung to the pole and the fish towed him about the channel until Robinson got near enough to catch into his trousers with the gaff hook and pull him to safety."[16] In many ways, this vignette illustrates how Judson approached life: with curiosity, ambition, an attraction to danger and aversion to warnings, and, most of all, by chasing exploits to make the basis for a great story.

As Reynolds said, if Judson was nothing else, he was the embodiment of the American capacity for imagination:

He had an innate understanding of the yearning of an emerging culture to anchor itself to something larger than itself and to claim it as its own. Europeans think all Americans are "cowboys" of one sort or another, even easterners who've never been west of the Jersey Meadows and never seen a horse that didn't have a policeman on it or a cow that wasn't packaged and resting comfortably in the butcher's cooler. It's a virus of sorts, and it's become part of our DNA. I think Judson created that. He may not have originated the infection, but he definitely spread it, and on purpose. And I sometimes think that if he could be somehow rejuvenated and made aware of how we regard the whole of American Western History today, he'd be pleased and probably a little sorry that he didn't do it bigger.[17]

Undoubtedly, Judson's family life and his paramours provided more drama than the average American ever experiences in his or her lifetime. "The tales of Judson's several marriages," notes Reynolds, "would make for a better story than he ever wrote."[18] This is true, and ironic: The man who wrote about the virtues and morals required for the ideal American family life was intrinsically lacking in them.

The Western genre owes a debt to Edward Zane Carroll Judson in spite of his flaws. And the man who created legends somehow became one himself: a red-haired, red-mustached, red-blooded American who might have been a hero in one of the tales he concocted.[19]

NOTES

AUTHOR'S NOTE

1. Kevin S. Blake, "Zane Grey and Images of the American West," *Geographical Review*, Vol. 85, No. 2 (April 1995), pp. 202–16.
2. Email from R. Clay Reynolds to the author, December 26, 2018.
3. Ibid.

INTRODUCTION

1. "Riot and Loss of Life," (New York) *Commercial Advertiser*, May 5, 1849, 2; "The Macready Riot in New York," *Longman's Magazine* (1884), 636–43.
2. *People v. Judson*, Historical Society of the New York Court, www.nycourts.gov/history/legal-history-new-york/legal-history-eras-04/history-new-york-legal-eras-people-judson.html.
3. "Trial of the Astor Place Rioters," (New York) *Spectator*, September 20, 1849, 3; "Court of General Sessions," (New York) *Evening Post*, September 19, 1849, 2.
4. "Riot and Loss of Life," 2.
5. Ibid.
6. Ibid.
7. *The Nashville Union*, July 16, 1846, 1.
8. Court of General Sessions, *People v. Hastings*, New York, New York, April 4, 1849.
9. Bennett moved with their baby to England, where she was born. She raised the boy with her maiden name.
10. Clay Reynolds, *Hero of a Hundred Fights*, xii.
11. Jay Monaghan, *The Great Rascal: The Life and Adventures of Ned Buntline* (Boston: little, Brown and Company, 1952). Though Monaghan's account of this meeting, featured in the first chapter of his biography, is highly embellished, it remains one of the most detailed descriptions and paints a very entertaining picture rooted in meticulous research.
12. Unsubstantiated stories say that at first Judson was looking for James "Wild Bill" Hickok, whose adventures in *Harper's New Monthly Magazine* highlighted his 1861 shoot-out with a member of the notorious McCanles gang at Rock Creek Station near Fairbury, Nebraska. Large, muscular, handsome, and a crack shot, Hickok would certainly make for a great dime novel protagonist. According to these stories, Judson found Hickok in a saloon, drunk and more eager to shoot his head off than to submit to an interview with him.
13. Monaghan, *Great Rascal*, 5.

14. Ibid, 6–7.

15. William H. Goetzmann and William N. Goetzmann, *The West of the Imagination*, (New York: Norton, 1988), 288.

16. In his autobiography, Cody lamented his mere $6,000 total earnings at the end of the season: *Scouts* grossed an average of about $15,000 per week and had run continuously for six months. In another example, the combination's one week of performances at the Boston Theater earned $16,200. This does not take into account the theater's take or payment for the other actors. But even half that amount multiplied by a conservative twenty weeks was an outstanding amount at that time. "I was somewhat disappointed," Cody wrote in his autobiography, "for, judging from our large business, I certainly had expected a greater sum." To be fair to Judson, newspapers reported that Judson, Cody, and Omohundro each earned $30,000 over the "eight-month run" of *Scouts*. As is usually the case with all of these people and numbers, the truth probably lies somewhere in the middle. William Frederick Cody and Frank Christianson, ed., *The Life of Hon. William F. Cody, Known as Buffalo Bill* (Lincoln: University of Nebraska Press, 1886, 383; *Carlisle* (PA) *Weekly Herald*, August 21, 1873, 2.

17. Author uses this site to calculate historical worth and takes both Real Price and Income Value into consideration: www.measuringworth.com/calculators/uscompare.

18. Letter from Anna Fuller Judson to Special Examiner of Pension Office, December 7, 1893, Edward Zane Carroll Judson pension file, National Archives and Records Administration.

19. Robert D. Pepper, "The 'Buntline Special' Reconsidered: The Case of Wilson H. Strickler, Ned Buntline's Friend in Dodge City, Kansas," Kansas History, www.kansashistory.us/buntlinespecial.html (accessed June 5, 2018).

20. Reynolds, *Hero of a Hundred Fights*, xi.

21. Ibid., xii.

22. Ibid., xi.

CHAPTER ONE: DEATH OF A LEGEND MAKER

1. "Death of Ned Buntline," *Delaware Gazette*, July 21, 1886, 3.

2. W. A. Croffut, "Ned Buntline: A Visit to 'Eagle's Nest,' and a Glimpse at the Life of a Remarkable Man," *Detroit Free Press*, June 28, 1885.

3. "New York Probate Records, 1629–1971," images, *FamilySearch*, May 28, 2014, https://familysearch.org/ark:/61903/3:1:3QS7-89HY-G55F?cc=1920234&wc=Q7RT-RM9%3A213304401%2C218111301; Delaware>Estate papers, image 744 of 1,226, county courthouses, New York.

4. "New York Probate Records, 1629–1971," images, *FamilySearch*, May 28, 2014, https://familysearch.org/ark:/61903/3:1:3QS7-89HY-G55F?cc=1920234&wc=Q7RT-RM9%3A213304401%2C218111301; Delaware>Estate papers, image 739 of 1,226, county courthouses, New York.

5. John William Schmidt, "Edward Zane Carroll Judson (Ned Buntline): The Granddaddy of Dime Novelists" (MA dissertation, University of Wisconsin—Madison, 1973), 133.

6. Shortly after Judson's death, contemporary Leon Mead estimated that "Ned Buntline accomplished more than Walter Scott and Dickens put together. In book form his serial stories which he has been almost incessantly penning for over fifty years would amount perhaps to more than two hundred volumes." I think it's safe to say that more Americans knew who he was and read him far more than they did Mark Twain or any of the more literary designates of the time. His work was distinctively lowbrow and appealed to workers, schoolboys, and people of limited education. It was also cheap to acquire. See Fred E. Pond, *Life and Adventures of Ned Buntline, . . . and Chapter of Angling Sketches by Fred E. Pond* (New York: Cadmus Book Shop, 1919).

7. Dale Walker, "'The Hero of a Hundred Fights': Clay Reynolds on Ned Buntline," *Roundup Magazine* (October 2011), 24.

8. Letter from Judson to unknown recipient dated April 10, 1885, William Henry Venable (Cincinnati, OH: Robert Clarke, 1891), 294–95.

9. Schmidt, "Edward Zane Carroll Judson (Ned Buntline)," 133.

10. Miriam Biskin, "Ned Buntline—Adirondack Image Maker," *Times Union* (Albany, NY), February 11, 1968, G-3.

11. Ibid.

12. *Pittsburgh Daily Post*, September 17, 1884, 1.

13. "Ned Buntline: A Visit to a Famous-Storyteller . . . ," *Delaware Gazette*, July 7, 1886, 3.

14. "New York Probate Records, 1629–1971," images, *FamilySearch*, May 28, 2014, https://familysearch.org/ark:/61903/3:1:3QS7-89HY-G55F?cc=1920234&wc=Q7RT-RM9%3A213304401%2C218111301; Delaware>Estate papers, image 740 of 1,226, county courthouses, New York.

15. Pension record, testimony of Anna Fuller.

16. Pension record, testimony of Anna Fuller.

17. Letter from Eben Locke Mason in Boston to Frederick E. Pond, Chicago, May 19, 1888.

18. Recollection of Mason's friend Clifford Champion. Dr. Robert D. Pepper, "Eben Locke Mason, Jr.—A Double Life," *Asylum: Quarterly Journal of the Numismatic Bibliomania Society* 17 (Winter 1999): 5.

CHAPTER TWO: CREATION OF A LEGEND MAKER

1. The elevation of the mountain is 3,214 feet above sea level. Today, as it did in Judson's day, it provides breathtaking hikes that provide a view of the Delaware Valley.

2. Ancestry.com, "New York, Military Service Cards, 1816–1979" [database online], Provo, UT, USA: Ancestry.com Operations, Inc., 2012; "Obituary: Colonel L. Carroll Judson," *New York Daily Herald*, January 15, 1865, 2.

3. Jay Monaghan tried to make a close estimate of Judson's birth. "A statement made by his father," the biographer wrote, "indicates that 1821 was Ned's birth year and this may be so. Ned himself believed all his life that he was born later." In two of his earlier semiautobiographical works, Judson said he enlisted in the navy at age fourteen, which would place his birth date in 1823. In the summer of 1850, Judson said he was nearly

twenty-seven, which also makes his birth date 1823. Twelve years later, the writer gave his birth date as 1825, but of course he wanted to be young enough to get into the service. His pension record file, W0 906 598, gives his age at death as sixty-four years and four months, which puts his birth date in 1822. In several instances throughout his lifetime, Edward refers to Irene as his younger sister, so we can be reasonably sure she was born a year or two after him. Still, Dr. Robert D. Pepper's assessment stands correct: "Regardless of what you may see in reference books, the birthdates of Ned and his sister are still a matter of conjecture; it's not even known who was older. 'Early 1820s' is really the best we can do for both Ned and Irene Judson." Robert D. Pepper, "Ned Buntline's Corner," *Dime Novel Roundup*, vol. 69, no. 2 (New York: J. S. Ogilvie Publishing Co.), 64.

4. Daisy R. Desilva and Anne Willis, "A Centennial History of Stamford," Delaware County NY Genealogy and History site, http://www.dcnyhistory.org/stamford-cenn1970_ts.html, accessed January 20, 2019; Anne Willis, "Ned Buntline's Stamford Revisited," *Stamford Mirror-Recorder*, July 3, 1986, 6.

5. Ibid.

6. David Torrey, *Memoir of Major Jason Torrey, of Bethany, Wayne, PA* (J. S. Horton, 1885), 92.

7. "Memories of Old Wayne County, by Ned Buntline," *Wayne County Herald* (Pennsylvania), March 30, 1982, 3.

8. "Trout Fishing in Wayne Half a Century Ago," *Wayne County Herald* (Pennsylvania), May 12, 1881, 2.

9. Jay Monaghan, *The Great Rascal: The Life and Adventures of Ned Buntline* (New York: Bonanza Books, 1951), 36. For some portions of his biography of Judson, Monaghan (and others) pulled from Frederick E. Pond's *Life and Adventures of Ned Buntline with Ned Buntline's Anecdote of 'Frank Forrester' and Chapter of Angling Sketches* (Cadmus Publishing, 1919). Pond was a late nineteenth-century conservationist and served as editor of *Turf, Field and Farm* from 1881 to 1886. He was friends with Judson, and interviewed him at length for the *Life and Adventures* portion of his fishing treatise.

10. "Incidents in the Early Life of 'Ned Buntline,' A Wayne County Boy, Number Three," *Hawley Times*, March 24, 1876, 1, courtesy Wayne (PA) County Historical Society.

11. This information also comes from Jay Monaghan's *The Great Rascal*. Monaghan, in turn, derived this information from Pond. Because Pond's information came straight from Judson, was then embellished by Pond, and then filtered through Monaghan's lens, we have to consider its veracity. But anti-Masonry was alive and well in the region, and Levi's responses to the alleged murder of Morgan are probable, given his staunch Masonic loyalty and his later writings of its tenets.

12. Monaghan, *The Great Rascal*, 35–37; Pond, *Life and Adventures of 'Ned Buntline*," 11–13; Milton W. Hamilton, "Anti-Masonic Newspapers, 1826–1834," *Papers of the Bibliographic Society of America*, vol. 32 (1938), 71–97. Again, both Pond and Monaghan had to wrestle with hyperbole from their subject, but these events are corroborated by the fact that by 1830, no fewer than thirty-one anti-Masonic newspapers existed. Also, many parts of Pennsylvania were populated with newer immigrant groups who were

typically fearful of secret organizations. Levi would not have let his neighbors' distrust of Masons get in the way of a vocal response to those who opposed them.

13. The senior Judson announced this to his creditors in the *Wayne County Herald* and *Bethany Enquirer*, as noted in Monaghan, *The Great Rascal*, 38.

14. Letter from Edward Z. C. Judson in Scranton, Pennsylvania, to his sister, Irene Judson McClintock, in Pittsburgh, Pennsylvania, October 4, 1863, NARA pension files.

15. Edward Z. C. Judson, "Ned Buntline's Life-Yarn," *Knickerbocker* (New York: John Allen Publishing, 1845), 432.

16. Ibid.

17. "Miscellaneous Records of the Office of Naval Records and Library, 1803–1859," Record Group 45, Roll 0005, National Archives and Record Administration, https://www.fold3.com/image/616712029.

18. "Register of the Commissioned and Warrant Officers," *Navy Cruise Books, 1918–2009* (Navy Department Library).

19. "Ned Buntline. . . . Some Account of Colonel Judson's Adventures and Varied Career," *Times* (Philadelphia, PA), June 28, 1885, 6. This account is suspect as anything but a vanity piece put out by a friend or Judson himself, not only because the reporter omitted his name on the piece and that of his subject, but because the dates of historical events are wrong.

20. Pond, *Life and Adventures of Ned Buntline*, 15–16.

21. Cooper Kirk, historian for Broward County, Florida (1920–1989), wrote an interesting, in-depth article about Judson and the Second Seminole War in the southeast Florida theater, 1838–1842. Cooper Kirk, "Edward Zane Carroll Judson, Alias Ned Buntline," *Broward Legacy* [S.l.], vol. 3, no. 3–4 (December 1979), 16, http://journals.fcla.edu/browardlegacy/article/view/79228/76573, accessed January 28, 2019.

CHAPTER THREE: THE SEMINOLE WAR

1. Ned Buntline, "Sketches of the Florida War, Number II: A Chase in the Everglades," *Western Literary Journal and Monthly Review*, Vol. 1 (Cincinnati: Robinson & Jones, 1844), 68.

2. See C. S. Monaco, "Whose War Was It? African American Heritage Claims and the Second Seminole War," *American Indian Quarterly*, vol. 41, no. 1 (University of Nebraska Press: Winter 2017), 31–66.

3. Cooper Kirk, "Edward Zane Carroll Judson, Alias Ned Buntline," 16.

4. "Declaration for Original Invalid Pension: Of Edward Z. C. Judson for services in the US Navy in Florida War," July 12, 1886, Federal Military Pension Application— Civil War and Later Complete File, National Archives and Records Administration. For a short time Judson also served on the frigate *Constellation*, as noted in the *Daily Commercial Bulletin* (St. Louis, MO), August 1, 1838, 2.

5. One of his most colorful and sweeping stories set in this time and place, all fifty-two chapters of it, was *The White Wizard, or, The Great Prophet of the Seminoles* (New York: Frederic A. Brady, 1862). It was set in South Florida—at that time almost unknown to most Americans—against the backdrop of the Second Seminole War.

The story ranges from the Ten Thousand Islands into the Big Cypress Swamp and the Everglades, and from St. Augustine to Havana to New York City. Its cast of characters includes a future president, Zachary Taylor, and such major Indian leaders as Chekika, Coacoochee, and Osceola.

6. Buntline, "Sketches of the Florida War, Number II: Chase in the Everglades," 169–70.

7. Ned Buntline, "Indian Key: It's Rise, Progress and Destruction," *Pensacola Gazette*, March 29, 1845, excerpted from the *Western Literary Journal and Monthly Review*.

8. Ibid. Decades later, Captain Francis Key Murray was featured in an article about Judson's time in the navy—an article Judson may have written about himself in the third person. Clearly Judson admired the man, whether he was his superior or a peer.

9. Letter from E. Z. C. Judson, New York, to Abel P. Upshur, Secretary of the US Navy, Washington, DC, November 21, 1841, Navy Officers' Letters 1802–1884, National Archives and Records Administration; "Florida, County Marriages, 1823–1982," Ancestry.com.

10. *The Knickerbocker*, xxiv, no. 6 (December 1844), 563.

11. Navy Officers' Letters 1802–1884, National Archives and Records Administration, Record Group 45, roll 0144.

12. Cooper Kirk, "Edward Zane Carroll Judson," 18.

13. Ibid., 17.

14. "Declaration for Original Invalid Pension: Of Edward Z. C. Judson for services in the US Navy in Florida War," July 12, 1886, Federal Military Pension Application—Civil War and Later Complete File, National Archives and Records Administration. The problem with this record, of course, is that it is partially composed of Judson's deposition in 1886, and thus subject to Judson's memory and license with facts—though there is nothing in Judson's navy record to dispute his account, and he was continually paid his full midshipman's salary until the end of his service in 1842. There was, in fact, a terrible outbreak of yellow fever among the Indian Key navy contingent in September 1839. For more about the men who served with Judson, see https://navy.togetherwe-served.com/usn/servlet/tws.webapp.WebApp?cmd=ShadowBoxProfile&type=Battle-MemoryExt&ID=209569, accessed February 3, 2019.

15. Pond, *Life and Adventures of "Ned Buntline,"* 18.

16. One former shipmate emphatically said that he never knew Judson to receive an injury, never mind engage in any duel that caused one. But this was only one person who served only a short time with him. Judson, though, claimed he received both a serious head injury and one in the groin due to ship mishaps—a common occurrence in the service at that time. The navy took Judson's claims of multiple duels seriously, because injuries sustained in those duels would have lent credibility to Judson's claims that he received them during service and therefore give the writer cause for an invalid pension.

CHAPTER FOUR: "THE CAPTAIN'S PIG" AND A PROBLEM IN NASHVILLE

1. James T. Callow, *Kindred Spirits: Knickerbocker Writers and American Artists, 1807–1855* (Chapel Hill: University of North Carolina Press, 1967), 104; Roderick F. Nash,

Wilderness and the American Mind, 4th edition (New Haven, CT: Yale University Press, 2001), 97–99. It is possible—even likely—that Judson got at least the title of his story from a previous work in *The Knickerbocker.* As Monaghan points out in *The Great Rascal,* the writing style of this anonymous story is not Judson's, and he generously notes that "even if he [Ned] did get the name 'The Captain's Pig' from the article, he copied nothing else." Monaghan, *The Great Rascal,* 296, n1.

2. Monaghan, *The Great Rascal,* 82.

3. Ibid., 83.

4. Ibid., 86.

5. Julia L. Dumont (1794–1857) is frequently billed as the earliest female writer of the West whose poems, tales, and sketches have been preserved.

6. Ibid., 88.

7. Diary entry of family friend George Allen as transcribed in "Ned Buntline and the Allen Family of Pittsburgh," *Dime Novel Round-Up* 84, no. 3 (Fall 2015): 116.

8. Ibid., 117.

9. Ibid.

10. George Tipton Wilson, "Part of Colorful Buntline Story Written at Smithland," *Paducah (KY) Sun,* September 15, 1965, 15.

11. William Henry McRaven, *Nashville: "Athens of the South"* (Chapel Hill, NC: Published for the Tennessee Book Co. by Scheer & Jervis, 1949), 83–87.

12. Ibid.

13. Charles Fenno Hoffman, et al., comps. and eds., *The Knickerbocker: Or, New-York Monthly Magazine* 27 (March 1846): 277. The text says, "new contributor from Natchez," but this is most certainly a mistake, as pointed out by Monaghan in *The Great Rascal,* 105. Nashville is almost exactly thirty miles from Gallatin.

14. *Tri-Weekly Nashville Union,* November 18 to December 27, 1845 (as noted by Monaghan, *The Great Rascal,* 299).

15. Monaghan, *The Great Rascal,* 103.

16. Ibid., 104.

17. Monaghan, *The Great Rascal,* 106; "A Report of the Proceedings of the First Baptist Church," *Nashville Union,* July 16, 1846, 2.

18. "A Report of the Proceedings of the First Baptist Church, continued," *Nashville Union,* July 18, 1846, 2.

19. Indeed, the boys could not even tell if the woman was black or white.

20. Monaghan, *The Great Rascal,* 106.

21. Ibid.

22. *Nashville Union,* August 11, 1846, 2.

23. *Nashville Union,* July 16, 1846, 2.

24. Monaghan, *The Great Rascal,* 107.

25. "Most Lamentable Occurrence," *Huntsville (AL) Democrat,* March 25, 1846, 2, reprint from the *Nashville Whig.*

26. Ibid.

27. "Awful Tragedy," *Tennessean* (Nashville), March 18, 1846, 1; "Most Lamentable Occurrence," 2.

28. "Most Lamentable Occurrence," 2.

29. Ibid.
30. "Report of the Proceedings," *Nashville Union*, July 16, 1846, 2.
31. "Rural Choice, Logan, Kentucky," *Nashville Union*, July 16, 1846, 2.

CHAPTER FIVE: "THAT ODIOUS RASCAL"

1. Anonymous, *The Private Life, Public Career, and Real Character of that Odious Rascal Ned Buntline! 1849* (New York: Thomas V. Paterson, Printer and Publisher, 1849), 50. This source is rich and full of details about Judson, his associates, and New York City in general. But it has to be mined carefully, because although many details in it can be corroborated elsewhere, the pamphlet is certainly sensational, and appears to be composed of reports from many different "detectives."
2. "Launched," *New London Democrat*, December 2, 1848, 3.
3. Monaghan, *The Great Rascal*, 117; Anonymous, *That Odious Rascal*, 46.
4. Ibid., 120.
5. Ibid., 121.
6. Ibid.
7. Ibid., 124–26.
8. Letter from John A. Aulick, Washington, DC, to E. Z. C. Judson, New York City, November 8, 1847, Virginia Historical Society, Correspondence, 1844–1859, of John Young Mason (1799–1859).
9. Letter from E. Z. C. Judson in New York to John Y. Mason in Washington, DC, dated November 11, 1847, Virginia Historical Society, Correspondence, 1844–1859, of John Young Mason (1799–1859).
10. Letter from E. Z. C. Judson in New York City to John A. Aulick, Washington, DC, November 11, 1847, Virginia Historical Society, Correspondence, 1844–1859, of John Young Mason (1799–1859).
11. I found no claims of misconduct in his navy files.
12. Mark Twain, *The Adventures of Tom Sawyer* (Mineola, NY: Dover Publications), 46 (more on 71–75).
13. Judson had a mutual friend with Colonel John McArdle and Colonel Michael K. Bryan. The friend, Fred Mather, later wrote about his fishing expeditions with all three men, and emphasized that they had all served together in both the Second Seminole War and the Mexican War. It is possible that age, drink, or the power of suggestion was at play here. See Fred Mather, *My Angling Friends: Being a Second Series of Sketches of Men I Have Fished With* (New York: Forest and Stream Publishing Company, 1901).
14. Monaghan, *The Great Rascal*, 133–36.
15. Ibid., 131–32.
16. Anonymous, *That Odious Rascal*, 50.
17. Streetby, *American Sensations*, 149.
18. Reynolds, *The Hero of a Hundred Fights*, Introduction, xix.
19. Anonymous, *That Odious Rascal*, 15.
20. Monaghan, *The Great Rascal*, 137; Anonymous, *That Odious Rascal*, 14–15; Reynolds, *The Hero of a Hundred Fights*, Introduction, xix.

21. "National Theatre," *New York Daily Herald*, September 10, 1848, 2.

22. For more on Judson's place in American pop culture, see Shelly Streeby, *American Sensations: Class, Empire, and the Production of Popular Culture* (Berkeley and Los Angeles: University of California Press, 2002).

23. Extracted from *Mysteries and Miseries of New York* by Jay Monaghan, *The Great Rascal*, 139.

24. Original source: Anonymous, "Ned's Introduction to Mr. Bennett's Family," *That Odious Rascal*, 16; Monaghan, *The Great Rascal*, 140–41.

25. *Flag of Our Union*, February 12, 1848, 4.

26. Anonymous, *That Odious Rascal*, 17.

27. "Nearly a Street Fight," *National Police Gazette*, September 9, 1848, 2.

28. Anonymous, *That Odious Rascal*, 31.

29. Monaghan, *The Great Rascal*, 159–60.

30. "Ned Buntline's Own," *New-York Organ & Temperance Safeguard*, September 20, 1848, 109.

CHAPTER SIX: LIBEL, NATIVISM, AND THE ASTOR PLACE RIOT

1. "Ned Buntline's Own," *Godey's Lady's Book*, October 1, 1848, 252.

2. Anonymous, *That Odious Rascal*, 54. It should be noted that although Bennett's testimony here in a libel case can be corroborated with other sources, Bennett was also preparing to testify against Judson in the latter's upcoming riot trial, just weeks away. At this point, Judson had not only wronged Paterson's daughter but had also pulled his son into the Astor Place Riot affair. Needless to say, Bennett had a proverbial ax to grind. He did begrudgingly admit that *Ned Buntline's Own* made profits and that in lieu of a salary, Judson gave him copyrights to his work for future royalties.

3. Summarized in Marilyn Wood Hill's *Their Sisters' Keepers: Prostitution in New York City 1830–1870* (Berkeley: University of California Press, 1993), 161.

4. Ibid., 162.

5. Ibid. For a full account of this trial, see New York Municipal Archives, Court of General Sessions (CGS), *People v. Hastings*, April 4, 1849.

6. Monaghan, *The Great Rascal*, 170; "Arrest of Ned Buntline for Libel," *Brooklyn Daily Eagle*, May 7, 1849, 2.

7. See "Account of the terrific and fatal riot at the New-York Astor Place opera house, on the night of May 10th, 1849, with the quarrels of Forrest and Macready, including all the causes which led to that awful tragedy! Wherein an infuriated mob was quelled by the public authorities and military, with its mournful termination in the sudden death or mutilation of more than fifty citizens, with full and authentic particulars . . . ," https://archive.org/stream/bub_gb_s9m_TmbOyT0C/bub_gb_s9m_TmbOyT0C_djvu.txt, accessed February 22, 2019.

8. For a short but clear summary of the riot and its main causes, see https://www.smithsonianmag.com/history/when-new-york-rivalry-over-shakespeare-boiled-over-deadly-melee-180964102/, accessed February 23, 2019.

9. Ibid.

10. Ibid.; Monaghan, *The Great Rascal*, 171.

11. *People v. Judson*, http://www.nycourts.gov/history/legal-history-new-york/legal-history-eras-04/history-new-york-legal-eras-people-judson.html, accessed February 23, 2019.

12. "The Great Theatrical War—Macready Yet in the Field," *New York Daily Herald*, May 10, 1849, 4.

13. *New York Daily Herald*, May 14, 1849, 2.

14. https://www.smithsonianmag.com/history/when-new-york-rivalry-over-shakespeare-boiled-over-deadly-melee-180964102/.

15. *New York Daily Herald*, May 14, 1849, 2.

16. Ibid.

17. *Account of the Terrific and Fatal Riot at the New-York Astor Place Opera House, on the Night of May 10, 1849 . . . ,"* (New York: H. M. Raney, 1849), 6.

18. "Alarming Riot at the Astor Place Theater," *Evening Post* (New York), May 11, 1849, 2.

19. "Court of General Sessions—Sept. 19th," *Evening Post* (New York), September 19, 1849, 2.

20. Ibid.

21. Ibid.

22. Ibid.

23. See http://www.nycourts.gov/history/legal-history-new-york/legal-history-eras-04/history-new-york-legal-eras-people-judson.html, accessed March 4, 2019.

24. *Buffalo Daily Republic*, May 16, 1849, 4.

25. Monaghan, *The Great Rascal*, 181.

26. Anonymous, *That Odious Rascal*, 54.

27. Judson may have suffered from syphilis, by the description of this malady. But it also describes any number of other illnesses, including mumps. Bennett—or Paterson—may have meant "mercury" instead of "lead"; mercury was used by those who could afford it then to cure syphilis. Notably, Judson did not appear to have carried any outward signs of venereal disease to his deathbed, but of course this would not have been noted in any public sources. Lastly, it is possible that Judson contracted a disease called tularemia while in Florida, which has similar symptoms.

28. "Tragedy on Board Ned Buntline's Boat," *Sandusky (OH) Register*, July 12, 1849, 2, reprinted from *New York Daily Mirror*; *Daily Post* (Pittsburgh), July 11, 1849, 1.

29. "Ned Buntline," *Wayne County Herald*, August 29, 1849, 1.

CHAPTER SEVEN: WESTERN EXPANSION AND THE ST. LOUIS RIOT

1. Letter from E. W. Hart, Special Examiner, New York to Green B. Raum, Commissioner of Pensions, Washington, DC, October 31, 1892, enclosed within pension file.

2. See, for example, Hendrik A. Hartog, "Marital Exits and Marital Expectations in Nineteenth Century America," *Georgetown Law Journal*, vol. 80, April 1991, 95–129.

3. "Attempt to favor 'Ned Buntline' by a Public Officer," *Sandusky (OH) Register*, October 9, 1849, 2.

4. Reprinted in *The Tennessean* (Nashville), October 10, 1850, 2.

5. Reprinted in *Fayetteville (NC) Semi-Weekly Observer*, September 30, 1851, 2.

6. Deposition of James Mulligan, files of Anna Fuller Judson, NARA.

7. Many political scientists point to some modern-day conservative branches as a natural outgrowth of the Know Nothing Party. See, for example, Jay Kiedrowski's blog: https://www.minnpost.com/community-voices/2016/09/trump-throwback-know-nothing-party-1850s/, accessed March 10, 2019.

8. *History of Marion and Clinton Counties, Illinois: With Illustrations Descriptive of the Scenery, and Biographical Sketches of Some of the Prominent Men and Pioneers* (Clinton County, IL: Brink, McDonough & Co., 1881), 110.

9. Monaghan, *The Great Rascal*, 196–98.

10. Soulard Market and Coffee-House remains one of the oldest farmers' markets west of the Mississippi.

11. The *St. Louis Republican* estimated the crowd to be less: 1,000–1,200. Reprinted article from April 7, *Hannibal (MO) Journal*, April 15, 1852, 2.

12. Monaghan, *The Great Rascal*, 199. "Lop-eared Dutch" was a common anti-German insult in the middle of the nineteenth century.

13. "The Riot on Monday—Detailed Accounts," *Hannibal (MO) Journal*, April 15, 1852, 2, reprinted from the *St. Louis Republican*, April 7, 1852, 1.

14. Monaghan, *The Great Rascal*, 199–201; Frederick Franklin Schrader, *"1683–1920": The Fourteen Points and What Became of Them—Foreign Propaganda* (Concord Publishing Company), 142–43; Heinrich Boerstein, *Memoirs of a Nobody: The Missouri Years of a Austrian Radical, 1849–1866* (St. Louis: Missouri Historical Society, 1997), 179; William Hyde and Howard L. Conard, eds., *Encyclopedia of the History of St. Louis, a Compendium of History and Biography for Ready Reference* (St. Louis: Southern History Company, 1899).

15. Monaghan extracted this quote from the *St. Louis Daily Globe*, December 27, 1872, n.p.

16. Monaghan, *The Great Rascal*, 202; *St. Louis Republican*, April 6, 1852, 1.

17. Monaghan, *The Great Rascal*, 202.

18. Testimony, James F. Milligan, April 30, 1887, pension file, Anna Fuller Judson.

19. Monaghan, *The Great Rascal*, 202.

20. "The Denunciation of the Mayor for the Arrest of Mr. Parsons," *New York Times*, December 16, 1853, 4.

21. Ibid.

CHAPTER EIGHT: THE WIDOW SWART

1. *Liberty (MO) Tribune*, May 7, 1852, 2; Ned Buntline, "The Widow's Wedding: A Tale of the St. Louis Masqueraders," *Gallipolis (IL) Journal*, 1.

2. "1900 United States Federal Census," Ancestry.com, Provo, UT: 2004, accessed March 19, 2019.

3. See, for example, "A Strange Story," *Kingston (NY) Daily News*, April 18, 1881, 1.

4. Testimony, Lovanche Kelsey Swart Judson, August 25, 1882, Anna Fuller Judson pension file, NARA.
5. Ibid.
6. Ibid.; Monaghan, *The Great Rascal*, 206.
7. Reprinted in the *Port Gibson Reveille*, June 8, 1853, 4.
8. The authorship of this phrase was later ascribed to Judson. Whatever its origin, the public began using it when it appeared in the *New York Times* on November 10, 1853. Louis Dow Scisco, *Political Nativism in New York State* (New York: Faculty of Political Science, Columbia University, 1901), 286.
9. Monaghan, *The Great Rascal*, 206–7.
10. "A Strange Story: Lovanche L. Judson's Statement," *Kingston (NY) Daily Freeman*, April 18, 1881, 1.
11. Ibid.; *Evening Star*, April 20, 1854, 2.
12. *Tennessean* (Nashville), July 29, 1854, 3.
13. *Lebanon (PA) and Semi-Weekly Report*, June 23, 1854, 2.
14. "A Know Nothing Leader," *Syracuse Daily Standard*, July 1, 1854, 2.
15. *Boston Herald*, July 1, 1854, 2.
16. "The Bath Riot," *Bath Independent and Enterprise*, December 1, 1906, 1. In this article, Ridley mistakenly conflates Judson as a Republican and his arrival as being in 1856; but the South Church burning was in 1854, and other sources name Judson as the instigator that year.
17. Ibid.; *Bath Independent*, August 18, 1900, 6.
18. Ibid.
19. "The Outrage on a Catholic Priest in Ellsworth, Maine," *New York Times*, October 21, 1854, 1.
20. Monaghan, *The Great Rascal*, 211.
21. Ibid., 211–13; "Arrest of Ned Buntline for Shooting a Colored Boy," *Brooklyn Daily Eagle*, October 26, 1854, 3; *Boston Courier*, October 30, 1854, 4.
22. Transcribed from the *Democratic Pioneer* (Elizabeth City, NC), October 17, 2.
23. Monaghan, *The Great Rascal*, 215.
24. "The Great Race! Painful Intelligence for the Lovers of Presidential Sports!" *Cooper's Clarksburg Register*, July 4, 1855, 3.
25. "That Extra," *Union and Eastern Journal*, August 24, 1855, 3.
26. Ibid.
27. For an excellent timetable on the political events leading up to the 1856 presidential election and similarities to modern-day politics, see Will Fenton's article "Free Quakers, Founding Fathers, and Native Americans: Ned Buntline's Nativist Historiography," https://buntline.hcommons.org, accessed March 23, 2019.
28. "Pennsylvania and New Jersey Town Records, 1669–2013," Ancestry.com, Ancestry.com Operations, Inc., Lehi, UT, 2011.
29. *Spiritual Telegraph*, June 23, 1855, 2. "Miss Judah" or "Hagar I. Judah" appears in this periodical frequently this summer of 1855, but after that seemingly disappears. There is a marriage record for her in Buffalo some years later, but what happened to the couple after this has yet to be discovered: "New York Marriages, 1686–1980," database,

"FamilySearch," https://familysearch.org/ark:/61903/1:1:F6SY-RNR, 10 February 2018, Charles Weston and Hagar Judah, 27 May 1861; citing reference 2:1HCZMDX; FHL microfilm 1,378,628.

30. "The 'Father of Know-Nothings'—Judson's Wife," *Portage (OH) Sentinel*, November 4, 1858, 3.

31. Testimony, Special Examiner, Commissioner of Pensions, Edwin B. [illeg.], August 27, 1892, Anna Fuller pension file, NARA.

CHAPTER NINE: ADIRONDACKS, EVA, SARAH, AND KATE

1. For example, the *Louisville Daily Courier*, March 9, 1858, 1.

2. Harold K. Hochschild, *Township 34: A History with Digressions of an Adirondack Township in Hamilton County in the State of New York* (New York: 1952). Philanthropist and conservationist Hochschild (1892–1981), a major contributor to the creation of the Adirondack Park Agency in the 1970s, wrote this extremely detailed volume about the Central Adirondacks using deeds, letters, and interviews with elderly residents to craft what it is probably the most reliable accounting of Judson's time there.

3. Ibid.

4. His tombstone epitaph: https://www.findagrave.com/memorial/61573438/chauncey -hathorn, accessed March 26, 2019.

5. Monaghan, *The Great Rascal*, 219–20.

6. "Buntline's Adirondack Life," *Post Star* (Glens Falls, NY), July 24, 1886, 4.

7. Fred E. Pond, *Life and Adventures of "Ned Buntline,"* 63–64.

8. Ibid., 64.

9. *Post-Star* (Glens Falls, NY), July 24, 1886, 4.

10. Ibid., 66.

11. For example: *New York Tribune*, February 8, 1859, 1; Judson's friend, writer Leon Mead, once described this as Judson's favorite way to write.

12. A remembrance in the *Berkshire County (MA) Eagle*, February 20, 1873, 2. Thankfully, Judson was a crack shot. There are dozens of anecdotes of his hunting skills and recreational shooting, such as the times he would hang a bottle by a string from a tree, run toward it on his pony, and cleanly cut the bottle from the string with a bullet.

13. "Ned Buntline," *Schenectady Reflector*, April 22, 1859, 4.

14. *Buffalo Daily Republic*, April 14, 1859, 3.

15. "Buntline's Adirondack Life," *Post-Star* (Glen Falls, NY), July 24, 1886, 4. It's unclear why the papers noted Eva Marie as being "German" or "Dutch"; her parents were born in Connecticut and Rhode Island.

16. "The Wife of Ned Buntline," *Buffalo Daily Republic*, April 18, 1859, 3.

17. Hochschild, *Township 34*, 123.

18. Gardiner's sister noted her death as March 4, 1860, but she was relying on Judson's word. Letter written to J. G. Thompson by Sarah Gardiner, Olmstedville, November 12, 1890, Adirondack Experience Archives; US Census Mortality Schedules, New York, 1850–1880; New York State Education Department, Office of Cultural Education, Albany, New York, Year: 1860, Roll: M3, Line Number: 10. In 1891 a later owner of the

Eagle's Nest property, William West Durant, had the bodies moved to a cemetery at Blue Mountain Lake and bought them a headstone. He—rightfully so—was afraid the bodies would be disturbed or lost if he did not.

19. Hochschild, *Township 34*, appendix D, 459.

20. *Schenectady Reflector*, September 7, 1860, 2.

21. For example, the *Burlington (VT) Weekly Free Press*, September 14, 1860.

22. *Post-Star* (Glens Falls, NY), July 24, 1886, 4.

23. For example, "Ned Buntline's Whereabouts," *Berkshire County (MA) Eagle*, August 11, 1859, 2.

24. John William Schmidt, "Edward Zane Carroll Judson," 57–59.

25. Ibid.

26. Ibid., 59.

27. Ibid.

28. Hochschild, *Township 34*, 127.

29. Monaghan, *The Great Rascal*, 233–34.

30. Diary entry, Edward Z. C. Judson, July 29, 1862, Adirondack Experience archives, Hamilton Lake, New York.

31. Diary entries, Edward Z. C. Judson, July 29–August 8, 1862, Adirondack Experience archives, Hamilton Lake, New York.

32. Diary entry, Edward Z. C. Judson, August 17, 1862, Adirondack Experience archives, Hamilton Lake, New York.

CHAPTER TEN: CIVIL WAR

1. Monaghan, *The Great Rascal*, 223–24. This was not Judson's first time away from Kate. Little more than two months after their marriage, he turned up in New York City and allegedly visited a house of prostitution, where his watch was stolen. *Buffalo Morning Express and Illustrated Buffalo Express*, January 18, 1861, 2.

2. *Detroit Free Press*, January 29, 1861, 2.

3. *Republican* (Ogdensburg, NY), May 21, 1861, 1.

4. "Ned Buntline," *Baltimore Sun*, May 14, 1861, 1.

5. "Ned Buntline," *Brooklyn (NY) Daily Eagle*, May 14, 1861; Deposition N, pg. 67, James S. Conlin, Case of Anna Judson, Widow, Pension File Nos. 580740 and 342879, NARA; "Doctors Will Disagree," *South* (Baltimore, MD), June 10, 1861, 2; *Clipper* (New York, NY), May 25, 1861.

6. "Chronicles of Camp Life . . . Letter to E. Z. C. Judson ("Ned Buntline") from an Only Sister," *Sunday Morning Chronicle* (Washington, DC), June 30, 1861, 1.

7. "47,000 Copies Sold," *Flag of Our Union* (Boston), May 18, 1861, 5. The misspelling of "Monterrey" was common in the mid-nineteenth century.

8. Letter from E. Z. C. Judson, Scranton, PA, to Irene Judson McClintock, Pittsburgh, PA, December 3, 1863, NARA pension files.

9. On his Declaration of Recruit form, Judson gave his age as thirty-seven; his age on the New York Registers of Officers and Enlisted Men Mustered into Federal Service, 1861–1865, lists it as forty-two. The discrepancy can be explained by the fact that the

latter index was often information gleaned from questionnaires sent to friends and family or local officials when the soldier could not be immediately found. In 1862 Judson likely gave himself a birth date that made him a little younger (born in 1825) and therefore more desirable as a recruit, while someone who was estimating made him older.

10. Deposition files of Anna Judson, NARA.

11. Deposition of John Dolan, files of Anna Judson, NARA.

12. "'Ned Buntlin' [sic] in Arms," *Petaluma Argus*, November 12, 1862, 1.

13. Dodge did not give dates in this testimony, so it's unknown which of Judson's families he was referring to. Deposition of Charles C. Dodge, files of Anna Fuller Judson, NARA.

14. Deposition of Charles C. Dodge, files of Anna Fuller Judson, NARA.

15. Deposition of John Dolan, files of Anna Fuller Judson, NARA.

16. Monaghan, *The Great Rascal*, 237.

17. Deposition of Charles A. Combes and deposition of Alexander Hunter, files of Anna Fuller Judson, NARA; deposition of Alexander B. Leggett, files of Anna Fuller Judson, NARA.

18. Monaghan, *The Great Rascal*, 237.

19. Company Muster Rolls, Form 85-D, pension files, NARA.

20. September 25, 1862–December 31, 1862, Company Muster Roll, Form 86, Military Service Records, Edward Zane Carroll Judson, NARA.

21. Depositions of Alexander Hunter and Captain Moses W. Cartright, files of Anna Fuller Judson, NARA.

22. Depositions of B. H. Engelke and Charles A. Combes, files of Anna Fuller Judson, NARA.

23. Depositions of John Elmer Mulford and John Dolan, files of Anna Fuller Judson, NARA.

24. "A Strange Story: Lavanche [sic] L. Judson's Statement," *Kingston (NY) Daily Freeman*, April 18, 1881, 1. Lovanche's account of this time in this newspaper article is consistent with her pension testimony.

25. Monaghan, *The Great Rascal*, 245. Monaghan derived these pieces of information from a letter Lovanche wrote to Fred E. Pond on April 23, 1887. That letter no longer exists, but there is strong evidence that suggests that at least Lovanche's assertion that Judson went to Westchester is correct: Kate and Judson's second daughter, Irene Elizabeth, was born on November 10, 1863. The normal human gestation period puts her conception squarely in the middle of the previous February.

26. Monaghan arrived at this conclusion based on Fred E. Pond's interview of Major Thomas P. McElrath (1808–1888), who had served both before and during the war as a business manager and copublisher with Horace Greeley of the *New York Tribune*. He had also held various state and city offices, and was later involved with sponsoring and promoting various world fairs. There is no reason to doubt the sincerity of McElrath's recollection except to say he dictated it to Pond from a distance of a quarter century later.

27. Monaghan, *The Great Rascal*, 244.

28. Edward Zane Carroll Judson, Company Muster Rolls, Compiled Military Service File, NARA.

29. Letter written by William Cauldwell and Horace Whitney to President Abraham Lincoln dated June 29, 1863; Compiled Military Service File, Edward Z. C. Judson, NARA.

30. Lieutenant John Dolan remembered seeing Judson in his company when chasing Longstreet. People who mentioned Judson's fall from a horse include Charles C. Dodge, his commanding officer, and fellow privates Thomas Place, Charles U. Combes, and others.

31. Letter from Edward Z. C. Judson to sister Irene Judson McClintock dated July 12, with no year, but in context must be 1863. Also, he wrote from Chesapeake Hospital, a ward commandeered for officers. It is not clear why Judson spent time at both Hampton Hospital, designated for enlisted men, and Chesapeake, except to say that all military hospitals were pressed for space as the war wore on.

32. Letter from E. Z. C. Judson to Kate Myers Judson, August 9, 1863, files of Anna Fuller Judson, NARA.

33. Letter from E. Z. C. Judson from Luzerne, PA, to Irene Judson McClintock in Pittsburgh, PA, September 4, 1863, pension files of Anna Fuller Judson, NARA.

34. Letter from George F. Browning, 1st Lieutenant, 73rd US Invalid Corp., Scranton, PA, to Irene Judson McClintock, Pittsburgh, PA, November 16, 1863, pension files of Anna Fuller Judson, NARA.

35. Letter from E. Z. C. Judson, Scranton, PA, to Irene Judson McClintock, Pittsburgh, PA, December 3, 1863, pension files of Anna Fuller Judson, NARA.

CHAPTER ELEVEN: CHAPPAQUA AND CALIFORNIA

1. "A Strange Story: Lavanche L. Judson's Statement," *Kingston (NY) Daily Freeman*, April 18, 1881, 1. Unfortunately, none of these letters appear to have survived.

2. There are several versions of this attempted suicide story. Lovanche gave her version to a *Stamford Mirror and Recorder* reporter; it no longer exists, but a version appears in Monaghan's *The Great Rascal*. A friend of Judson's, Fred Mather, later told *Forest and Stream* magazine that he saw Judson slip on an orange peel on the docks, and the "powerfully built" man managed to hang onto the rudder of a steamer until Mather fished him out (Fred Mather, "Men I Have Fished With," *Field and Stream* [Forest and Stream Publishing Co., 1897], 69). We may safely dismiss this account as a highly flattering one given by an admirer. According to contemporary newspaper accounts, two policemen fished Judson out around half past one in the morning. That Lovanche was obviously nearby lends credence to an account in which Judson was drinking heavily and perhaps threatening that he would do himself harm if she did not let him in ("A Strange Story: Lavanche L. Judson's Statement," *Kingston Daily Freeman*, April 18, 1881, 1).

3. Testimony, Kate Myers Judson Aitcheson, October 1892, Edward Zane Carroll Judson pension file, NARA.

4. Ibid. There's no mention of this residence as being a known house of prostitution in any of the New York City newspapers 1855–1865, but "higher class" establishments were often able to escape notoriety.

5. Monaghan, *The Great Rascal*, 249.

6. Ibid., 250.

7. As improbable as this sounds, especially when one factors the "25 feet above the ground" height of the tree mentioned later in this article, the Greeley farm was built on two water sources: a "very accessible spring" and a "brawling brook," two things Mrs. Greeley insisted upon, along with the planting of evergreens among the older mixed woods already there.

8. Monaghan, *The Great Rascal*, 250.

9. Robert D. Pepper, "Horace Greeley's Raffish Neighbor: or, Ned Buntline, the Westchester County Truant," *Westchester Historian*, vol. 71, no. 2 (Spring 1995): 35.

10. Ibid.

11. "Ned Buntline, Creator of Buffalo Bill Novel . . . ," *New Castle Tribune* (Chappaqua, NY), April 23, 1937, 11.

12. Monaghan, *The Great Rascal*, 250.

13. Myers's testimony in Judson's pension file is peppered with references to his publishers.

14. *Lawrence (KS) Tribune*, February 23, 1865, 1.

15. *Harrisburg Telegraph*, December 19, 1867, 3; Pepper, "Horace Greeley's Raffish Neighbor," 35.

16. "Love—Human, Divine and Infernal—Lecture by Ned Buntline," *Brooklyn Daily Eagle*, February 19, 1868, 1.

17. "The Temperance Movement . . . ," *Brooklyn Daily Eagle*, January 6, 1868, 2; "What the Dashaway and Temperance Legion Did Last Night," *San Francisco Examiner*, May 18, 1868, 3.

18. "Farewell to Ned Buntline—Mr. E. Z. C. Judson," *New York Times*, April 13, 1868, 2.

19. Ibid.; Jack S. Blocker and David M. Fahey, et al., *Alcohol and Temperance in Modern History: An International Encyclopedia, Vol. 1* (Santa Barbara: ABC–CLIO: 2003), pp. 573.

20. *Weekly Rescue* (Sacramento, CA), June 6, 1868, 2; "Ned Buntline," *Santa Cruz Weekly Sentinel*, June 27, 1868, 2; "Ned Buntline," *San Francisco Chronicle*, August 19, 1868, 2.

21. Reprinted in the *San Francisco Chronicle*, August 11, 1868, 2.

22. "A Card to Temperance Men—E. Z. C. Judson," *San Francisco Bulletin*, June 2, 1868, 3.

23. Monaghan, *The Great Rascal*, 255–56.

24. Monaghan, *The Great Rascal*; "Ned Buntline!" *San Francisco Chronicle*, December 27, 1868, 2; "New Serial Story," *Daily Alta California*, December 31, 1868, 2; *Weekly Alta California*, February 22, 1869, 7.

25. *Vallejo Chronicle*, January 16, 1869, transcribed by Vallejo Naval and Historical Museum, http://vallejomuseum.blogspot.com/2009/01/ned-buntline.html, accessed April 18, 2019.

26. Thomas Duncan, ed., *E. Clampus Vitus: Anthology of New Dispensation Lore* (Morrisville, NC: Lulu Press, 2009), 29.

27. For example, "A Card from 'Ned Buntline,' Unionville, Humboldt Co., Nev., May 17," *Pomeroy's Democrat*, June 9, 1869, 3.

28. *Deseret News* (Salt Lake City, UT), July 7, 1869, 1.
29. "Ned Buntline," *San Francisco Chronicle*, September 5, 1869, 2.

CHAPTER TWELVE: THREE WIVES AND BUFFALO BILL

1. "Ned Buntline," *Deseret News* (Salt Lake City), July 21, 1869, 281.
2. Monaghan, *The Great Rascal*, 3–4.
3. Don Russell, *The Lives and Legends of Buffalo Bill* (Norman: University of Oklahoma Press, 1979), 150.
4. Monaghan, *The Great* Rascal, 4–5.
5. Unsubstantiated stories say that at first, Judson was looking for James "Wild Bill" Hickok, whose adventures in *Harper's New Monthly Magazine* highlighted his 1861 shootout with a member of the notorious McCanles gang at Rock Creek Station near Fairbury, Nebraska. Large, muscular, handsome, and a crack shot, Hickok would certainly make for a great dime novel protagonist. According to these stories, Judson found Hickok in a saloon, drunk and more eager to shoot his head off than submit to an interview with him.
6. Monaghan, *The Great Rascal*, 5.
7. William F. Cody, *The Life of William F. Cody—Buffalo Bill* (reprint by the Board of Regents of the University of Nebraska, 2011), 305–07.
8. Testimony, William F. Cody, March 24, 1887, pension file, E. Z. C. Judson, NARA.
9. Ibid.
10. *Atchison (KS) Daily Champion*, August 14, 1869, 2.
11. His thoughts about the platform that did emerge are not recorded, but they would have been interesting to know. The final tenets of the Prohibition Party, which remains a third-party alternative today, include suffrage for women and the wholehearted inclusion of immigrants.
12. "Ned Buntline, Temperance, and California," *Oakland Daily Transcript*, September 4, 1869, 3.
13. *Commerical Advertiser* (New York), October 6, 1869, 3.
14. "Now Ready in the *New York Weekly* . . . ," *Sun* (New York), February 16, 1870, 4.
15. Testimony, Kate Myers Judson Aitcheson, October 17, 1892, pension file, E. Z. C. Judson, NARA.
16. Joy Kasson, *Buffalo Bill's Wild West* (New York: Hill and Wang, 2000), 21.
17. Monaghan, *The Great Rascal*, 19–21; William Frederick Cody and Frank Christianson, eds., *The Life of Hon. William F. Cody, Known as Buffalo Bill* (Lincoln: University of Nebraska Press), 373–83.
18. Monaghan, *The Great Rascal*, 22.
19. Ibid., 23–26. According to Monaghan, the play's name was changed from *Scouts of the Plains* to *Scouts of the Prairie* when it left St. Louis, so Judson could avoid any liability should debtors chase him for bond money. But contemporary newspaper advertisements for the play show that it was originally labeled *Prairie*. Historian Nellie Yost writes that the name only changed when Cody and Judson later parted ways (*Buffalo Bill: His Family, Friends, Fame, Failures, and Fortunes* [Chicago: Swallow Press, 1972, 72]). In any event, it made little difference; it was practically the same show no matter the name.

20. "Salmagundi," *Chicago Tribune*, April 7, 1873, 8.
21. "Amusements," *New York Herald*, April 1, 1873, 12.
22. *New York Herald*, April 3, 1873, 6.
23. Joy Kasson, *Buffalo Bill's Wild West* (New York: Hill and Wang, 2000), 28; Sandra Sagala, *Buffalo Bill on Stage* (Albuquerque: University of New Mexico Press, 2008), 31.
24. James Monaghan, "The Stage Career of Buffalo Bill," *Journal of the Illinois State Historical Society (1908–1984)*, vol. 31, no. 4, December 1938, 415–16; "Amusements," *New York Herald*, April 1, 1873, 12.
25. The exact words of Judson's temperance lecture at this particular performance aren't recorded, but he tended to preach some version of this one, which can be found in "The Temperance Movement," *New York Times*, January 24, 1870, 8.
26. *Brooklyn Daily Eagle*, May 28, 1873, 2.
27. No serious examination of *Scouts of the Prairie* and other William F. Cody/Edward C. Z. Judson collaborations is complete without reviewing Sagala, *Buffalo Bill on Stage*, and Louis S. Warren, *Buffalo Bill's America: William Cody and the Wild West Show* (New York: Vintage Books), 2005.
28. *Rochester (NY) Democrat and Chronicle*, May 1, 1873, 2. In his autobiography, Cody lamented that he was disappointed in his mere six-thousand-dollar total earnings at the end of the season. *Scouts* grossed an average of fifteen thousand dollars per week and had run continuously for six months.
29. For example, the combination's one week of performances at the Boston Theater earned $16,200. This does not take into account the theater's take, nor payment for the other actors. But even half that amount multiplied by a conservative twenty weeks was an outstanding amount at that time. "I was somewhat disappointed," Cody wrote in his autobiography, "for, judging from our large business, I certainly had expected a greater sum." To be fair to Judson, newspapers reported that Judson, Cody, and Omohundro each earned thirty thousand dollars over the "eight-month run" of *Scouts*. As is usually the case with all these people and numbers, the truth probably lies somewhere in the middle. Cody and Christianson, *The Life of Hon. William F. Cody*, 383; *Carlisle (PA) Weekly Herald*, August 21, 1873, 2.
30. Russell, *The Lives and Legends of Buffalo Bill*, 201.
31. *Paterson Daily Guardian*, August 26, 1873, n.p., as recorded in Monaghan, *The Great Rascal*, 30.

CHAPTER THIRTEEN: HAZEL EYE

1. "'A Strange Story,' Lavanche L. Judson's Statement," *Kingston (NY) Daily Freeman*, April 18, 1881, 1; Testimony of Lovanche L. Kelsey Swart Judson, E. Z. C. Judson pension file, NARA.
2. Schmidt, "Edward Zane Carroll Judson (Ned Buntline)," 98.
3. "'A Strange Story,'" *Kingston (NY) Daily Freeman*, April 18, 1881, 1; Testimony of Lovanche L. Kelsey Swart Judson, E. Z. C. Judson pension file, NARA.
4. "'A Strange Story,'" *Kingston (NY) Daily Freeman*, April 18, 1881, 1.
5. Ibid.

6. Ibid.; Letter of Divorce, Edward Zane Carroll Judson and Lovanche L. Judson, November 15, 1871, pension file, E. Z. C. Judson, NARA.

7. "Ned Buntline, Creator of Buffalo Bill Novel, Wrote in Oak Tree In Chappaqua," *New Castle Tribune*, April 23, 1937, 11.

8. Ibid.

9. Testimony, William F. Cody, March 24, 1887, pension file, E. Z. C. Judson, NARA.

10. Deposition of William F. Cody, files of Anna Fuller Judson, NARA.

11. *Edward Z. C. Judson v. Kate M. Judson*, State of Indiana, Scott County, pension file, E. Z. C. Judson, NARA.

12. Later in life, this child would claim his birthday as September 1, 1873, or 1874, but he is clearly eight years old in the US Census taken in June 1880.

13. Deposition of Catherine [*sic*] M. Aitcheson, October 15, 1892, pension file, E. Z. C. Judson, NARA.

14. Deposition of Thomas C. Glynn, March 19, 1887, E Z. C. Judson pension file, NARA, summarized by Schmidt, "Edward Zane Carroll Judson (Ned Buntline)," 92. This amount also jibes with the testimony of Anna Fuller's father, John, in the same file.

15. Schmidt, "Edward Zane Carroll Judson (Ned Buntline)," 95–96.

16. "Local Village Library Notes 100th Anniversary," *Stamford Mirror Recorder*, June 21, 1972, 2; "The Penitentiary on Blackwell's Island," *Herald* (New York), June 5, 1852, 7.

17. Testimony of John Fuller, December 7, 1893, E. Z. C. Judson pension file, NARA.

18. Will Wildwood, "The Life and Adventures of Ned Buntline, Part VI," *Wildwood's Magazine* (Chicago: Wildwood Publishing Company, 1888), 280.

19. "'A Strange Story,'" *Kingston (NY) Daily Freeman*, April 18, 1881, 1; divorce decree, *Lovanche Judson v. E. Z. C. Judson*, August 23, 1876; E. Z. C. Judson pension file, NARA.

20. Ibid.

21. Ibid.

22. Monaghan, *The Great Rascal*, 260–61; the couple's daughter, Irene, was born April 4, 1877.

23. Ned Buntline, *Scouts of the Plains* (1873).

24. Tom Clavin, *Wild Bill: The True Story of the American Frontier's First Gunfighter* (New York: St. Martin's Press, 2019), 222.

25. Monaghan, *The Great Rascal*, 264–65.

26. Ned Buntline, "In the Toil; or, The Lottery Gambler's Victim," *Plymouth (PA) Weekly Star*, November 15–29, 1876, 1, 8.

27. Monaghan, *The Great Rascal*, 265; *Delaware Gazette*, July 4, 1877, 3.

28. *Pittsburgh Daily Post*, November 23, 1877, 2.

29. Monaghan, *The Great Rascal*, 268–69.

30. Ibid.

CHAPTER FOURTEEN: EVER THE FOURTH OF JULY

1. Monaghan, *The Great Rascal*, 108.

2. *Stamford Mirror*, March 15, 1881, 3.

3. *Windham (NY) Journal,* January 20, 1881, 1.

4. Ibid.; http://findagrave.com, accessed October 6, 2019, Stamford Cemetery, Stamford, NY, Irene Judson memorial, memorial number 109943404.

5. *Evening Gazette* (Port Jervis, NY), April 23, 1881, 2.

6. For example, *Stamford Mirror*, March 15, 1881, 3.

7. Monaghan, *The Great Rascal*, 276; "'A Strange Story,'" *Kingston (NY) Daily Freeman*, April 18, 1881, 1.

8. Ibid.

9. *Stamford Mirror Recorder*, September 17, 1980, 3.

10. Ibid.; Monaghan, *The Great Rascal*, 272.

11. Monaghan, *The Great Rascal*, 274–75.

12. "The Will of the Late Samuel Judson," *Bloomville Mirror*, September 13, 1870, 1; Will, Samuel Judson, Wills, 1797–1926; New York, Surrogate's Court (Delaware County); Probate Place: Delaware County, New York.

13. Ibid.

14. Monaghan, *The Great Rascal*, 257.

15. "Blaine as a Know-Nothing?" *Buffalo Evening News*, September 19, 1884, 3, reprinted from *New York World*.

16. "'Ned Buntline's' Opinion of Whittaker," *Kingston (NY) Freeman*, April 17, 1880, 1.

17. Monaghan, *The Great Rascal*, 281; "Safe Bind, Safe Time: Ned Buntline's Daughter Has to Tie a Hawser to Her Lover," *Trenton Evening Times*, September 18, 1884, 5.

18. Monaghan, *The Great Rascal*, 281.

19. Reprint from the *Morning Journal* (New York) in scrapbook at *Stamford Mirror* office circa 1950; Monaghan, *The Great Rascal*, 281.

20. Monaghan, *The Great Rascal*, 281.

21. Testimony of William F. Cody, March 24, 1887, pension file of E. Z. C. Judson, NARA.

22. "Ned Buntline's Wild Days," *New York World*, Sunday Supplement 2, June 28, 1885, 1.

23. W. A. Croffut, "Ned Buntline: A Visit to 'Eagle's Nest,' and a Glimpse of the Life of a Remarkable Man," *Detroit Free Press*, June 28, 1885, 4.

24. Ibid.

25. Ned Buntline, "Thoughts of an Invalid," reprinted in *Delhi Republican*, May 15, 1886, 1.

26. Ned Buntline, reprinted in *Wildwood's Magazine* (Chicago: Wildwood Publishing Company, 1888), 108.

CHAPTER FIFTEEN: NED BUNTLINE'S AMERICA

1. *Hobart (NY) Independent*, July 22, 1886, 1.

2. Beverly Schwartzberg, "'Lots of Them Did That': Desertion, Bigamy, and Marital Fluidity in Late-Nineteenth-Century America," *Journal of Social History* (Spring 2004): 574.

3. W. A. Croffat, "Ned Buntline: A Visit to 'Eagle's Nest' and a Glimpse of the Life of a Remarkable Man," *Detroit Free Press*, June 28, 1885, 4. Unfortunately for Judson and many others, there was no law calling for the distribution of a pension for the widows of those who had served in the Indian Wars (1818–1898) until 1892. See

Claire Prechtel-Kluskens's very helpful article "For Love and Money: Pension Laws Affecting Widows of Military Veterans," National Archives newsletter, vol. 42, no. 1 (January–March 2016): 35–39.

4. Testimony of Ezekiel W. Gallup, MD, July 12 and 16, 1886, and November 14, 1887, pension file of E. Z. C. Judson, NARA.

5. Testimony of John Frelinghuysen, May 9, 1887, pension file of E. Z. C. Judson, NARA.

6. Special Examiner George H. Ellis to Honorable William Lochren, December 14, 1893, pension file of E. Z. C. Judson, NARA; Special Examiner Edwin B. Smith. to Hon. Green B. Raum, August 25, 1892, pension file of E. Z. C. Judson, NARA.

7. "Attempted Suicide: A Well Known Numismatist Cuts His Throat with a Razor," *Morning Post* (Camden, NJ), 1.

8. "New York Probate Records, 1629-1971," images, FamilySearch (https://familysearch.org/ark:/61903/3:1:3QSQ-G9HY-4T1G?cc=1920234&wc=Q7R5-3TL%3A213304401%2C214217101: 28 May 2014), Delaware, estate papers, proceedings 1797–1900 no 1J image 992 of 2044, county courthouses, New York.

9. Testimony of Irene A. McClintock to the Clerk of the US District Court, Western District of Pennsylvania, June 9, 1887, pension file of E. Z. C. Judson, NARA.

10. The source for this information wishes to remain private.

11. Testimony of William F. Cody, March 24, 1887, pension file of E. Z. C. Judson, NARA.

12. William Leon Mead, "How 'Ned Buntline' Turned from Runaway Boy to Writing Genius . . . ," *Binghamton (NY) Press*, section 2, 10.

13. Ibid.

14. Don Russell, *The Lives and Legends of Buffalo Bill* (Norman: University of Oklahoma Press, 1973), 150–55.

15. Mead, "'Ned Buntline'," *Binghamton (NY) Press*, section 2, 10. Mead, an author and reporter, also born in Delaware, was just twenty-five years old when his idol, Edward Zane Carroll Judson, died. His appraisal of Judson must be taken with the smallest grain of salt, because Mead absolutely idolized his hometown celebrity. But Mead also spent a lot of time with Cody and people in the publishing industry, so his assessments must at least be considered a reasoned and authentic point of view.

16. Schmidt, 140–141.

17. Charles E. Belknap, *The Yesterdays of Grand Rapids* (Grand Rapids, MI: Dean-Hicks Company, 1922), 88–89.

18. E-mail from R. Clay Reynolds to author, May 17, 2019.

19. Reynolds, *The Hero of a Hundred Fights*, 421.

20. Miriam Biskin, "Ned Buntline—Adirondack Image Maker," *Times-Union* (Albany), February 11, 1968, G-3.

INDEX

About the Author

Julia Bricklin is the author of the only biography of female sharpshooter Lillian Frances Smith (April 2017) and of trailblazing reporter Nell Campbell, aka "Polly Pry" (TwoDot Books, September 2018). She is also the author of *Blonde Rattlesnake: Burmah Adams, Tom White, and the 1933 Crime Spree That Terrorized Los Angeles*. She has authored a dozen articles in well-respected commercial and academic journals, such as *Civil War Times*, *Financial History*, *Wild West*, *True West*, and *California History*.